AN ECONOMIC ECLIPSE

AN ECONOMIC ECLIPSE

SHIFTING TOWARD A SUSTAINABLE
FUTURE BY ELIMINATING WASTE

BY ALEXA SMITH

NEW DEGREE PRESS

AN ECONOMIC ECLIPSE
Shifting Toward a Sustainable Future by Eliminating Waste

ISBN   978-1-63676-705-5   *Paperback*
         978-1-63730-062-6   *Kindle Ebook*
         978-1-63730-164-7   *Ebook*

Tomorrow's Child © Glenn C. Thomas 1996
Used by permission of the Ray C. Anderson Foundation

This book is dedicated to my wonderful family, friends, and mentors who gave me the courage to unleash my inner voice and passion to become the introverted activist I always dreamed of being.

CONTENTS

INTRODUCTION   **11**

A CELESTIAL CALLING   13

AWAKENING TO WASTE   25

PHASE ONE.   **WASTE OBSCURATION**   **29**

CHAPTER 1.   TIPPING THE SCALES   31

CHAPTER 2.   RECIPE FOR SUSTAINABILITY   53

CHAPTER 3.   THE PURCHASER'S DILEMMA   75

PHASE TWO.   **PENUMBRAL BUSINESS STRATEGY**   **89**

DESIGN

CHAPTER 4.   CHANNELING COPERNICUS AND CURIE   91

CHAPTER 5.   TAPPING INTO CREATIVITY   113

ENGAGE

CHAPTER 6.   COMMUNITY MATTERS   131

CHAPTER 7.   PASSION FOR TRASH   153

CHAPTER 8.   SEEING IS BELIEVING   175

CONNECT

CHAPTER 9.   RIDING TRENDS   195

CHAPTER 10.   SIX DEGREES OF CIRCULARITY   213

PHASE THREE.   **EMBRACING ETHEREAL CHANGE**   **233**

CHAPTER 11.   CONSUMER CONNECTION   235

CHAPTER 12.   COMING FULL CIRCLE   253

AFTERWORD   265

BIPOC ZERO WASTE DIRECTORY   269

ACKNOWLEDGMENTS   275

APPENDIX   283

"Eclipses upset the natural order as day becomes night and night becomes day. An eclipse has historically acted as a symbolic portal for exponential growth, a time of rapid change, internally and externally… It's a time to harvest and reap what we've sown, throw out the weeds! A solar eclipse is a time to focus on internal change."

~VICKI FOREMAN

INTRODUCTION

A CELESTIAL CALLING

———

Scrolling through my YouTube recommended page and hunting for offbeat TED Talks is one of my favorite pastimes. My passion has helped me scout everything, from preventing global health pandemics to using human gut bacteria as emotional Adderall. One of my most treasured talks, however, led me down an intriguing rabbit hole from which I have yet to resurface. That talk was entitled "Saving the Planet by Running a Dating Site."[1]

As an environmental science major, it is sometimes hard to resist the temptation to click on content with the words "save" and "planet." Instinctively, I gravitated my cursor toward the thumbnail of this presentation by Maayke-Aimée Damen. The twelve-minute discussion of her "dating site," better known as Excess Materials Exchange (EME), left me captivated by her reinterpretation of waste in our modern society.

---

1   *TED*, "Maayke-Aimée Damen: Saving the Planet by Running a Dating Site," January 2, 2020, video, 2:50.

AN INDUSTRIAL MATCHMAKING SERVICE

Rather than viewing waste as inevitably destined for the landfill, Damen shone a spotlight on the vigor of repurposing excess production materials to give them a new life. EME allows companies to advertise their waste to businesses in other sectors.[2] For example, used coffee grounds from the restaurant industry need not be tossed in the trash and immediately sent to landfill, never to see the light of day again. With the help of EME, these grounds can be made available to other companies, perhaps in the fashion industry. Instead of "dying" in the landfill where they end up six feet under, coffee grounds might be used to "dye" in a different way as a natural alternative to synthetic colorants in textile manufacturing.

Similar to traditional dating sites eharmony or Bumble, EME unites complementary users through its complex algorithms. The result is a circular setup where nothing is left unused and waste is completely eliminated through the collaboration of market participants. These partnerships are determined by matching waste and input streams.[3] In other words, the needs and desires of stakeholders are perfectly paired to build material relationships, like an industrial matchmaking service.

This transformative business sees waste as a beginning rather than an end, unlike most other participants in the consumer goods industry. Aside from EME's stewardship for the planet, their work is also driven by profitability. If all

---

2   Ibid.

3   *TED,* "Maayke," 8:01.

goes well, outputting businesses avoid lofty landfill fees and inputting businesses acquire recycled resources at a reduced price compared to virgin raw materials.[4] When I first learned about this innovative approach, I wanted to see if this large-scale waste repurposing was idiosyncratic or part of a larger entrepreneurial tendency.

As it turns out, there is widespread support for creating a circular system in the consumer goods sector, be it fashion, food, or other single-use items. The goal of this rebellion is to eradicate all wasteful derivatives through responsible production and consumption practices. Accelerating a waste-free movement could impart just the tipping point our world needs to actualize its fantasy of sustainability and unravel the abusive entanglement between our economy and our planet.

THE AMBUSH OF OUR PLANET

By now, your daily news outlet has certainly informed you that our planet is in a complete state of emergency. Earth has been ambushed by the woes of climate change, biodiversity loss, ozone depletion, coral bleaching, deforestation, desertification, and, most relevant to this book, trash proliferation. The unfortunate consequence of our daily habits and expenditures is an accumulation of waste, which sits in our landfills and ecosystems and degrades our environment.

Our waste seems to be coming from every possible direction, from the plastic packaging on our online shopping binges to the rotting fruit in the back of our refrigerators. As such,

---

4   Ibid.

the World Economic Forum projects there will be more plastic waste in the ocean than fish by the year 2050.[5] And our waste supply goes far beyond just plastic, even infiltrating our closets and refrigerators. The Ellen MacArthur Foundation estimates one garbage truck full of clothes is incinerated or landfilled every second.[6] Plus, nearly 40 percent of food in the United States is wasted, due to "ugly" produce, improper household storage, and uneaten leftovers.[7]

All these forms of waste have a hefty impact on the environment. Food, textiles, and single-use plastics, all of which fall under the consumer-packaged goods (CPG) industrial category, constitute a notable portion of the western waste stream. Together, they amount to obscene amounts of trash. An average American produces about 4.9 pounds of trash every single day, according to the United States Environmental Protection Agency (EPA).[8] At this rate of trash production, our wasteful world is in for a lot more trouble than sore eyes from highway litter. The Great Pacific Garbage Patch, which you may have heard of, is an island of rubbish in the middle of the Pacific Ocean twice the size of Texas. The gyre is a death trap for birds and marine life feeding on bits of plastic and aluminum. *National Geographic* even obtained evidence

5   Anna Bruce-Lockhart, "More Plastic in the Sea Than Fish? Not If We Do These 3 Things," World Economic Forum: Agenda, January 16, 2017.
6   "One Garbage Truck of Textiles Wasted Every Second: Report Creates Vision for Change," Ellen MacArthur Foundation, November 28, 2017.
7   Dana Gunders et al., *Wasted: How America Is Losing up to 40 Percent of Its Food from Farm to Fork to Landfill* (New York City, NY: Natural Resources Defense Council, 2017), 4.
8   US Department of the Interior, Environmental Protection Agency, *National Overview: Facts and Figures on Materials, Wastes and Recycling* (Washington D.C., 2018).

of ocean plastic lurking in the Mariana Trench, the deepest explored part of the ocean.[9] It seems our wasteful operations have caressed every nook of our world in some shape or form. Correspondingly, several unique natural habitats and eco-systems have deteriorated beyond repair.

Industrialized exchange has also exacerbated the effects of climate change. According to the EPA, over 40 percent of our greenhouse gases come from the industrial, commercial, and agricultural sectors facilitating single-use consumerism.[10] Both the manufacturing of goods themselves and their irresponsible disposal lead to catastrophic emissions. This issue intensifies global warming and all its noxious effects including, but not limited to, severe flooding and natural disasters, increased vector-borne diseases, and blows to agricultural and fishing industries.

Besides the widespread environmental impacts, *Scientific American* described the tumultuous effects of trash on humanity itself. Their research revealed that as plastic breaks down and accumulates in our bodies, organ damage and hormone disruption ensue.[11] The Natural Resources Defense Council (NRDC) also cites microplastics, an unfortunate result of our waste (mis)management, as human carcinogens—as they absorb and carry toxic compounds that

---

9   Sarah Gibbens, "Plastic Proliferates at the Bottom of World's Deepest Ocean Trench," *National Geographic,* May 13, 2019.

10   US Department of the Interior, Environmental Protection Agency, *Inventory of US Greenhouse Gas Emissions and Sinks: 1990-2018* (Washington D.C., 2020), 4-4.

11   Andrea Thompson, "From Fish to Humans, a Microplastic Invasion May Be Taking a Toll," *Scientific American,* September 4, 2018.

have lasting health effects when ingested.[12] Plastics are omnipresent in our daily lives, and because most of the different types of plastic are not able to be efficiently recycled, they end up in our environment, harming human health. Even when we try to get rid of plastic through means such as incineration (often in low-income communities), devastating respiratory disease and skin rashes make themselves known.[13]

SHORTCOMINGS IN COMPASSION

This phenomenon and all its ramifications are not something we usually learn about (either formally or informally) in our western society. Speaking from my perspective as a citizen of the United States, the majority of us never choose to question or even fully understand our tossing of items in the trash. But as that complacency builds up day by day through our "out of sight, out of mind" mentality, so too do our landfills. This is a major problem. Heaps of waste yielded everyday sit in landfills, causing the environmental and human health detriments just described. Parasitic trash is wreaking havoc on our health and planet in ways we may not even be able to imagine.

The most disheartening aspect of this whole scenario, though, is the lack of exertion around changemaking. Even the small proportion of individuals who comprehend the gravity of this issue tend not to act on their concerns as a result of their own self-inefficacy in overcoming existing institutions. For example, many individuals who are considerate of their

---

12   Courtney Lindwall, "Single-Use Plastics 101," *Our Stories* (blog), *NRDC*, January 9, 2020.

13   Ibid.

environmental impact may not have access to recycling programs that accept paper or plastic. Even if these people may
happen to live within driving distance of a recycling center,
they may not have access to a car, and this additional transportation (and therefore emissions) may even offset some of
the benefits of recycling in the first place.

Many industries are also ignorant obstacles to reducing
waste and refuse to reduce it through their business models.
A "Grade A" example would be corporate giants like Amazon, who are consistently ridiculed for their incessant plastic
packaging, yet for the most part choose to ignore cries for
change. Even small businesses like local coffee shops often
fail to contemplate the end of life of their used coffee grounds
and plastic to-go cups, which end up in their own local landfills. This leaves enthusiastic individuals with an extremely
limited, if at all existent, array of alternatives to single-use,
resource-intensive products. At the end of the day, we are
faced with an ultimatum: rejecting all industries for complete self-sufficiency (which is essentially impossible given
our current situation) or violating our values by continuing
down the path of wastefulness set out by society.

THE TIPPING POINT WE NEED

Why is the commercial world so insistent on maintaining this
single-use lifestyle for consumers? Why are they so hesitant
to endorse waste-reducing devices and move toward a more
sustainable future? As the saying goes: fear of the unknown
is the greatest fear of all. Waste awareness has been a decades-
old awakening, but it wasn't until 2003 that a flagship com-
mencing this crusade, called the Zero Waste International

Alliance, was formed. But even at that time, only three hundred individuals across the globe were involved in its work. Since then, zero-waste has resided mostly within the lifestyle blog community and has yet to reach the tipping point of industrial acceptance. In essence, "zero-waste" is still a newborn buzzword with a minute cult following.

This small but persuasive group of individuals stands by its mission of:

> Conservation of all resources by means of responsible production, consumption, reuse, and recovery of products, packaging, and materials without burning and with no discharges to land, water, or air that threaten the environment or human health.[14]

As socially and economically optimal as this philosophy may be, the standing majority continues to neglect the possibility of eliminating waste, especially in a business context. These major doubts and misconceptions are rooted in the idea that eliminating waste equates to limiting economic growth. Business101 teaches us that since our economy historically flourished through vigorous extraction of precious resources, that must be the best and only strategy.

Through my extensive, multi-disciplinary research spanning from single zero-waste families in Tanzania to South African engineers to Dutch circular economists, I can assure you that this is completely and utterly untrue. Creating a world

---

14   "Zero Waste Definition," Zero Waste International Alliance, last modified December 20, 2018.

that repudiates waste and embraces renovation can ensure a valuable and sustainable future for humanity.

Waste is an untapped asset.

With a model that treats waste as a valuable resource, we won't need to worry about "running out" of raw materials as we eventually will in our current linear order. Redefining waste means enhancing industrial efficiency and increasing value to producers, sellers, and consumers across the board utilizing creative capabilities.

A UNIFIED FRONT

Converting to a waste-reduced economy requires the commitment of both businesses and their clientele. In a wealthy democracy such as the United States, we have the fortunate opportunity to mobilize these groups. Companies can and should reinvent their manufacturing processes and business models to spark systematic change, which is possible given our technological advancement and access to resources. Purchasers can and should educate themselves on the issue of waste, and they should act upon that education by choosing goods designed and expended with reuse and recycling in mind. This is once again possible by the access we have to education on environmental issues and sustainable alternatives to everyday products. Both of these analogous passages are made possible by the trailblazing zero-waste community's demand for sustainability.

In writing this book, I take pride in identifying myself as one of these trailblazers. My studies in natural resources and environmental economics, along with my experience crafting sustainability initiatives for my university of forty thousand students, have enabled me to deliver this message to you. Through deeply understanding issues of environmental externalities and current hurdles to recycling and waste management, I have made it my mission to reverse these toxic trends and uplift a future devoid of their influence. My creation of this book also coincides with my research addressing plastic waste in my own city through a student organization advocating social entrepreneurship. My expertise and commitment to managing waste at both an individual and societal level have served me well as a liaison for this ever-important development.

Never did I imagine this would be my calling until Earth Day 2020.

On this day, I watched a virtual summit guest-starring Lauren Singer, a respected zero-waste activist known for her little mason jar of trash. During her popular TED Talk, Singer displayed a sixteen-ounce jar comfortably fitting the entirety of her three years' worth of trash.[15] Her eloquent, simple, and well-reasoned lifestyle instantly hooked me. As an environmental studies major who failed to recognize her own plundering practices, Singer's story of hypocrisy mirrored my own, giving me even more reason to dip my toe into zero-waste. Her daily life did not entail obsessive minimalism, intense dietary restrictions, or obscenely expensive alternatives to everyday products. Rather, it marvelously

---

15   *TED,* "Lauren Singer: Why I Live a Zero Waste Life," May 27, 2015, video, 0:10.

reflected a conscious, enjoyable life with a low environmental footprint. Realizing all of this, I was inspired to follow in her footsteps.

Given my education and values, seeing my garbage load lighten through my new deliberate consumption made my heart sing. I also noticed a weight lifted off my bank account because the investments I make are limited yet long-lasting. Indulging in meaningless single-use items that slowly but surely deplete my money, space, and peace of mind no longer interests me. Although my individual growth has been substantial, my ultimate goal is to spread awareness of how these personal gains of trash reduction can translate to the business sector in industrialized societies, especially the United States and western Europe. By resculpting the business model of waste, we can develop personal and professional synergies on a grand scale. Individuals can live and work in alignment with their values, practicing mindfulness in the impact their life has on others and the environment.

The contents in this book may inspire ambitious environmentalists and college students interested in sustainability and entrepreneurship. For those diagnosed with an unfulfilling, bleak career path, the opportunities for purpose-driven work demonstrated through these stories could be life-altering. For young innovators, you may be compelled to fill in particular gaps in waste mismanagement by activating entrepreneurial skills and creating value for society.

A complete vision of circularity becomes clear throughout this book, as I highlight both activists and business leaders advocating for waste-reduced growth. As such, whether you are involved in procurement, consulting, activism, or sustainable business at large, the principles of zero-waste described in this book will provide unique insights to boost your career and give you a competitive edge in your professional life. Consumers, too, will derive value from this environmental exposé that will surely impact your daily purchasing choices.

This book is a compilation of stories appealing to an array of diverse backgrounds and characters. If you are amazed by lustrous designer bags out of torn and worn fire hoses, look no further than the story of Elvis & Kresse. If you are intrigued by bold activists wearing every food wrapper, flyer, pizza box, and coffee cup they generate for a whole month, then Rob Greenfield's journey will encapsulate your attention. If you are curious about economists turning a doughnut from an indicator of poor dietary choices to a model of economic health, let Kate Raworth's story be your muse.

No matter your discipline or experience, I can ensure that you will encounter a resonating waste-warrior whose footsteps you can follow (or at least roughly trace). By identifying that point of resonance, we can all work together to declutter our lives and clean up our society's way of doing business.

AWAKENING TO WASTE

Saturday afternoons were my artistic retreat. No expertise or particular direction involved—just free-wheeling, euphoric creativity. Throughout middle and high school, I would spend my 120-hour, jam-packed school week with my head stuck inside textbooks or, more likely, in front of a laptop screen. I fell into a routine of cramming my brain to the brim with tidbits of history, geometry, and biology, leaving my conscience throbbing by the week's end. Like an overflowing Chipotle burrito with black beans, fajita veggies, medium salsa, lettuce, and guacamole, my tortilla brain could barely accommodate the information it was being force-fed.

For years I accepted my inability to decompress. But after recognizing my desire to treat this almost permanent headache, I finally found the perfect Tylenol to ease my pain: upcycling. Going through my wardrobe of over-sized, secondhand men's T-shirts surged me with a rush of unmatched adrenaline. My mind was free to craft whatever it desired, turning bulky sweatshirts into delicate tees and frumpy dresses into chic skirts. I had a collection of patches, strings, buttons, and dyes I could depend on to transform any drab piece into a work of art. Back in middle school, when I would revamp these washed-up items, I never saw it as a way of saving our planet. Pure and simple, I found enjoyment from uncovering beauty in unlikely places.

A WORLD WITHOUT TRASH

It wasn't until almost ten years later that my hobby transformed into a dedication for reducing waste. Several life-altering escapades nudged me along the way toward the epiphany that I should become an advocate for this important cause. On a vacation in fifth grade with my worldly best friend, my spiritual bond with nature was built in a place called Sacred Monkey Forest Sanctuary in Bali, Indonesia. Stepping into this lush scenery was like crossing the threshold into an alternate universe where humans and nature were indivisibly one. Without an inkling of hesitation, monkeys would hop on the shoulders of their human brothers and indulge themselves in sweet, sun-ripened bananas. After polishing off their afternoon snack, the hooligans would graciously comb through the manes of visitors, checking for parasitic vermin. Beyond the main attraction of monkeys, the subtleties of this biological bliss were equally as striking. The humming of cicadas was intoxicating, and the hushed rustling of foliage carried a sense of groundedness I had never felt before.

There was one thing missing from this encounter, though, that left me pondering the world as I knew and accepted it: trash.

Not a single plastic bag, water bottle, ketchup packet, or packing peanut littered the sacred ground. Without the distraction of litter and corporate byproducts, I was able to fully immerse myself in a green, untainted wonderland. Witnessing the respectful, devoted relationship the indigenous Balinese people had with their sacred forests made me rethink my own values and nexus with the environment. I recognized my desire to learn from this culture and their harmony with the planet. Other cultural awakenings, including my brush with Ramadan, also ushered my admiration for a non-materialistic and reflective life. This newfound appreciation became my North Star in choosing my academic and professional career path. It also brought me to the gut-wrenching realization that others did not share this same appreciation for Mother Earth. But instead of letting that deter me, my awareness of this unfortunate fact fiercely motivated me in the fight against our wasteful world.

A COMMON SORT OF CATASTROPHE

My developing activism came to a head on Earth Day in 2018. For an honors research project in a class called Environment and Society, two of my classmates and I constructed a booth covered in trash. Our table was decorated with greasy pizza boxes, empty yogurt cups, crumpled office paper and cellophane, among other odds and ends. Sounds just stunning, doesn't it? Overlooking the aesthetically underwhelming nature of our project, the intent was to invite passersby to sort the waste into recyclable and trash containers based on our municipality's standards.

To my utter dismay, not a single person, out of the fifty-plus participants of our booth, correctly sorted the trash. Often times cardboard pizza boxes, which were covered in grease, were incorrectly placed in the recycle pile. Flimsy plastic packaging was also a point of contention, with many visitors wishfully hoping this material so frequently used for convenient snacks and sanitary items could be recycled (which it unfortunately cannot). This worrying incident sent me on a rampage to promote reducing, reusing, and recycling. From changing my own shopping habits to stimulating others to properly dispose of their trash, I became fixated on the world of waste.

Although personal habits are absolutely important when it comes to reducing waste, my fascination with this topic lead me to seek answers beyond personal practices. As a capitalist citizen, I am aware of the corporate sector's capacity to hypnotize their patrons into following the agenda of its choosing. In that respect, industry can choose whether to commend relentless purchasing or—alternatively—mindful investment. Since realizing the urgency of waste reduction, I propose that businesses take on this responsibility to facilitate an inevitable changeover to sustainability. By reducing waste, businesses of all sizes in many sectors have an opportunity to test the limits of creativity while simultaneously conserving the very sources of life on Earth.

PHASE ONE

WASTE OBSCURATION

Obscure: "Shrouded in or hidden by darkness"

MERRIAM-WEBSTER

CHAPTER 1

TIPPING THE SCALES

———

Bulk piles of apples, sweet potatoes, and onions decorate the produce section of a local grocery store. Eye-catching prices accompany the whole foods, announcing sales such as fifty-eight cents a pound for organic bananas or twenty-one cents a pound for watermelons. These incredible deals may stimulate frantic customers to stock up on fresh food like it's going out of fashion, stuffing every corner of their carts with colorful fruits and vegetables. As wonderful a deal as these discounts may be, something to pore over is what these prices are actually paying for. Of course, the delicious and sweet interior of these fruits is included, but so are the bits of waste that inherently come with them. Himkaar Singh, founder of South African company the Compost Kitchen, clarifies and explains this fruit phenomenon which can be analogized to most other single-use items. For example, he says, if a bunch of bananas is three dollars, when the peels are discarded nearly one-third the weight of the bananas is lost, which means that you essentially spent one dollar on material which will instantly be thrown away. Now, one dollar might not be a very compelling incentive to reevaluate one's banana-purchasing habits, but by extending the frame of view to a whole year, this amounts to losing fifty-two dollars and about fifteen pounds of banana peels!

If six to seven hours-worth of hourly wages could be lost from the scraps of just one food item, imagine the financial burden from the wastage of potato peels, nut shells, carrot stems, and most pervasively, plastic packaging. The endless supplies of waste purchased from the grocery store are associated with baffling costs. Plus, the direct monetary costs of this waste are just a small squadron in comparison to its impact on the environment.

This grocery store demonstration is a stellar example of the science of compounding, a discipline central to the study of waste. When examined in the short term, bits of unused material are insipid and insignificant. When examined in the long term, they become mountainous and expensive, which adds a compelling argument for the zero-waste philosophy. Capturing small assets like banana peels or plastic food wrap over time, especially apparent in consumer-packaged goods (CPG) industries—including food, fashion, and various sources of single-use plastic—can harvest value monetarily and environmentally. Whilst attempting to reduce waste and obtain value from each of these sectors, it is important to first understand the complexities of the issues themselves and their effects on our daily lives.

DREDGED EDIBLES

It was August 25 and the blistering Midwest sun was nearly unbearable. As I moseyed across my campus's main quad in the one-hundred degree heat, I began to lose traction. My mission for the day was to find new student organizations to join based on their rehearsed pitches and booths, which were aligned like ducks in a row along the sidewalks feeding into our Alma Mater. It had been two hours before I finally accepted my dehydration and heat exhaustion were not worth a spontaneous introduction to a new club. I was about to head back to my dorm when I saw a shining beacon decorated with Earth-shaped laptop stickers and a sign "Project4Less: less for more, more for everyone." Their captivating spiel roped me in as they proclaimed themselves:

"A student-run food recovery operation helping bulk food producers get their pre-consumer food waste to food pantries and other food assistance programs."

When I attended their first meeting, I was astonished to hear about the indigestible amount of food waste on our campus. Over half a million pounds of food were dumped from our dining halls to the landfill in 2012, which was still significantly less than it had been a few years earlier (about 2.5 million pounds in 2009).[16] Considering the fact that the average human eats around four pounds of food per day, over 375,000 prepared meals were ordered to landfill without the chance to nourish hungry community members. Before versing myself in these statistics, I was

---

16   "Reduce Foodwaste," Institute for Sustainability, Energy and Environment, accessed December 22, 2020.

distantly aware of students who voluntarily piled massive portions onto their plate simply to toss a large amount of it. What I didn't know was that nationally, some estimates equate this source of food waste to 140 pounds per student per year.[17]

So much time, energy, and resources were being spent just for the food to end up in the trash bin. Juxtaposed with the fact that 15 percent of people in my county were food insecure, with a much higher percentage on campus, I was determined to do something about the absurdity of it all.[18]

Seeing the industrial-sized vats of potatoes, biscuits, and fried chicken now made me feel nauseous, and not just because of the grease. This unleashed a new sense of urgency within me to tackle this problem.

As a public university with a goal of serving the community, the dining service consistently provides more food than necessary to ensure that no student seeking a meal goes hungry. While this may be a noble mission, the precaution creates equally large problems in the form of wasted meals. Whether the school staff threw away meals that were never eaten or the students picked at their too-full plates and tossed the rest, every step in the food supply chain on campus— from the refrigerator to the plate—wasted food. Multiplied by the fact that my school hosts around forty-thousand students,

17   "Food Waste Estimation Guide," Recycling Works Massachusetts, accessed January 21, 2021.
18   "Map the Meal Gap," Eastern Illinois Food Bank, accessed December 22, 2020.

with many eating at university facilities, the environmental impact is unfathomable.

Food waste of this scale is not an anomaly. After learning about my university's situation, personal reflection brought me back to my first job in the dish room at a local pizza joint. Hours of my time were spent staring at dirty plates and kitchen equipment. Visualizing this scenario may be distasteful to the average person, but what really made me uneasy was witnessing all the uneaten food that fell straight into my sink. At least once an hour, the drain would clog with lumps of lettuce, pizza crusts and French fries hitching a ride on the used dishware even after the servers "cleared" them. A running joke with my coworkers formed around the "dish room soup" brewed in the sink from the food remnants I had rinsed away. My dish stew in the sink served a hypothetical meal for four by the hour.

This does not even compare to the food we wasted for sanitation reasons, as ingredients were rotated and discarded if they had gone past their prime. The running list we kept for food wasted, dropped, or thrown away, whether it be six ounces of tomatoes or two barrels of sauce, filled up at least once or twice a week, despite the simple prevention that could have come from better kitchen management and stricter employee training.

Alas, the sources of food waste go far beyond the extent of pizza crusts at a mom-and-pop restaurant or the dining hall at a university. In the United Nations Food and Agriculture Organization's food waste campaign, farms, markets, and household trash cans are all portrayed as villains in the war on food waste.[19] Attesting to the expanse of this problem in America, the EPA passed the first ever domestic goal in 2018 to reduce wasted food by 50 percent by 2030.[20] The group ReFED, a national non-profit combating food waste, even quantified current inefficiencies, citing that sixty-three million tons of food are wasted annually with "nearly 85 percent occurring downstream at consumer-facing businesses and homes."[21]

This food waste correlates to the exploitation of 21 percent of all fresh water, 19 percent of all fertilizer, 18 percent of cropland, and 21 percent of landfill volume. It also generates to a $218 billion financial weight distributed among farms, manufacturers, consumer-facing businesses, and to the highest degree, homes.[22] With such an enormous amount of food waste being generated, costs are also weighed upon waste management facilities, as the usable lives of landfills are limited. Once we fill one hole, we've got to dig another, and increasingly those landfills encroach on natural landscapes. This is becoming a more prominent and expensive issue in areas where the amount of land and air space needed to build and sustain landfills is shrinking. In these scenarios, the addition of food waste indisputably contributes to costly disposal.

---

19 Food and Agriculture Organization of the United Nations, "FAO Policy Series: Food Loss & Food Waste," June 30, 2016, video, 0:40.

20 "United States 2030 Food Loss and Waste Reduction Goal," United States Environmental Protection Agency, accessed January 21, 2021.

21 Mark Cirilli et al., *A Roadmap to Reduce US Food Waste by 20 Percent* (Berkeley, CA: ReFED, 2016), 5.

22 Ibid.

Food (especially fruits and veggies) may decompose rather quickly in open-air natural environments, but the suffocation of garbage in the landfill creates an environment where oxygen-fueled decomposers (i.e. earthworms, bacteria) cannot survive. In that event, the breakdown occurs very slowly and releases the greenhouse gas methane, which has a warming potential about twenty-five times higher than carbon dioxide. The energy and resources required to grow and prepare all the uneaten food, from fertilizer to harvesting equipment, is another large emissions source. Therefore, according to Project Drawdown, a manual by environmentalist author Paul Hawken describing the one hundred most promising methods of reversing climate change, food waste reduction is ranked the number three solution.[23]

Clearly, the very substance nourishing our bodies and providing us with the fuel of existence has been dragged into an unhealthy relationship with first-world inhabitants. We don't think twice when we trash a half-eaten sandwich or fruit we let rot in the back of our refrigerator. As these oblivious habits compound, the effects of food waste on the environment and economy escalate as well.

The bad news: food waste is a contributor to three of our world's most complex and dire problems: climate change, world hunger, and landfill overcapacity. The good news: a remedy to these three problems exists in a single solution. The compounding of wasted food may seem overwhelming,

---

23   Paul Hawken, *Drawdown: The Most Comprehensive Plan Ever Proposed to Reverse Global Warming* (New York: Penguin Publishing Group, 2017), 42–43.

but so would be the benefits if we gather the courage to address this problem. Our future is limitless, so why not start now on a mission to eliminate the waste that lies on our plates?

TEXTILE TRASH

What starts on our plates continues into our closet, where fashion is a disguised culprit in product waste. While exploring my own wasteful habits, seeds planted by my AP Environmental Science teacher blossomed into my renewed understanding of this industry. I vividly recall her strutting into our classroom one day, boasting prAna and Patagonia from head to toe. By the end of our class discussion, I envied her intentional attire.

We started things off with a chat on our favorite clothing brands. As environmentalist high school students, many of us admitted to spending most of our fashion budget at Dick's Sporting Goods or Lululemon. Some students, including myself, revealed an interest in Forever 21 and H&M for more affordable options. After answering the question, I looked down at my medium-washed, distressed American Eagle skinny jeans. Simultaneously, my teacher posed the question, "How many gallons of water do you think it takes to make a pair of jeans?" Classmates shrugged and looked to each other for some ounce of insight, but these unspoken exchanges were met by equally blank stares.

"I don't know... ten?" one student guessed.

"Try again," my teacher responded.

"Um, one hundred fifty?" another student proposed.

"Higher."

"Four hundred?" ventured the last brave soul.

With a sympathetic but defeated grin, she finally answered, "Two thousand."

At first, a wave of shock washed over me. Two thousand is a pretty large number, regardless of the context. Two thousand students could fit in my high school. Two thousand ants could cover a distance of about thirty feet. But two thousand gallons? I had no comparison to make this number meaningful; so I took to Google. Surprisingly, two-thousand-gallon water tanks commonly exist on semi-truck beds. An entire semi-truck full of water was required to manufacture a single pair of jeans. Imagining the number of jeans in just one trendy California-inspired teenage clothing store and the amount of water it would take to produce them was too much to handle. I didn't even dare to ponder the water resources needed to fulfill the jean demand throughout America or the world. Besides water usage, denim also depletes human resources. For example, sandblasting practices often used to distress jeans release silica particles into the air and cause lung damage to underpaid workers.[24]

On a quest to purge myself of these water-guzzling, unjust pieces of fabric, I ransacked my closet with a vengeance. My

---

24 Cordelia Hebblethwaite and Anbarasan Ethirajan, "Sandblasted Jeans: Should We Give Up Distressed Denim?" *BBC News*, September 30, 2011.

intent was to clear things that I "didn't want" or "didn't wear" in addition to garments that violated my values of sustainability and green living. During my first go, I emerged with a trash bag full of clothes. As a closet-cleaning enthusiast, this was not terribly atypical; I usually purge twice a year yielding similar outcomes.

A couple weeks later, I decided to reevaluate. Digging through and scrutinizing my closet, I conceived three more full bags of clothing, making a total of four kitchen-sized trash bags within a two-month span. I had no emotional attachment to these piles of fabric that I had barely worn. Nonetheless, their volume was quite staggering.

Catching sight of my haul, my mother asked me, "Where did all these clothes come from?"

To which I sheepishly replied, "My closet."

After donating these mounds of clothes to a local consignment shop, I embarked on an adventure to educate myself on the causes and implications of fashion waste. Initially, I stumbled across an article titled: "One Garbage Truck of Textiles Wasted Every Second."[25] Even the title was grotesque. To contextualize its message, while just reading this paragraph so far, five to seven garbage trucks of textiles have been landfilled or burned somewhere in the world. Reinforcing that concept, a TED Talk by fashion enthusiast Amit Kalra revealed that 85 percent of garment

---

25　"One Garbage Truck of Textiles Wasted Every Second: Report Creates Vision for Change," *Ellen MacArthur Foundation*, November 28, 2017.

waste ends up in landfills every year, averaging about two hundred shirts per person for a total of ten million tons. Kalra also disclosed that the fashion industry trails only the oil and gas sector in globally-polluting industries.[26] These devastating environmental effects correspond with economic implications, with *an estimated $500 billion value lost every year due to clothing that's barely worn and rarely recycled.*[27]

Similar in principle to food waste, fashion waste's volume, cost, and environmental impact are absolutely massive, especially in a global context. So expansive, in fact, that a collaborative campaign by select governments and industries has recently introduced an entirely new economic model for fashion deemed the "New Textiles Economy." This arrangement is made up of collective projects and partnerships with brands such as Stella McCartney and H&M. Motivated by this new model and frustrated by her own industry's trends, Stella McCartney herself preached, "What really excites me about [a new textiles economy] is that it provides solutions to an industry that is incredibly wasteful and harmful to the environment."[28]

Perhaps inclined by this new demand, other luxury fashion brands have stepped up to the plate, including a move by Alessandro Michele, Gucci's creative director. Michele released a series of diary entries on his Instagram

---

26 *TED*, "Amit Kalra: 3 Creative Ways to Fix Fashion's Waste Problem," March 9, 2018, video, 1:28.

27 "One Garbage Truck of Textiles Wasted Every Second: Report Creates Vision for Change," *Ellen MacArthur Foundation*, November 28, 2017.

28 Ibid.

account titled, "Notes from Silence." This pandemic-induced awakening led him to cut Gucci's annual runway appearances from five to two by desegregating menswear and womenswear and getting rid of mid-season shows in an effort to "[purify] the essential by getting rid of the unnecessary."[29]

Michele's artful preach for purification was justified by his evidently eco-centric values, as revealed by another one of his entries, "Our reckless actions have burned the house we live in. We conceived of ourselves as separated from nature, we felt cunning and almighty. We usurped nature, we dominated and wounded it."[30]

Alessandro Michele's change of heart, while noble, is not even close to enough to completely extinguish the twenty billion items of clothing bought by Americans each year. Nor does it negate necessary waste-reduction strategies highlighted by Amit Kalra, such as intentional product design to easily dismantle and recycle materials.[31] Nonetheless, these fledgling steps by industry are a promising start. Taken together, all these baby steps lead to a fertile breeding ground for a wholesome solution to textile trash. Now comes the hard part: putting these promises into action and getting more people on board.

29 Oscar Holland, "Gucci Abandons 'Worn-Out Ritual' of Fashion Seasons as the Industry Looks Inward," *CNN*, Updated May 26, 2020.

30 Ibid.

31 *TED*, "Amit Kalra: 3 Creative Ways to Fix Fashion's Waste Problem," March 9, 2018, video, 3:39.

PLASTIC PIFFLE

The sneaky presence of synthetic material and other waste is not confined to the items we flaunt on our bodies, but instead infiltrates many common household items. Even as an environmentalist, I find myself victim to the disposability of single-use products. For instance, like many twenty-year-old college students, I relish basking in the rich aroma of coffee in the morning. The rhythmic sound of my coffee machine combined with the warm, engulfing beverage make it a comforting start to a calm, relaxed day. I had religiously praised my Keurig machine since the admittedly premature age of ten years old, so when I moved away to college, it was one of the first items I secured for my dorm room. Heart-wrenchingly, this staple of mine concealed hidden evils I only recently become aware of.

One weekend, my brother came home to visit and brought along a container of strange-looking, half-spherical pods labelled "SF Bay." Intrigued, I asked him what the little capsules contained.

"They're compostable coffee pods. You've never heard of them?" he exclaimed.

As his competent, environmentalist sister, I felt a bit ashamed to admit that I had never even contemplated coffee pod waste. Regular pods typically contain a mix of plastic, aluminum, and of course, coffee granules.[32] Due to their mixed-materials and food contamination, most recycling

---

32   Paula Poots, "What Goes Into a Keurig K Cup Pod?" *Expert Advice* (blog), *Office Barista*, December 7, 2017.

facilities do not accept them. SF Bay, on the other hand, is attempting to reduce single-use plastic in these morsels that many of us drink down daily, if not multiple times a day. Since switching to compostable pods (and even more recently old-fashioned coffee beans), I have become much more aware of the amount of plastic I use on a daily basis. Most of the plastic waste I generate is very hard to avoid due to the lack of alternatives to disposable options. From food packaging to personal care, cleaning supplies and shipping material, plastic is omniscient in our current society. Despite this, I aim to reduce my plastic footprint in any way I possibly can. But again, it is not easy.

The popularity of this disposable material is partially explained by the fact that it is derived from fossil fuels. Essentially, plastic is made from crude oil, which is part of an industry run on bottomless investments from governments and multi-national corporations. What's worse is the petrochemical plants running the operations (and the toxic emissions accompanying them) have historically been built in communities of color, manifesting a culture of environmental injustice. Because our society is predominantly fueled by the broken values of oil and gas companies, it has been quite difficult to substitute its use and divest into other sources of energy and material input.

This is especially true given the innovation in plastic surrounding industries such as healthcare, which relies on sanitary single-use tools and machinery to tend to their patients. Given this moral dilemma of whether to prioritize the health of our people or our planet, the responsibility of reducing plastic is turned onto single-use consumerism. Individual purchasers, therefore, have the efficacy and obligation to change their daily habits to mitigate the detriments of plastic on our earth.

At this point, the plastic pandemic is no longer just a people problem. Its impact has transcended the human society and reached into the realm of wildlife and ecosystems all around the world. One such exhibit of plastic's virality can be seen in the stomach of the majestic bird, the Laysan albatross. Amazingly, this species is able to "go years without even touching land, live for more than half a century, and [...] stick with a single mate for their entire lifespan."[33]

While albatross can evade land for years, their encounters with plastic are much more persistent. These black and white Hawaiian fowls mistakenly eat the stuff, deceived by its bright coloration which mimics bait. Chicks are unable to regurgitate the manufactured material, so it sits in their stomachs and makes them feel full.[34] Over time, this causes them to slowly starve and waste away until they meet their long, insufferable death. While performing autopsies on these beautiful creatures, researchers have uncovered a plethora of plastics in their stomachs ranging from bottle caps and cigarette butts to drink lids, straws, and stirrers.[35] The red, green, white, and clear plastic bits are parasitoids that slowly kill their host from the inside. Once they have killed their victim through starvation, they wait in their

---

33 "Laysan Albatrosses' Plastic Problem," Smithsonian Institution, accessed December 22, 2020.

34 Ibid.

35 Ibid.

decomposing bodies to emerge once again and infect yet another host.

Distant tropical birds are simply a proxy for the pervasiveness of plastic waste, which is unpacked in a mockumentary entitled *The Majestic Plastic Bag*.[36] This masterpiece displays a plain old plastic bag as it traverses through city parks, neighborhoods, skyscrapers, and forests "on its migration to its home, the Pacific Ocean."[37]

Images of a Teacup Yorkie nibbling and playing with the bag and night vision sequences demonstrate the scale and longevity of this common household item after its typical single use. After traversing streams and rivers with its "natural buoyancy," the bag makes it to its eternal resting place, the Great Pacific Garbage Patch.[38] This environmental horror scene contains millions of tons of plastic trash and covers an area twice the size of Texas. Dominant currents keep the mound in place as a colossal amoeba-like island in the middle of the Pacific Ocean.

The patch is constantly being fed by the eight million metric tons of plastic which enter the oceans each year, as estimated by the National Oceanic and Atmospheric Administration (NOAA). This mass is equivalent to the weight of about ninety aircraft carriers, only it is made entirely of wispy plastic material of various sizes and weights from the marine surface to

---

36   *HealtheBay*, "The Majestic Plastic Bag—a Mockumentary," August 14, 2010, video, 0:21.

37   Ibid.

38   Ibid.

the sea floor.[39] Sadly, the Great Pacific Garbage Patch is just one of several garbage gyres located in the world's oceans.

This is not to say there have not been massive expenditures to attempt to mitigate these environmental impacts. Clean-up costs in the state of California alone amount to over five hundred million dollars annually.[40] Like an open wound on a hemophiliac, however, the source never seems to stop flowing. The birthplace of plastic spans the homes of billions of people worldwide, as well as their workplaces and institutions. It seems that the very existence of every living being exudes plastic, so much so that one day the Great Pacific Garbage Patch could become its own continent.

Figuratively and literally, the Garbage Patch is only the tip of the iceberg when it comes to the expanse of ocean plastics. As larger pieces begin to break down, they release microplastics which nestle themselves into the furthest nooks and crannies of the aquatic system, from deep ocean trenches to arctic ice cores. A recent *National Geographic* feature describes the venture of a Dallas businessman, Victor Vescovo, to the 35,849-foot-deep Marianas Trench. As a part of his "Five Deeps" expedition to the deepest points of each of Earth's oceans, his four-hour journey led him to an unusually familiar sight: a plastic bag.[41] This confirms findings from a

---

39 National Oceanic and Atmospheric Administration, "A Guide to Plastic in the Ocean," *Hazards* (blog), *National Ocean Service,* updated August 14, 2020.

40 Serena Ingre, "New Report: California Communities Spend Nearly $500m Annually in Keeping Trash Out of Waterways," *Natural Resources Defense Council,* August 28, 2013.

41 Sarah Gibbens, "Plastic Proliferates at the Bottom of World's Deepest Ocean Trench," *National Geographic,* May 13, 2019.

previous *National Geographic* study, which found ingested microplastics in amphipods (crustaceans) in 100 percent of investigated deep-trench sites. Seventeen percent of the plastic documented in these isolated locations was in close interaction with marine life.[42]

Life we haven't even discovered yet has acknowledged human existence by ingesting the very life force of our society: plastic.

Although it may be discouraging to realize that nearly every existing ecosystem has been touched by plastic in one form or another, equally as evident is our ability to reduce these intrusions through human behavior. Undoubtedly, we were the ones who created this mess. According to the Ellen MacArthur Foundation:

> More than forty years after the launch of the first universal recycling symbol, only 14 percent of plastic packaging is collected for recycling. When additional value losses in sorting and reprocessing are factored in, only 5 percent of material value is retained for a subsequent use.[43]

Plus, since losing China as a purchaser of plastic waste in America, that dismal recycling rate has only plunged. But if we, as a species, take a moment (or several) to weigh the ramifications of our daily habits, we have the opportunity to

---

42 Sarah Gibbens and Laura Parker, "Creatures in the Deepest Trenches of the Sea Are Eating Plastic," *National Geographic*, February 28, 2019.

43 Michiel De Smet et al., *The New Plastics Economy: Rethinking the Future of Plastics & Catalysing Action* (Cowes, United Kingdom: Ellen MacArthur Foundation, January 2016), 19.

restore natural ecological processes to at least some degree of normalcy.

We have the capability to release our planet from its plastic body bag.

Simple fixes like using reusable shopping bags and coffee cups can have a great impact in the long term. Not only that, but those changes can be profitable by recapturing the value of all the tiny bits of waste which accumulate on an international scale. Currently, the Ellen MacArthur Foundation has estimated that 120 billion dollars is spent annually on plastic packaging around the world. On top of that, there are eighty billion dollars in externalities, or indirect costs of the industry on the environment.[44] Turning these debts into assets could present an unmatched financial opportunity.

Luckily, numerous geniuses around the world are already on the quest to manifest it.

One such innovator is Boyan Slat, a Dutch engineering student who designed and crafted a two thousand-foot waste collection barge for his organization, the Ocean Cleanup. After a scuba-diving trip in Greece where he saw more plastic bags than fish, he was inclined to invent a ship that could ease the burden. While he discussed in a CBS interview that traditional skimming ships would impose a whopping seventy-nine-thousand year wait time for an ocean clear of the Pacific Garbage Patch, his coastline-shaped infrastructure could collect half the patch using six barges in just five

---

44 Ibid.

years.[45] Slat's invention is definitely a variable that will allow us to address the immediate threat of plastic pollution. It will not, however, medicate our plastic addiction.

MENDING INDIFFERENCE

Making that change is up to individual consumers like you and me in the items we choose to purchase. Much of the failure to address this issue stems from the indifference we have with waste on both a societal and personal level. Undeniably, contributions of infrastructure and regulations by governments are obligatory to enabling our responsible behavior, but by personally educating ourselves first (with the help of the private sector) the use of these institutions will become much more productive.

By confronting and analyzing waste head on, we can begin to lighten our load on the landfill.

Even in situations we may not expect, covert waste is created. For example, washing polyester fabrics in the washing machine sheds microplastics that ultimately end up in our oceans. Even supposing that currently-available technologies, such as filtration systems, could prevent pollution from entering our aquatic environment, many of us are unaware the issue exists in the first place.

Nothing quite awakened me to my personal synapse with waste like a post on my LinkedIn feed that read: "What if

---

45   CBS *This Morning*, "Device Developed by Young Entrepreneur Collecting Pacific Ocean Litter," September 10, 2018, video, 1:12.

every piece of trash you produced this month was not taken away but was dumped back in your front yard?"[46]

Several moments passed as I reread the profound question staring back at me many times over. Sitting in my at-home office, my eyes darted toward my overflowing waste basket brimming with torn notebook paper and bits of tape. Instead of activating defense mode, I allowed myself to submerge into inquiry.

If there wasn't a facility for me to ship my waste to, how much would I be left to sit and deal with? Why had I so easily accepted the sheer volume of trash that I generated on a daily basis?

Shedding light onto this fact, I become hyperaware of my consumptive habits and committed to waste tracking. I have since been very conservative, only filling up my mailbox-sized bin in my office once every six to seven months. By making small, incremental changes to my daily routine, I have diminished the small scraps that ultimately add up over time.

Yet even as an individual aware of the science of compounding and actively choosing to lessen its impact, I still find myself generating trash. In some instances, it seems inescapable. How is one supposed to avoid plastic safety seals or disposable medicine containers?

---

46   Vishnu Vardhaan, "What if every piece of trash you produced this month was not taken away but was dumped back in your front yard?" LinkedIn, June 16, 2020.

Undoubtedly, the hurdles and tactical solutions facing each of the unique sources of waste needs to be analyzed and formulated individually. Fruit peels are not the same as clothing scraps, which are not the same as plastic packaging. What unites them is the fact that these bits of trash are elicited by end use resulting from product design and mindless purchasing. Accordingly, their similar complexities require similar solutions.

While the amount of waste in consumer product industries may seem infinite and demoralizing, a glass-half-full enthusiast such as myself sees these wasted resources as a spawning point for impressive entrepreneurship. We have already seen some of the prospective business-oriented solutions. Whether that be creating flour from the derivatives of plant-based milk, designing clothes that are easily dismantled for recycling, or surrogating compostable coffee pods, the horizon is limitless. Ultimately, we need this relationship between purchaser demand and entrepreneurial innovation to address our compounding of waste. While it will be no easy feat, lessons from the sustainability evolution at large and early steps taken to exalt the circular economy are promising footholds to make this vision a reality.

CHAPTER 2

RECIPE FOR
SUSTAINABILITY

———

Sustainability: A word that has been thrown around so much in recent years you might be caught dead searching for a brand *not* claiming to be "sustainable." Vouching that claim to fame, a recent study of Gen Z participants by Cone Communications showed that 92 percent care about sustainability issues and 89 percent express worry for the overall state of our planet.[47] But underneath all that uninformed usage and alleged concern, what does sustainability actually mean? In sum, it is the premise that our actions today should not compromise the livelihoods of future generations.[48] Traditionally, sustainability has had an environmental undercurrent, coaxing natural resource conservation and protection.

---

47 "Cone Communications Gives Companies a Lesson on How to Speak Gen Z," *Sustainable Brands*, September 12, 2017.

48 Brundtland Commission, Our Common Future: Report of the World Commission on Environment and Development (Oxford: Oxford University Press, 1987), 42.

Nowadays, sustainability has extended to encompass a slew of other important social agendas.

Regardless of sustainability's terminological perplexity, its environmental angle has brimmed the point of trendiness, especially on social media. Despite heavy promotion of fast-fashion and other unnecessary goods on these websites, the number of people posting "#plasticfree" on Instagram has risen to almost three million as of February 2021. The postage count for "#earthday," almost five million.[49] This increased awareness makes sense given the concerning state of our planet. As our world spirals into deeper and deeper devastation; as wildfires and hurricanes seem to be a weekly occurrence; as the number of record-breaking temperatures in recent years is a record in and of itself, people have slowly started to take notice of our planet's sickness. With each passing month, it becomes more and more clear that, as Swedish professor Johan Rockström expressed:

"We have transitioned from being a small world on a big planet, to a big world on a small planet."[50]

---

49   "#Plasticfree," Instagram, accessed February 15, 2021; "#Earthday," Instagram, accessed February 15, 2021.
50   Johan Rockström, Mattias Klum and Peter Miller, *Big World, Small Planet: Abundance Within Planetary Boundaries* (London: Yale University Press, 2015), 12.

BIG WORLD, SMALL PLANET

This ecologically destructive oxymoron (which has piqued interest in sustainability) is driven by a decades-old model, serving as the foundation for our global economic growth. The Kuznets curve, a hump-shaped graph displaying a country's environmental impact along a continuum of economic development, has unintentionally led to a disjunction between the wellbeing of Earth and the affluence of nations residing upon it.[51] As explored in the field of development economics, the theory explains that in the preliminary stages of a nation's economic growth, their environmental impact will also compound. At a certain tipping point, upon attaining a "sufficient" amount of prosperity, the economy begins to utilize its wealth to decrease environmental impact.

Logically and historically, this theory makes sense. How can a country afford state-of-the-art solar panels and carbon-sequestering technology if it can barely afford to feed its population?

But this theory begins to fall apart when you account for the externalities of production and dynamics of the global interface. We are now beginning to realize, for the first time in economic history, that our actions have consequences on the planet. Producing items in a factory releases carbon emissions. Distributing plastic-wrapped goods leads to material pollution. And most importantly, these unintended consequences associated with "developed economies" also incur costs. We have to pay to clean up trash. We have to

---

51   Prateek Agarwal, "The Environmental Kuznets Curve," *Intelligent Economist*, March 1, 2018.

pay to sequester carbon. While these payments are currently voluntary, given our political climate in America, at some point they will become mandatory expenditures.

Which begs the question: Is it really worth it to invest in cheap, unsustainable technology and business now just to inevitably pay mountainous costs later?

A HISTORICAL INTERFACE

This is not a novel or profound question that has only been proposed with the onset of unprecedented technology or social media interchange. In the industrialized western culture, political demands began back in the 1960s with reformists of the environmental movement. Now that the pesky minority of environmentalists have attracted a roaring crowd, these abstract clamors have formulated into concrete steps for implementation. According to Fred Krupp, the president of the Environmental Defense Fund, there are four steps that businesses need to take to advance sustainability:[52]

1. Commit to the sustainable development of their company—publicly.
2. Secure partnerships between businesses in the global supply chain to execute the mission holistically.
3. Advocate for environmental policy objectives in order to promote a broader transition.
4. Invest in and accelerate environmental innovation.

---

52 Fred Krupp, "CEOs Need to Fill the Leadership Void on Climate Policy," *Fortune,* February 21, 2019.

For most companies, that journey ends at step two or maybe even one. However, Interface, one of the world's largest commercial carpeting companies creating America's first free-lay carpet tiles, was a leading force abiding these steps to dignify the sustainable business movement. Despite their establishment as a traditional corporate giant, in 1994 (twenty years into their operations) they were jolted into taking responsibility for their impact due to an epiphany by their founder, Ray Anderson.

Anderson's awakening came as he delved into the literature of Paul Hawken, an environmentalist, entrepreneur, and sensational author. His numerous books, including *Project Drawdown* (discussed earlier), expose the afflictions of our global environment, the instigators creating them, and the solutions to reverse them. *Ecology of Commerce* was his first work emphasizing the apparent controversy between business and the environment. Rather than defensively criticizing Hawken's claims, in a time when "green business" had not yet gained its bearings, Anderson was able to steep and reflect in them—creating what he calls a "spear in the chest" experience. He was forced to look in the mirror to see his own plundering, and he came to accept the fact that his business was partially responsible for the wreckage of our planet.[53]

Immediately, he formed his own "Eco Dream Team" to execute the company's new mission—Mission Zero. This green vision laid out seven initiatives, or "fronts," needed to reach

53   *TED,* "Ray Anderson: The Business Logic of Sustainability," May 18, 2009, video, 1:28.

"Mount Sustainability." Through Mission Zero, Anderson transformed Interface into a cutting-edge design corporation with a mission of "unplundering" the environment using technological modernization.[54] Specifically, his proposals included:

- Eliminate waste
- Benign emissions
- Renewable energy
- Close the loop
- Efficient transport
- Sensitizing stakeholders
- Redesign commerce

In 2000, they made tenacious headway on these goals when they released the first recycled nylon carpet in the industry, with 100 percent recycled vinyl backing. That year they also delivered a used corn-based collection called the Great Plains.[55] Over the fifteen-year period since his demonstrable value shift, step one of Fred Krupp's framework, Interface jumped straight to step four, technological advancement. Interface cut waste by 80 percent while still managing to increase sales by 66 percent. Meanwhile, 175 million pounds of used carpet were diverted from the landfill and 400 million dollars were saved in landfill costs.[56]

---

54   Ibid.

55   "Ray's Life," Ray C. Anderson Foundation, accessed December 23, 2020.

56   Ray Anderson and Robin White, *Confessions of a Radical Industrialist: Profits, People, Purpose: Doing Business by Respecting the Earth* (New York: St. Martin's Press, 2009), 4.

Interface's newfound profit is a "Grade A" example of the benefits of Mission Zero, an admirable reinterpretation of sustainability. Fortunately, their success was not a one-off occurrence, nor a past bubble that has since been popped. Even in the face of the COVID-19 pandemic, green businesses have prevailed. According to JUST Capital, a sustainable business tracking agency, during the first four months of the COVID pandemic, green companies tended to be more resilient, reaping 10 percent higher returns than traditional businesses on average.[57] Clearly, besides the obvious environmental returns, there is a monetary incentive to be sustainable.

To much bewilderment, however, only 24 percent of CEOs believe that climate change is extremely concerning.[58] Apparently the burning forests, drowning shorelines, and disease influx aren't convincing enough to change the way they do business. Whilst my sustainability mentors have observed an increased awareness among investors and venture capitalists around Environmental, Social and Governance (ESG) practices, inaction is still a notable defect transcending the corporate sector.

A study by GlobeScan surveyed twenty-five thousand consumers from across twenty-five countries worldwide. The overwhelming consensus showed that while 54 percent of

---

57   Charlie Mahoney and Steffen Bixby, "Chart of the Week: America's Most Just Companies Are Bouncing Back More Quickly During the Current Recession," *JUST Capital News*, May 21, 2020.

58   Bob E. Moritz et al., 23rd Annual Global CEO Survey: Navigating the Rising Tide of Uncertainty (London, United Kingdom: PwC, 2020), 37.

respondents believed sustainable living was a top priority, only 37 percent of those people actually lived in alignment with their belief.[59]

With such a hefty amount of evidence supporting the shift to sustainability, the question remains: why does this cognitive dissonance still exist? Why haven't we fully committed to emerging our economy away from environmental destruction? And I don't mean taking half-baked tiptoes like carbon offsets or using partially recycled plastics. I mean Interface-level change. I mean *real* change. Change in the *way* we produce and consume things. Change in the *way* we think about businesses' interaction with the environment.

Some will say the incentive is not large enough for big business. Others will say that governments are not doing enough to foster this behavior. Additional critics blame the public who fails to partake in activism forcing businesses to care. While I agree to some extent with each of these statements, the overarching dilemma is the intersection of these three, or rather the fact that they are being treated as mutually exclusive issues. Instead of placing the blame on one particular group, there needs to be cohesive participation from all stakeholders to make this vision a reality. A common goal for green is necessary to do this.

---

59 Eric Whan and Stacy Rowland et al., *Healthy & Sustainable Living: A Global Consumer Insights Report* (Toronto, Canada: GlobeScan, 2019), 5.

CREATING A COMMON VISION

Creating that common vision starts with a thorough comprehension of how sustainability looks in action and what it will take to get there. Currently, there seems to be a lot of confusion and inconsistency on the actual meaning of sustainability, as I alluded to earlier. John Elkington's affair inventing the "triple bottom line" concept, a core theory to the movement, suggests the memo was destined for failure from the get-go. His book, *Cannibals with Forks*, published in 1997, introduced this concept which urged companies to look at their profit, their environmental impact, and the effects on relevant communities when making business decisions.[60] Colloquially, his idea was deemed "People, Planet, and Profit." Elkington's original intent was to curtail the public into thinking about capitalism in a new light. Ideally, green industries could thrive, economic growth could be replaced with environmental regeneration, and a paradigm shift denoting businesses as a force for good would ensue. Rather than demolishing the profit-driven motive of business, Elkington unknowingly enhanced it and turned sustainability into a branding opportunity.

Many unsustainable enterprises have since claimed to be "sustainable" or "green" to reap patronage without putting in the work to create real, lasting change. For example, Tide's "plant-based detergent" actually contains around 25 percent petroleum-based ingredients.[61] The Body Shop, while it heavily advertises its botanically-based products, also uses

---

60 John Elkington, Cannibals With Forks: Triple Bottom Line of 21st Century Business (Oxford: Capstone Publishing Ltd, 1997).

61 "Tide Clean," TruthinAdvertising Blog, TruthinAdvertising.org, September 16, 2020.

synthetic, petroleum-derived fragrances and preservatives.[62] Tide, the Body Shop, and so many other companies have perpetuated a culture of greenwashing, or "fabricated sustainability," which takes away from the companies doing meaningful work. These include companies like PUR Home (who fully committed to a sustainable future for detergents after eighteen months of research and development by their founder) or BLK + GRN (who omits petroleum, synthetic fragrances, parabens, phthalates, triclosan, and a host of other nasty chemicals).[63]

So why are truly green companies like PUR Home and BLK + GRN being neglected? Perhaps part of this stems from the fact that these are both BIPOC-owned companies. On top of that, the dusty haze surrounding industry and standards of sustainability inhibits their recognition. As clientele have pushed for more sustainability, some companies have felt no choice but to project a fantasized version of their environmental valuation. To "undo" this, we need to acclaim actionable solutions for our planet rather than exasperated mission statements and drawn-out intentions.

How can this be done?

One incentivizing measure could be tax programs for truly sustainable companies or more strictly enforced certification schemes. A few obstacles come with these programs. First,

---

62   Diane Small, "5 Brands You Think Are Eco Friendly... but Really Aren't," *Eluxe Magazine,* November 15, 2019.

63   Candice Georgiadis, "Angela Richardson of Pur Home: 5 Things I Wish Someone Told Me before I Became a CEO," *Authority Magazine,* January 18, 2021; "Toxic Twenty List," BLK + GRN, accessed February 4, 2021

the definition of sustainability, as we have seen, is constantly contested. Because "sustainability" encompasses so many priorities and agendas, even beyond Interface's seven fronts to Mount Sustainability, a single certification scheme for consumer goods could be an impossible undertaking.

Additionally, practices that one aspect of the scientific community sees as sustainable may be deemed environmentally harmful by another group. Solar panels are a wonderful example of this. Whilst they detract from the toxic fossil fuel industry, solar panels have a limited lifetime after which they must be replaced, creating material waste and toxic pollutants such as cadmium.[64] Even if these differences were hashed out to a cohesive certification scheme, similar to the Leadership in Energy and Environmental Design (LEED) green building model, there would still be regulatory trammel to ensure businesses claiming to meet these criteria were in fact doing enough for the planet.[65]

DECLUTTERING WITH ZERO-WASTE

Luckily, a more transparent solution to greenwashing hypocrisy exists: zero-waste. As previously mentioned, the Zero Waste International Alliance defines zero-waste as:

The conservation of all resources by means of responsible production, consumption, reuse, and recovery

---

64 Michael Schellenberger, "If Solar Panels Are So Clean, Why Do They Produce So Much Toxic Waste?" *Forbes*, May 23, 2018.

65 "LEED Rating System," United States Green Building Council, accessed February 10, 2021.

of products, packaging, and materials without burning and with no discharges to land, water, or air that threaten the environment or human health.[66]

This comprehensive definition leaves little room for interpretation but also gives some insight into how to achieve this goal.

Let's break it down.

The basis of zero-waste is to conserve resources. With this, it is not only seen as an end-of-the-line strategy, it must be consciously assumed throughout all stages including the "production, consumption, reuse, and recovery."[67] This includes low-waste design, take-back programs, use of recyclable and compostable alternatives, and several other protocols to prevent byproduct from entering our landfills.

According to presentations I attended at the National Zero Waste Conference, the most important component of maintaining a zero-waste business is having an all-in approach.[68] Without everyone involved in the process being in full support of the mission, the leap is near impossible. Because many zero-waste businesses today are entangled with environmental conservation, this is not necessarily an issue. But as more and more brands accept their duty of reducing waste, it is important to keep in mind this company culture. Having

---

66 "Zero Waste Definition," Zero Waste International Alliance, last modified December 20, 2018.

67 Ibid.

68 Mandi McKay, "Building a Circular Economy with Zero Waste Businesses" (panel, 2020 National Zero Waste Conference, December 1, 2020).

complete buy-in is not only essential in house for things like metric tracking and source sorting, but it also builds the integral relationship with sentient, green consumers.

This collaborative methodology covers the bases that "sustainability" lacks. Zero-waste can't be achieved just by designating a single team member as "Sustainability Officer." It requires the whole team, from CEO to foreman, from producers to users, to make things happen.

Take Ray Anderson's "Eco Dream Team" as a prime example.[69] Interface's first company-wide strategy in achieving Mission Zero was eliminating waste. Considering their success in "People, Planet, and Profit," we should view their work as a model of lasting, sustainable change. Since eliminating waste is much more actionable in a business sense, it can also be quite a large task. Overnight, it is impossible to cut all production waste and effectuate waste-free design. This is not the intent of the movement, and in fact it took Interface over fifteen years to completely reform as a company.

As overwhelming and foreign as this transition may seem, the priority of waste reduction has been long in the making. Excessive waste is essentially a twenty-first century problem.[70] Even in the early 1900s, our economic and social frameworks did not tolerate it. Excess threads were turned into new fabric, and food scraps were turned into compost for home gardens. Following World War II, units that were

---

69 Ray C. Anderson Foundation, "Ray's Life."
70 *Ray Grunders*, "Zero Waste in Business: Documentary on Business and Environmental Waste (Full Documentary)," January 15, 2016, video, 1:40.

once personally delivered by the milkman in glass containers became mass-produced in plastic bottles. At the same time, our obsession with consumption caused disposable options to be favored to durable ones.

If we can progress back to the sustainable connections developed with the milkman model utilizing modern technology, zero-waste is within our reach.[71]

THE REGULATORY STRUGGLE

To enhance the private sector's shift toward a zero-waste model, governmental intervention is also an important contribution. Over the past few decades, there have been numerous legislative attempts to curb toxic waste, which outline a reputable structure for mandating waste reduction in the business setting. For example, the Resources Conservation and Recovery Act (RCRA) regulates the disposal of hazardous waste and sets landfill standards for municipal waste sources, and the Comprehensive Environmental Response, Compensation, and Liability Act (CERCLA) identifies hazardous waste clean-up sites for responsible parties to remediate. Both these federal regulations demonstrate attempts to protect human health and the environment from industrial disposal. While they largely concentrate on the relatively small segment of hazardous waste, these statutes are a step in the right direction of providing administrative control over waste management.

---

71   Sean Fleming, "Here's How One Company Is Championing the Circular Economy," *World Economic Forum Agenda*, February 25, 2020.

Taken by themselves, though, these US laws fail to deliver incentives for sustained waste reduction on an individual basis. For example, in most cases the only incentive for bringing reusable cups to a coffee shop is a good conscience. There may be small discounts for continued practice of these green actions, but for many short-sighted guests they are too small to instill habitual change.

To recoup America's lack of action, multinational bodies such as the World Economic Forum, Zero Waste International Alliance, and Ellen MacArthur Foundation have accelerated advocacy. The European Commission has even made a Circular Economy Action Plan to increase our world's circularity beyond its current 8.6 percent. Its tactics include redesigning more energy-efficient alternatives, shifting to product-as-a-service models, setting up take-back schemes, repurposing waste, and encouraging the use of renewable materials.[72] Additionally, the United Nations devised a compilation of Sustainable Development Goals (SDGs) to guide international growth. The twelfth goal on the SDG list, "Responsible Production and Consumption," pinpoints the reduction of waste through evolution to a circular economy. From an administrative standpoint, the undertaking is just starting to turn heads.

The large political brush strokes at this point are not much more than words on a page.

---

72 Carolina Schmidt et al., The Circularity Gap Report 2020 (Amsterdam, Noord-Holland: Circle Economy, 2020), 15.

Summarily, they enact lofty national or international targets without the clearest actions to reach them. Thus, standards and certifications have become fundamental guidance tools. One of the most prominent, TRUE Zero Waste certifications, was acquired by the Green Building Certification Institute (GCBI) and is based off the LEED model. As I discovered from interviewing one of their representatives, Stephanie Barger, TRUE was instated to rank resource-use efficiency for signatories. Their evaluations don't bank on large financial investment, though; eligible companies are only explicitly required to achieve 90 percent or more waste diversion from landfill and incineration, likely into a cycle of reuse, recycling, composting, or other forms of recovery.[73] In that way, waste reduction can take many forms, from centralized recycling to devising takeback schemes.

The benefit of engaging businesses in such a maneuver has become increasingly apparent. Many major companies such as Colgate and Microsoft have already made impressive progress, with Colgate achieving TRUE Zero Waste in Latin America, mainland Europe, India, China, and Vietnam. Being integrated internationally, with increased subjugation to environmental policies and values around the world, it makes sense that these globally focused organizations are taking the first steps toward zero-waste. Other reporting agencies such as the Global Reporting Initiative (GRI) and Sustainability Accounting Standards Board (SASB) have also conceived waste standards and reporting to further expand the operation.

---

73 "TRUE Program for Zero Waste Certification," TRUE Zero Waste, accessed February 10, 2021.

Albeit select companies have demonstrated their drive and ingenuity in tackling these certifications, they are not mandatory by any means. Given the extremity of our circumstances, with the volume of our nation's annual trash output equivalent to fifty times the distance to the moon, it is preposterous that more is not required.[74] In this complex circumstance, without harsh guidelines by higher ups, the power of business—the interaction between suppliers and demanders—comes center stage.

Together, we, as responsible producers and consumers, can authorize more companies to go beyond the bare minimum and create long-lasting TRUE greenness.

AN ECONOMIC ECLIPSE

How do we do this?

Well, it's no secret that businesses function to make money. Fortunately, the zero-waste initiative is also a huge penny pincher, so by advertising the economics we can begin a snowball effect. To calculate these savings, though, we must evaluate the holistic costs of a product as a baseline. By simply comparing the retail price of a traditional good versus its zero-waste counterpart, the zero-waste option may actually impose a higher short-term expense, but when looking at the longevity of less wasteful alternatives and the lessened costs to the environment, this swap becomes abundantly logical.

---

74   "Land of Waste: American Landfills and Waste Production," SaveOn-Energy, accessed December 23, 2020.

The father of this cost-oriented analysis is a man by the name of William McDonough, in his book *Cradle to Cradle: Remaking the Way We Make Things.*[75]

Nowadays, "Cradle to Cradle" is common vernacular in sustainability conversations, symbolizing the responsibility of producers to quantify their environmental impact from manufacturing of the virgin material through disposal to remanufacturing of the captured waste. If companies own responsibility for the "after-life" of their products, they will naturally begin to manufacture in a way that is less polluting and detrimental to nature.

An economic tool called "Life-Cycle Analysis" has been derived to weigh the internal and external costs of every stage of a product's lifecycle. Bearing in mind the carcinogenic and other effects of product breakdown on human and environmental health, among other impacts, the costs of industry have become much more than just its receipt value.

For example, in a recent scientific article from Environmental Deterioration and Human Health, it was found that about 40 percent of textile dyes contain organically-bound chlorine, which is a known human carcinogen.[76] When effluent from textile manufacturing then enters drinking water sources, it can have huge impacts on the value of human life. So, if

---

75   William McDonough and Michael Braungart, *Cradle to Cradle: Remaking the Way We Make Things* (New York: Farrar, Straus and Giroux, 2002), 6.

76   Sana Khan and Abdul Malik, "Environmental and Health Effects of Textile Industry Wastewater," *Environmental Deterioration and Human Health*, (December 8, 2013): 55-71.

fashion labels were to take responsibility for these human health costs caused by their manufacturing, it would incentivize them to reduce waste and other harmful effects.

McDonough not only sheds light on the costs of waste ignorance, but he also explores trash's regenerative properties which can be utilized to a company's advantage:

"A tree produces thousands of blossoms in order to create another tree, yet we do not consider its abundance wasteful but safe, beautiful, and highly effective."[77]

Essentially, by treating waste as the asset it is, innovative new products and ideas can blossom to boost our economy. The reuse of trash is a beautiful artform and recycling should be viewed as a beginning rather than an end. This perspective loops perfectly into the novel concept of the circular economy. Defined by the Ellen MacArthur Foundation through three tenets, the circular economy is a new-age economic model which runs by:

- Designing out waste and pollution;
- Keeping products and materials in use; and
- Regenerating natural systems.[78]

---

77 McDonough, *Cradle to Cradle*, 92.
78 "What Is a Circular Economy?" Ellen MacArthur Foundation, accessed December 23, 2020.

A continuous cycling of resources in manufacturing and packaging prevents waste at the outset. The manifestation of this system comes through recycling programs, intentional design, reuse models, and durability. It does not hamper our economic growth. Instead, it enhances it by boosting technological revolution and building interdependence.

Communication between stakeholders is a critical component of this form of organization, analogous to zero-waste. Private businesses are motivated to maximize technological innovation to maintain a shared understanding. Individual consumers are roped in by voting with their dollar to support circularity. Their fit in this model is a keystone piece of the puzzle, because even if companies were to boycott producing disposable goods or espouse dematerialized models, the expenditures are futile if correspondents don't buy.

Without prospective input in circular proposals, there is a missing link in the chain.

It is precisely this coaction between responsible production and consumption, outlined by the Sustainable Development Goals, which can be utilized to fuel the circular economy. Despite growing momentum, the world is still only 8.6 percent circular. According to a Circle Economy report, our global resource use has exceeded 100 billion tons annually. By 2050, without our help, that number will surpass 184 billion tons. A transition to a circular economy, on the other hand, could bring in $4.5 trillion dollars in profit while simultaneously freeing our economy from unsustainable resource dependence.[79]

Clearly, our society is ripe and desperate for nurturing this conversion. The general culture of sustainability is reaching a fever pitch. Greenwashing is becoming rampant, indicating the need for transparent environmental change. Resource use is maxing out at unsustainable levels. Recent thought leaders and economists have laid out reliable tools and models to trailblaze a successful upheaval. It seems all the cards are in order to make real, untainted change. So, what exactly is holding people back?

---

79 Carolina Schmidt et al., *The Circularity Gap Report 2020* (Amsterdam, Noord-Holland: Circle Economy, 2020), 15.

CHAPTER 3

THE PURCHASER'S DILEMMA

A cliff-laden, pumice-lined cave by a sea of glistening aqua water and ragged volcanic stalagmites. A slightly salty breeze and blistering sunshine. A stone-encrusted throne crafted from cave walls and a posse of dolphins at my side. This was my childhood realm; my happy place. Nobody else ever laid eyes on this imaginary world, but whenever I drifted off into trance or sashayed away to dance and play, this is where I would end up.

It's strange looking back. I could vividly picture this fantasy that quite literally absorbed my life. As endearing as it may be as a child, most of us would reckon it inappropriate and concerning to languish in such a mental realm into adulthood. Surprisingly, though, these dreamt-up versions of reality are the basis of a lot of societal change. The momentous modifications necessary to realize a zero-waste economy often lead us to a fantasy realm of euphoric environmentalism. This matter of thinking may dangerously cause us to hypothesize ideas and possibilities endlessly without physical adaptation.

POPPING THE GREEN BUBBLE

Despite recognizing this hazard, I continue to concentrate my wishful thinking into what is referred to as the "green bubble," an ideological realm where environmentalists exchange ideas. I was first introduced to the bubble whilst interviewing one of my close mentors, sustainability director Patty Lloyd. At first, I didn't quite understand what she meant by this foreign terminology. But as she elaborated, I came to grasp the green bubble as an intellectual faction sharing novelties in sustainability and general environmental issues. To outsiders, a peer into the conversations and ongoings of the bubble might seem incomprehensible.

Before our conversation, I was aware of this exclusivity, but I had only previously understood it from an outsider perspective. I would think to myself:

Those activists and sustainability professionals are so competent and well connected.

Decisively, I discredited my own knowledge and experience, and instead relied upon the royalty of this bubble for environmental advice and expertise. While getting the opinion of others (especially competent, well-researched others) is almost never a bad idea, I developed an unhealthy "me versus them" mindset, which depleted my self-confidence and disconnected me from my passion. I never felt brave enough to make myself a part of this clique and develop my own insights. That is until Lloyd, who has been a front-running woman in the sustainability industry for the past few decades, made me realize that I have valid insight when it comes to zero-waste. I can help make the green bubble bigger by inviting more people into the conversation, and I can help nudge on-the-fence environmentalists into full-fledged contributors to a sustainable future.

While my awakening made me feel confident, it also gave me a sense of discomfort. If I, a third-year environmental studies student with hours upon hours of research into waste management, still felt wary about my ability to promulgate zero-waste, how on earth would my potentially unfamiliar readers feel? Presumably, they would not be fierce activists right out of the gate, and not everyone has the time or motivation to research themselves into subject matter experts on the circular economy. Not everyone identifies with a community to distribute relevant information and effectual solutions. This insinuates a recipe for disaster for newbies intimidated by the extremities of zero-waste.

ONE STEP AT A TIME

When anyone hears the term "zero," automatic discouragement inevitably follows. Think about the treadmill of failed dietary fads that have captured our culture the past few decades. Telling yourself you can have "zero sugar," "zero carbs," or "zero fat" concludes in an unhealthy, pointless cycle of restricting and indulging. Registered dietitians Rachel Kleinman and Mary Condon, from the University of Chicago, denounce diets like keto (a zero-carb diet) as unsustainable and weight-compounding in the long term.[80] Perhaps we can apply these human health lessons to the health of our economy and planet. Perhaps this stigma around "zero" is another fundamental reason for the maintenance of our consumerist society. People feel discouraged by the fact they need to give up something major that used to constitute such normalcy in their daily lives, especially without a clear direction or series of steps to follow in order to achieve their end goal. They turn it into a non-existent "all or nothing" scenario.

Surely, the zero-waste migration requires dramatic shifts in our habits. Without making changes, no advancements can be made in any situation. That is not to say, however, that zero-waste is a one-size-fits-all, instantly-turn-your-world-upside-down maneuver. Rather, the intent is to modify existing institutions, behaviors, and habits to become less waste-dependent over time, which could lead to more dramatic improvements in the future. What we need are "imperfect environmentalists." That being said, in the early stages of progress, awareness deficiencies and societal infrastructure can cause some bumps in the road.

I have witnessed these difficulties first-hand as I tried to transition my family to be more conscious with recycling. This journey was an uphill-both-ways sort of project for my family, who did not even own a recycling bin before my intervention. My mom is a daily grocery store shopper with an entire closet-full of plastic shopping bags. My dad, while he tends to shop in bulk, is a department store fiend with a tendency

---

80   Natalie Helms, "Ketogenic Diet: What Are the Risks?" *UChicago Medicine*, June 20, 2019.

to update his wardrobe on a more-than-consistent basis. Needless to say, neither of these households were sustainable models in any respect and, before proposing my concerns, had no intent to change their behaviors. Fortunately, they were also both open to listening to my upward generational influence educating them on waste.

As their environmentalist daughter, I began to inform them of the consequences of their actions. I had a discussion with my mom about the repercussions of placing greasy pizza boxes in the recycling bin that I had sneakily installed despite her hesitation. My dad, with whom I took a more subtle approach, learned about the horrors of take-out food service through my refusal of plastic cutlery and straws and inclination for dining in. These inceptive steps were mandatory to creating behavior change for my family members, but (especially in my mom's case) it left a sense of inadequacy as they were left to sit with their guilt and try to formulate solutions to shift their habits. Following trips to the grocery store where plastic bags snuck their way in, my mom would turn to me with a hopeless sigh, "I know, I forgot the bags again."

Luckily, I directed them toward sustainable behavior and responsible waste management. For example, I proposed a plan for my mom to use reusable grocery bags and return them to her car after unloading so she wouldn't forget them. I also gifted my dad a set of reusable food lids to cover bowls and containers in lieu of plastic wrap. Paving these pathways in the lives of my loved ones gave me unimaginable joy and fulfillment, which I hope to draw out through more interventions in the future.

But not everyone has an environmentalist daughter—or sister, cousin, friend, schoolmate or coworker—to educate them on the urgency of the situation and the small habit changes that can reverse its destructive effects. Complete ignorance and inaction infect those who never cross paths with the magnitude of the problem. When I went to a Hawaiian island called Molokai over one summer, I faced the ramifications of consumer incompetency head on.

As I was tasked with mulching paths on my friend's property with compostable material from the waste processing facility, I scouted plastic wrappers of all shapes and sizes. Buried underneath heaps of shredded wood and grass lay aluminum cans and old clothing. From one angle, this careless sorting is a despicable defiance of civic responsibility. More realistically, these inefficiencies stem from gaps in individual knowledge of proper disposal. It's no shameful matter that novices on the subject matter go into a state of manic confusion. Even aspiring sustainability professionals such as myself encounter difficulty and uncertainty when trying to reduce personal waste. This knowledge disparity can then translate to a negligence of waste reduction in the commercial sector because, ultimately, people run business.

THE ROAD LESS TRAVELLED

Patty Lloyd, my previously mentioned mentor, is a sustainability director at a construction contractor in the Chicagoland area. Construction is one of the most waste-intensive industries, largely because demolition projects leave tons of cement, drywall, and planks that often end up in the landfill. In fact, Lloyd revealed to me that in Chicago, 25 percent of the waste sent to landfill comes from demolition projects. The precision needed to design sturdy and reliable infrastructure also inevitably offshoots scrap material that gets left out of the recycling and reuse cycle.

Compared to other areas of the country without ordinances or recycling infrastructure, Chicago is actually a leader in construction and demolition debris recycling. Nonetheless, these sources of waste nationally equate to more than double the amount of cumulative household waste according to the EPA.[81] In other words, the tearing down of buildings creates substantially more waste than the combined sources we as individuals generate from our Amazon purchases, refrigerator tosses, fashion waste, and all other sources (which I hope you know by now is a lot). On top of the material waste, other resources such as energy, water, and ambient air impacts from diesel-fueled equipment are major concerns that increase the environmental footprint of construction.

Being a sustainability professional in a field so synonymous with resource exploitation has understandably presented its frustrations and dilemmas. Proposing ideas to invoke new construction recycling programs or other initiatives around healthy, sustainable materials has often been met with limited enthusiasm. Resistance from the industry at large comes from the fact that intensive waste management and circularity are extremely new concepts in the context of business—especially construction. Recently, there have

---

81 US Department of the Interior, Environmental Protection Agency, *Advancing Sustainable Materials Management: 2017 Facts and Figures (2019)* (Washington D.C., November 2019), 19.

been ambitions such as All for Reuse, an organization which accumulates excess construction materials to resell for new uses.[82] This and other programs in their early stages of operation have still yet to gain publicity and acceptance. Without an extensive knowledge base of successful construction groups who rendered this approach or infrastructure to enhance materials reuse, hesitation surrounds the construction industry. In this way, industry and individuals face similar difficulties preventing them from validating circularity.

Just as companies will maintain their business as usual without a spearheading example in industry, passive patrons without a connector to sustainability are left up to the constructs of society to guide their actions. If there is no recycling collection service in a municipality, the citizens are almost certain to toss these items in the trash. If plastic bags are given for free in grocery stores, shoppers will take advantage of the fact they don't have to contribute their own carrying devices.

These infrastructure concerns are not only present in rural or less privileged areas, but even the progressive grounds of college campuses. On my campus, there has been some headway in programs like plastic bag recycling and waste transfer station tours. For reasons unclear, the publicity and use of these programs is extremely underwhelming, and most students are oblivious to their existence. As a consequence, our diversion rate of municipal solid waste was around half of our

---

82   "All for Reuse Vision," All for Reuse, accessed February 10, 2021.

45 percent target for 2020.[83] Evidently, recycling campaigns and other programs on a campus-wide spectrum have been ineffective. Perhaps this stems from the fact that students and community members are blissfully unaware of the monstrosity of the problem—let alone how to toss their recyclables.

Engaging, educational student activities for waste reduction have been successful mechanisms to stimulate change. For example, Enactus, a student organization I am involved in, vitalizes circular ideation through projects such as soap made of leftover coffee grounds and glass upcycling. Enactus, which stands for Entrepreneurial Action and Us, is a non-profit entity aiming to spawn a generation of social entrepreneurs through local projects that eventually de-link to become independently run by the community. Student members have accumulated knowledge and taken action in their own lives by becoming involved first-hand with the process of addressing waste. One of my fellow members of this organization commits to religiously composting in her apartment despite a lack of infrastructure in her city. Hence, experiential learning has enforced a sustainable culture among students.

Besides the opportunities and enthusiasm college communities supply, the peer-to-peer impact expedites revolution toward sustainable behaviors. Emulating fellow peers who are striving for similar goals makes these lifestyle transformations much more meaningful and attainable. Ultimately, these educational relationships can start a ricochet effect of

---

83 "MSW Diversion Rate," Institute for Sustainability, Energy, and Environment, accessed December 22, 2020.

habit change and increase participation in existing waste-reducing infrastructure. But how can we mimic this same experience for the rest of the population—without access to the resources of a college campus?

HEDGING WITH EDUCATION

Clearly, many roadblocks exist. Most importantly, on a scale greater than that of campus communities, a general lack of awareness coupled with cracks in societal constructs has maintained irresponsible consumerism and trash compounding. The intimidation of statistics and condescending experts have only hampered progress. Could you imagine reading about human-caused microplastics in American rainfall and trying to cope without prior knowledge?[84] Many social media users face this overwhelming ordeal reading through their feeds festered with environmental woes and bereft of concrete solutions.

By educating broader communities on the circular economy, successful zero-waste intervention can occur outside of the green bubble. For Patty Lloyd, her children's acceptance demonstrated a mountain of hope for upcoming generations. Their upbringing in a home that preached composting and buying second-hand made waste reduction behaviors a normal part of their daily lives. Rather than seeing these habits as intrusions or inconveniences, they have become second nature. Today, they deliberately process their purchasing decisions and esteem thrifting platforms like Poshmark a

---

84 Jacob Duer, "The Plastic Pandemic Is Only Getting Worse during COVID-19," *World Economic Forum: Agenda*, July 1, 2020.

first order of business. Their sports gear hauls come from Play It Again Sports, where rather than paying absurd prices for designer "athleisure" wear, they can obtain more affordable pieces and sell them back when they are done to keep the cycle going. The Lloyd boys were reared in a home that invited sustainable behaviors, but this is obviously not the case for everyone. Most households in America are not keen on protecting the environment, which is why we are in this conundrum in the first place.

LESSONS FROM BUSINESS

Utilizing business as an avenue to fortify this outlook can be enormously constructive for those crowds, especially with the emergence of values-based purchasing decisions of young people. B-corporations, also called "benefit corporations," are companies who specialize in this idea of "business as a force for good." Many certified B Corps have sustainability at the forefront of their operations, whether that be for the planet or the stakeholders involved. Some of these include Ben & Jerry's, Klean Kanteen, and Eileen Fisher. Advertisements for these companies are often soundbites of education. For example, one Klean Kanteen ad displayed a simple white background with bold black font reading, *Americans trash 160 million to-go cups everyday #BringYourOwn*.[85] Eileen Fisher has used taglines such as, *REconsider the lifecycle of your clothes* and *wear blue, think green*.[86] Customers of these

---

85 "Klean Kanteen: Bring Your Own," Stephanie Sizemore, accessed February 10, 2021.
86 "Marketing," Librett Creative, accessed February 10, 2021.

brands are not just purchasing items themselves—they are purchasing the values and education behind them.

Given the significance of business in our daily lives and the failure of regulatory mandates, business should be deemed the launch point moving forward.

Surely with time, the confluence of governments and civil society groups will be fundamental additions, but to get things off the ground and pique education and engagement, business is a core pawn. Using this institution, which is already so entangled with our capitalistic society, as a platform for education is a brilliant solution to our environmental problems. This information can go directly to consumers by the traditional culprits of resource exploitation themselves.

Public education of the economic benefits of more durable, circular alternatives is necessary. Once the financial benefits are recognized, this environmental development will fall into place. Money is a muscle that needn't be exercised to be leveraged. Any reasonable individual will make decisions that reduce the stress on their bank account. Whether that be through purchasing less or investing in circular options, learning about the economic advantages of this passage can induce individuals to vote with their dollar without the need for an active burst into the green bubble.

On the opposing front, businesses themselves could also capitalize on this behavior to earn profits. Unlike the fallacy of greenwashing tyrants, true proponents and participants in the circular economy have accountability from diverse partners to ensure their claims are not all talk. Nike, for example, has reduced their need for virgin rubber inputs through their Reuse-A-Shoe program, which recaptures rubber from old shoes brought in by customers.[87] Old sneakers are returned to the manufacturer, taken apart, and revamped in the manufacturing of new designs. They transform the rubber, foam, fiber, leather, and textile grains into a material they call "Nike Grind." This mixture is so durable, it can not only be "incorporated into performance products ranging from new Nike footwear and apparel, [but also to] sports and play surfaces."[88]

Nike Grind and other existing pilots have demonstrated the long-term financial benefits of a circular, waste-free enterprise, which can be a strong motivation for more resistant audiences. Many of those rebels come from older generations without much time left to deal with the consequences of their actions or middle-aged demographics who grew up without a concern for the planet.

That time for concern is now upon us. Especially in the wake of the COVID-19 pandemic, the fragility of wasteful product markets in comparison to the adaptability and strength of service-focused, sustainable businesses has come to light.[89] By educating society on these benefits, we can motivate entrepreneurship and responsible purchasing.

---

87 "What Is Nike's Reuse-A-Shoe Program?" Nike, accessed December 23, 2020.

88 "Nike Grind: A Legacy of Innovation," Nike, accessed December 23, 2020.

89 Piergiuseppe Fortunato, "How COVID-19 Is Changing Global Value Chains," *United Nations Conference on Trade and Development News*, September 2, 2020.

Tactical development is possible if we choose to acknowledge the challenges of zero-waste and preemptively target them.

The fact of the matter is the massive amounts of food waste coming from the household are not going to magically disappear due to acknowledgment confined to the activist circle. Garbage trucks full of unwanted clothing can't be dumped out of existence if individuals keep textile trash out of mind. Single-use plastics will continue to traverse our waterways until concrete, informed steps are taken to prevent them. To transform sustainable anomalies into new normalities, we need widespread awareness and knowledge of simple, actionable solutions. The way to distribute this, most beneficially, is through a systematic mobilization of business.

PHASE TWO

PENUMBRAL BUSINESS STRATEGY

*Penumbra: "a space of partial illumination
(as in an eclipse) between the perfect
shadow on all sides and the full light."*

MERRIAM-WEBSTER

CHAPTER 4

DESIGN

CHANNELING COPERNICUS AND CURIE

"Once designed, it's hard to reverse: 'We can't unscramble an omelette.'"

~ELLEN MACARTHUR FOUNDATION

Many a time I have found myself sitting at a cafe with friends from college discussing our roses and thorns of the week. Listening to some of my engineering friends fret about coding and computer science has left me with an unsettling regret on more than one occasion.

Was I missing out by not taking this constitutional course? If not in school, why had I not taken it upon myself to learn this sort of technology in my free time? I spend enough hours sitting in front of my computer anyway. It would only make sense.

Oh yeah, that's right. Because it's computer science, something I have absolutely no background in, not to mention it is one of the most competitive and difficult majors on my college campus. Getting started on this venture is not particularly intriguing to me either. All the foreign acronyms, programs, and acumen, from my perspective, seem out of reach. Even if I did have the urge to become a computer science whiz, my incompetency would surely stunt my progress.

Fortunately, research has proven otherwise. "The First 20 Hours—How to Learn Anything" is a TED Talk by number one best-selling author Josh Kaufman detailing the astounding capacity of the human brain.[90] Clearly, human intellect is a distinguishing factor between us and other organisms, but in the hectic motions of daily life it can be easy to forget just how capable our minds truly are. So capable, in fact, that we can learn just about any skill in twenty hours of practice. Do you want to learn how to speak French? Bake a perfect macaron? Play the saxophone? Setting aside just twenty hours will allow you to progress steadfastly toward these aspirations.

Although I most likely won't apply this boat of confidence to my shortcomings in computer science, the learning capabilities we inherit as humans nonetheless demonstrate our staggering capacity to adapt to new, unknown scenarios by relying on science. Even in the face of uncertainty, humans can adjust themselves and respond in a way that is efficient and logical.

---

90   *TED,* "Josh Kaufman: The First 20 Hours—How to Learn Anything," March 14, 2013, video, 9:35.

In his talk, Kaufman discussed the free time he lost after having a child, which ate away at his capacity to learn new things. This is quite a common dilemma faced by new parents, especially entrepreneurs with an entirely other "child" to take care of. As a tool to combat this time crunch, Kaufman described a simple procedure he used to concentrate his energy for efficient learning:

1. Deconstruct the skill;
2. Learn enough to self-correct;
3. Remove barriers that prevent practice of the skill; and
4. Commit from the start to set aside twenty hours.[91]

This four-step process can be applied to many scenarios besides baking or coding. Since we urgently need to transition to a circular economy, we should employ any procedure which can get us there faster, including Kaufman's methodology. For example, if you were to follow this sequence in attempting to go zero-waste, the shift could be much more manageable. Your Kaufman strategy may go something like:

1. Identify different areas of your life where you can reduce your waste. Auditing your trash contents for a week is a great way to get started.
2. Do some research on zero-waste bloggers, activists, and businesses in your area who can teach you about specific tactics to use in your local region.
3. Stop purchasing single-use items and invest in reusable alternatives where possible. Make sure your friends and

---

91   Ibid.

family are aware of your lifestyle change so that they can support you in any way possible.

4. Commit to going at least twenty hours (or maybe even twenty days) without using plastic as a way to get your feet wet and fuel your long-term motivation.

While individuals may feel overwhelmed by completely changing their ways of consumption and production, our species has the capability of overcoming it with a bit of brain-power and systems-based analysis. The Industrial Revolution is evidence of this. Prior to the late 1700s, horses and carts were the main form of transportation, and primitive looms defined the textile industry. Within just a few short decades, with the invention of the steam engine and other spearheading technology, a complete economic eclipse transpired.[92] The foundation and function of business was metamorphosed. From farms to factories, blue collar workers were thrust into a foreign habitat of business with a new way of designing and distributing their products. They had to think on a larger, more technological scale and revise their processes to accommodate their new clientele.

This is kindred to the proposed undertaking of circularity. Stakeholders in the production system, notably designers, are being called upon to base their assessments on an even larger scale—one that transcends humanity and encompasses our environment. Tools such as "Life-Cycle Analysis" promote this thoughtful design. New technology and apparatuses based upon these standards intend to draw in

---

92 History.com Editors, "Industrial Revolution," *History*, updated September 9, 2019.

fervent purchasers during the early stages of action. Utilizing the confidence that our ancestors possessed in redesigning their economy and business culture, we can echo the calls of these consumers and progress toward a zero-waste regime.

A TRIANGLE OF OPPORTUNITY

This whole systematic process begins with analyzing the problem. For Carl Hodges and his company Seawater Works, that issue was sustainable food production. Currently, farmers, scientists, policymakers, and other professionals in the field of agriculture are battling over next steps to grow a prosperous, bountiful future of food. From organic farming to eliminating tillage, many schemes have been proposed. Seawater Works's promising solution relies on Earth's natural cycles and attempts to mimic these ecological relationships. This way, we can not only sustain agriculture, but also regenerate the surrounding environment.

The plot: "Use the Other 97 percent of the World's Water."[93]

Saltwater farming is not necessarily a novel idea; cultures have been trying to make use of the ocean's bottomless waters in their plots for years, but none have successfully scaled their blueprints. That is, until an atmospheric physicist from the University of Arizona by the name of Carl Hodges came along. Prior to finding a solution to wastage from resource intensive crops, he built an educational sustainable agriculture ride called the "Land Pavilion" at Walt Disney World's Epcot and contributed to the development of algae biofuel,

93 "Seawater Works," Seawater Works, accessed December 23, 2020.

a renewable plant-based alternative to traditional diesel.[94] These projects demonstrate the diversity of his structural expertise, which he would then apply to Seawater Works.

Narrowing his focus to sustainable agriculture, Hodges decided to intervene in NASA's proclaimed "triangle of conflict," which is outlined by power, water, and food.[95] This geometric hazard sparked food riots throughout Eritrea, a small state in eastern Africa. Hodges's analysis of the triangle unveiled a logical, wasteless model for farms. His model repurposes materials traditionally seen as offage, such as shrimp excrement and salinized water, to organize a flourishing food system. Integrating these components allows for the growth of plants, animals, and ecosystems without resource-intensive inputs like fertilizer, even in traditionally deserted landscapes with little hope for life.

The construction of Hodges's 250-acre saltwater farms begins with a canal dug inland from the sea. The water is then pumped to a higher elevation, where gravity allows it to nourish a meticulously organized, circular living apparatus downhill. First, the water disperses into branched canals and lakes where fish, shrimp, and mollusks reside. Then, the effluent from these animals is collected and used as a fertilizer for crop fields. The water is also used to irrigate salt-tolerant Salicornia plants as a food staple and NASA's nominated "Biofuel of the Future." Lastly, any remaining water runs off to recharge underground aquifers and replenish dried out

---

94   Adam Spangler, "The Future's Farmer," *Vanity Fair*, April 23, 2007.

95   Carl Hodges, "Eco-Scientist," filmed at CUSP Conference 2008 in Chicago, IL, video, 9:30.

wetlands, attracting up to two hundred species of birds and many other forms of wildlife. With all these environmental benefits and the employment and education of eight hundred people in this impoverished nation, the farm's construction swiftly targeted the issues comprising the triangle of conflict.[96] Vanity Fair explained that Hodges turned this triangle into one of opportunity:

"By injecting life into the earth's proliferating desert landscapes, projects like the seawater farms of Carl Hodges may turn out to be just the kind of magic act the world sorely needs."[97]

Hodges's magical model in Eritrea was erected during a time of border conflict with Ethiopia, creating a rocky start for his project. This caused many of his partners to back out. Hodges remained committed to the process until the project's end in 2003, when political upheaval again destabilized efforts at stabilizing the food and environmental crises.[98] Nonetheless, Carl Hodges's seventy-one years of experience defined him as a giant upon whose shoulders younger generations could stand to adapt and refine his dreams of a zero-waste agricultural system. Recently, a school in the United Arab Emirates called Khalifa University replicated his model to produce

---

96   Spangler, "The Future's Farmer."
97   Ibid.
98   Ibid.

biofuel for the aviation industry.[99] Both Seawater Works and its recent adaptations demonstrate the competence of systems-oriented, or ecological, agriculture in reducing the resource waste that starts on our farms.

A similar scenario unfolded in Sonoma County, California, where the Singing Frogs Farm has taken root. Since recognizing the detriments of conventional agriculture on wildlife and the environment, the Singing Frogs Farm has become a flourishing plot of diverse life. Lush broccoli, cauliflower, cucumbers, winter squash, peppers, and over thirty varieties of tomatoes color the landscape. Dogwood, purple flowering aster, and native buckwheat scatter the fields, drawing in pollinators from all corners of Sonoma County. These precious creatures help apple, pear, and guava trees blossom and yield their ripe, juicy fruits.[100]

Not a single inch of land is wasted in their operation. All sparse or bare patches are segmented with ground clovers and deer grass to harbor millions to billions of beetles and spiders serving as natural pesticide. By covering the land so densely, soil moisture and organic matter is conserved, thus reducing the need for resource-intensive irrigation and fertilization practices.[101] Plus, the harvests are more bountiful than previously thought possible. The 250-plus species of vegetables, herbs, flowers, and fruits not only boost the income

---

99 Ilima Loomis, "Jet-Setting: Turning Aquaculture Wastewater into Aviation Fuel," *Global Aquaculture Advocate*, June 3, 2019.

100 *SpaciousEconomy*, "Farmshorts Northbay—Singing Frogs Farm," May 9, 2013, video, 0:07.

101 Todd Oppenheimer, "Sustainability on Steroids," *Made Local Magazine*, May 2015.

and variety of the Singing Frog harvests (equivalent to eight times the state average), but they also yield a load of other ecological benefits.[102] Agriculture on their operation is not perceived in a hue of destruction, but rather as an oasis of life and regeneration.

By designing intentional structures, these farms have shown we can eliminate waste in a way that is socially beneficial and profitable.

This not only applies to ambiguous supply chains such as agriculture, but it is also relevant for household items. Our current course of product design already puts a lot of pressure on manufacturers to be intentional and unique. In fact, a 2015 Ketchum Innovation Kernel global study revealed that on average, 68 percent of customers are willing to pay 21 percent more for ideas and brands that they personally regard to be "innovative."[103] To appease this demand, businesses have established intensive modeling schemes, testing everything from their comfort to their practicality.

SOLE TO SHINING SOLE

What many designers fail to consider is their design's waste footprint, from its birth in the factory to its death in the landfill. This is a fundamental design flaw, as Ellen MacArthur points out:

---

102 *SpaciousEconomy*, "Farmshorts Northbay," video, 0:07.
103 Ketchum, "Innovation Is More Than a Buzzword—Consumers Are Willing to Pay 21 percent More for Innovative Brands," *PR Newswire*, March 24, 2015.

Waste and pollution do not happen by accident—they're a result of the way we design things. If we can change our mindset to view waste as a design flaw, and embrace new materials and technologies, we can ensure that waste is not created in the first place.[104]

These design flaws are not unavoidable. Waste-free, nature-centered design is actually commonplace in many cultures and has been for many generations. For example, Leilani Unasa, Systems Design lead at Cause Collective with a Pacific island heritage, described the promise of "a design approach based on wairua [spirit, soul] to complement co-design methods and make space for a wider range of considerations."[105] In other words, by integrating her cultural values and practices to a broader industrial landscape in a respectful and honest way, the western world can "catc[h] up" in cultivating a waste-free future.[106]

Supplementing with "Life-Cycle Analysis" and other tools for circular design to analyze industrial practices could also make zero-waste businesses extremely plausible. Accordingly, there is hope for product-based industries to take notes of these sustainable swings and prosper on the zero-waste front.

---

104 Ellen MacArthur (@ellenmacarthur), "Waste and pollution do not happen by accident—they're a result of the way we design things. If we can change our mindset to view waste as a design flaw, and embrace new materials and technologies, we can ensure that waste is not created in the first place," Twitter, July 7, 2020, 5:29 a.m.

105 Nelson Meha, "Indigenous Worldviews and the Circular Economy," *Scion Connections*, June 2019.

106 Ibid.

In fact, this redefinition is completely justified and necessary, as 80 percent of the ecological impacts of a product are locked in at the design phase.[107] In other words, the waste that stems from textiles and packaged goods is not at all haphazard. This is not to say that designers are intentionally creating goods that maximize waste, but it is certainly under their responsibility to minimize it.

Chief Design Officer of Nike, John Hoke III, has personally taken on this responsibility. His atypical design practices stem from childhood curiosity. In his early years, he would often exercise his mind by cutting open his worn-out Nike trainers and observing their internal structure. One summer, floating on a pool raft after a tennis shoe dissection, a question came to him.

"What would happen if you took a raft and shrunk it to the size of the sole of your foot? Would it improve the heel-to-toe running transition and improve comfort?"[108]

This inquiry landed him a job at Nike two decades later. Adolescent Hoke wrote a letter presenting his youthful idea to President Phil Knight, who extended a job offer when he

---

107 "Sustainable Product Policy," European Commission, updated December 13, 2018, accessed December 23, 2020.

108 Valeriya Safronova, "Nike's Chief of Design Doodles All Day," New York Times, October 16, 2017.

reached working age.[109] Soon thereafter, Hoke was recognized as Chief Design Officer at the multinational company. Fueled by his unique thought processes instilled in him as a dyslexic child, Hoke also became an advocate for circular design in the shoe industry. Notably, as we mentioned previously, he enacted a Reuse-A-Shoe program where old sneakers can be recycled into new footwear, apparel, and play surfaces.[110]

John Hoke's relentless mission to cut out waste began with a curious problem-solving mentality, which prompted him to initiate change through products delivering the greatest performance and least environmental impact. Preserving resources in this way is especially relevant to the activewear industry, as users are oftentimes outdoor recreators who endure the degradation of natural environments firsthand.[111] Without clean air and room to move freely, the enjoyment of the outside world, and therefore equipment needed to thrive in it, would severely diminish. Responsively, John Hoke widened his scope of analysis for design by not only accounting the attributes of the end user but also the attributes of the location the product would be used in. He incorporated the quality of the natural environment, which is requisite to the end use of his product, into the design phase.

As a scripture, he released Nike's Circular Design Guide in May of 2019, which outlines a set of principles to be sanctioned by the fashion industry to ensure a system where

---

109 Ibid.
110 "Nike Grind: A Legacy of Innovation," Nike, accessed December 23, 2020.
111 Edgar Alvarez, "Nike's Chief Design Officer on Why the Company Is Going All in on Sustainability," *Input*, February 2, 2020.

wearable items become a renewable investment. Among the focus areas are material choices, durability, circular packaging, disassembly, and green chemistry, all of which Nike has incorporated into their designs.[112] If correctly implemented, long-lasting sneakers and garments with a transparent life cycle will become the new norm.

Nike's circular design principles have already been given life since their distribution, inspiring other industry participants to take a stand against wastefulness in their supply chain. For example, Adidas has committed to making shoes entirely out of ocean plastic and eliminating their use of virgin plastic by 2024.[113] Fast-fashion symbol H&M recently built a machine in their store in Stockholm, Sweden, to dismantle, shred, and ultimately remanufacture garments into new sweaters, baby blankets, and scarves—all within a matter of five hours per use.[114] These strides already taking place align perfectly with Hoke's guiding philosophy:

> "We strive for balance, knowing that no one piece stands alone and that everything needs to exist in harmony with everything else."[115]

---

112 Ibid.

113 "Adidas Aims to End Plastic Waste with Innovation + Partnerships as the Solutions," *News* (blog), Adidas, January 28, 2020.

114 "From Old to New with Looop," *H&M Magazine,* October 8, 2020.

115 John Hoke, "John Hoke on Design," *Nike News* (blog), Nike, Inc., April 11, 2016.

The "Cradle to Cradle" ideology underlying Hoke's design is a harmonious muse for anyone in the design or fashion space. Nike's pathway for responsible fashion sparked fantastic progress.

Not only has their philosophy been a logical course of action for the planet, but it also prompted economic benefits. Unused material is part of traditional design and product development. Money is lost from input inefficiency. But by conscientiously designing items free of waste from cradle to grave, or rather "Cradle to Cradle," operations can be completely circular and efficient, creating a large monetary incentive.

WHERE DEATH AND DECAY MEET LIFE

Replicating redesign such as Nike's, while theoretically attractive, will take more than just removing labels for enhanced recyclability or switching from plastic to paper packaging. Instead, we will need to analyze and revise the full production method. A novel recipe for this design procedure comes from Kresse Wesling, CEO of British luxury brand Elvis & Kresse. As a company that produces bags and accessories from miscellaneous waste materials, she preaches a step-by-step process by which she:

1. Searches for accessible waste streams;
2. Chooses a material;
3. Understands the material and its properties; and
4. Gets creative with possible uses.

In her case, she utilizes waste itself as her input material, which is an incredibly sustainable and viable option for some businesses.

In the case of Elvis & Kresse, waste culminated in luxury design. As couture as this may be, the waste transformation needn't always be so glamorous. South Africa native and founder of the Compost Kitchen, Himkaar Singh is a visionary who perfectly displays the attractiveness of a less-than-picturesque output. His forward-thinking composting operation runs on literal dirt itself.

Interestingly, Singh's journey with composting began in third grade, when an individual came into his class to discuss recycling and overpopulation issues in South Africa. After the depressing environmentalist monologue, this keynote speaker supplied Singh and his peers with tips on how they could reduce their own impacts: things like avoiding plastic water bottles and throwing aluminum cans in the recycling bin. This may seem a mundane motif for most elementary-aged students, but the mind-boggling aspect is that twenty years later, "things have just gotten worse."

Decades later, there has been little to no progress on the problem of waste management. Seeing as such immense energy has been exerted trying to educate children on environmental issues and responsible behavior, it would be reasonable to expect these practices to become commonplace in South African society. In reality, those interventions downright failed. Perplexed by this inconsistency, Singh set off to do something about it.

For his higher education, he earned a bachelor's and graduate degree in civil engineering from the University of Witwatersrand. His engineering work on water-related infrastructure at a time when South Africa was experiencing severe drought led him to leave his home country to find alternative solutions through an international degree program. The master's in Integrated Water Resource Management program included intense, immersive five-month projects in Jordan, Vietnam, and Germany. He was able to explore the infrastructure of water treatment facilities, approaches to water harvesting and purification, and, most importantly, the impact of healthy soils on water retention. This international scope, he believed, would allow him to understand water from all different aspects. Basically, he was trained to solve society-wide problems using an informed, system-based approach.

Country-hopping gave Singh more than just a cultured view of water management. During a lucky encounter with Vietnamese adolescents cleaning up trash at a river, Singh was exposed to the linkage between water and waste. As a part of his time in Vietnam, Singh volunteered to clean up trash through the Green & Book Ambassadors program.[116] The organization, according to their Facebook page, spreads awareness of social and environmental injustices "by teaching children about love, listening to the homeless, and laughing while picking up smelly trash."[117]

Singh's vision of a sensitive bonding experience with the homeless immediately pulverized when he recognized the insurmountable trash produced in this rapidly developing

---

116 "Our Story," The Compost Kitchen, accessed December 23, 2020.
117 Green & Book Ambassadors, "by teaching children about love, listening to the homeless, and laughing while picking up smelly trash," Facebook, July 23, 2020.

nation. The World Bank estimates Vietnam is one of the top five plastic polluting countries in the world, with about 2,500 tons being dumped into the oceans every single day.[118] To address this pollution situation, many youth-led organizations have begun clean-up, which escalated Singh's hope to drive environmental change in South Africa.

Upon completing his training and returning home with a shifted, holistic mindset, he was uplifted by his new set of possibilities in which to take his career. As an engineer, Singh describes he often pigeonholed himself to a career as "a contractor, which builds infrastructure, [or] a consultant, which designs those infrastructure and gives design advice."

Based on the lack of progress on waste management issues from his home country over the past two decades, plus the clear consequences of inaction he encountered abroad, Singh knew he needed to make a bold choice. A consulting position or involvement in a non-profit organization would simply not cut it. He needed to directly drive change himself to get society to understand the possibilities of a sustainable future.

It was during this phase of contemplation he built his competency in food waste and composting. His apartment in Durban, South Africa, had no easily accessible garden or composting facility nearby. To cope, he devised a scheme to reduce his food waste impact. Every week he collected his scraps, and when he went to work, he snuck them into the

---

118 "Meet the Innovator Battling Plastic Waste in Vietnam: Trang Nguyen,"
     The World Bank: News, May 31, 2019.

garden at his office and dug them into the soil when everybody had left for the day. It was only a matter of time before his own personal obsession with food waste turned into a business model.

After much research and analysis, Singh realized the financial benefits, water security and greenhouse gas mitigation stemming from the food waste reduction—which could be possible through a widespread composting program. Composting is a widely known but surprisingly misunderstood practice whereby organic waste, like fruit and veggie scraps, is broken down into a dirt-like material which can be used as a natural fertilizer. This multi-faceted solution reduces the amount of food waste sent to landfill, where it otherwise releases the extremely potent greenhouse gas methane into the atmosphere. It also has a regenerative property on the soil. The organic matter content skyrockets, which captures rainwater and holds it in the soil's pores, reducing the effects of drought. According to Singh, composting is:

> "A beautiful metaphor where death and gross, disgusting, decaying matter comes to life again, and feeds us with the richest of fruits and vegetables we could find."

A true embodiment of circularity, though it may not be advertisement-worthy, composting is the ultimate waste-reduction tool when it comes to our food. It reduces the need for resource-intensive fertilizers and puts nutrients back into a natural cycle which can be eternally upheld so long as organic matter continues to return.

Recognizing the eventuality of this solution, Singh founded the Compost Kitchen, a service-based company providing subscribers a container to store their food waste that is then picked up and turned into compost. Specifically, a vermi-composting facility is utilized, which is run by worms that digest and excrete nutrient-rich material. Then, the compost is returned to the customer to use on home gardens. Through this exchange, subscribers incrementally add compost to the soil and organic matter slowly becomes fixed, contributing to Singh's ten-year plan to reduce drought effects on the country. Singh's promotion of constituent participation allows citizens who historically distrusted the recycling industry to restore confidence in their sustainable efforts. Through the Compost Kitchen, they receive proof in the form of compost that their food waste was in fact recycled.

This very newly formed company currently has over two-hundred devoted customers, but its overall imprint is far greater. In Chicago, a similar organization called the Urban Canopy offers a variable-priced Compost Club where subscribers receive a bucket that can be picked up one to four times a month to reduce food waste in landfills in the metropolis.[119] In South Africa, Singh's company has reduced the amount of water wasted from food production in the country, which is equivalent to the amount of water held by the Gariep Dam, the nation's largest reservoir. His progressive attempts to reverse soil degradation were a direct

---

119 "Residential Composting," Urban Canopy, accessed December 23, 2020.

corollary of his solution and systems-based approach to food waste—beginning during his master's program abroad. Now, his company dispenses numerous external benefits directly combatting the cost of waste.

Singh's composting project demonstrates a nuanced scientific model which required an outside-the-box lens to execute. Similarly, Ray Anderson, founder of Interface carpet company and self-recognized "plunderer" of the environment, modified a broadly popularized environmental theory called the Ehlrich equation to kick start a solution to waste. The Ehlrich model is typically used in population and developmental studies, and it quantifies environmental impact (I) as a factor of population (P), affluence (A) and technology (T), mathematically delivered as I=PAT. As an industrial engineer, this model resonated with Anderson, but his analytical mind saw fundamental discrepancies. The model inherently blames technology (T) as a driving force for environmental destruction. Otherwise stated, more complex technology equals a higher environmental impact.[120]

Upon hefty analysis, Ray Anderson concluded that in fact I=PAT should be revised to I=PA/T, meaning that technology could be a source of enhancing sustainability. This hypothesis led him to transform his carpet company, Interface, into a cutting-edge design corporation with a mission of "unplundering" the environment using technological improvement in materials processing.[121] During this organizational change,

---

120 *TED*, "Ray Anderson: The Business Logic of Sustainability," May 18, 2009, video, 1:28.

121 Ibid.

Interface cut waste by 80 percent and increased sales by 66 percent.[122]

As technological masterminds, Singh and Anderson proved that utilizing scientific analysis can be essential to decreasing waste and increasing profit margins. Eloquent narration in *The Rise of Sustainability* documentary reinforces this procedure stating, "We can't solve problems by using the same thinking that caused them."[123]

Thus, our food, fashion, and other consumer-based industries need to take the plunge and invest in circular design. Miraculous work has already been done in this field, whether it be the transforming products themselves (as evidenced by Nike) or creating systems that intercept waste from the get-go. Even though Seawater Works and the Compost Kitchen were formed by trained scientists, you don't necessarily need to be an engineer to use this line of thinking. For example, Vanina Howan, host of a podcast called the *Ecopreneur Show*, learned about "Life-Cycle Analysis" and supply chains through personal research for her reusable bag venture. Despite the fact she didn't have the "technical skills" to execute a proper, numerically based report, her understanding of her operation's environmental footprint at all stages of the process was exponentially greater than that of most business executives. Her curiosity led her to rely on her own methodology, which analyzed

---

122 Ray Anderson and Robin White, Confessions of a Radical Industrialist: Profits, People, Purpose: Doing Business by Respecting the Earth (New York: St. Martin's Press, 2009), 4.

123 *ISS SRPS*, "The Rise of Sustainability," July 13, 2017, video, 30:30.

everything from the dying of threads to the degradation of her bags over time.

Regardless of technical expertise and background, as Howan and so many entrepreneurs have proven, relying on schematic analysis can propel the zero-waste industry to previously unknown heights. It's also no secret that not everyone interested in sustainable design is a math whiz or organizational fiend. Luckily for those right-brained rebels, the quest for circularity may follow a more artistic route.

"Design is not just how it looks like and feels like. Design is how it works."

~STEVE JOBS

CHAPTER 5

TAPPING INTO CREATIVITY

"The creative act, the defeat of habit by originality, overcomes everything."

~GEORGE LOIS

My bedroom is what some might call a hermit's dream. I prefer to think of it as a "part of Ariel's world," filled with whozits and whatzits galore.[124] My desk is a rainbow collage of old cereal box logos, newspapers, birthday cards, and colorful scraps I've carefully pieced and glued together to form a cohesive vintage-esque art piece. Fake flowers dispersed throughout the room are cradled in old Harney &

---

124 Ron Clements and John Musker, dir, *The Little Mermaid*, 1989 (Burbank, CA: Walt Disney Pictures) Blu-ray Disc, 1080p HD.

Sons tea tins. My decor even includes an old Soap & Glory gift set box which perfectly complements my aesthetic. Sure, these decorations are not very conventional (most people may prefer to secure their waste-free decorations from a thrift store rather than their trash bin), but the creative liberty I relished while upcycling this space was extremely empowering. Not to mention, in my humble opinion, the end piece is nothing short of an HGTV ad.

Pushing the creative bounds of one's mind in this way can be important leverage for designing zero-waste solutions. Regarding zero-waste, there tends to be a lack luster stigma around restriction. Much of the professional zero-waste community tends to fixate on regulation, certification, and metrics. Even though all these institutional mechanisms are important for the zero-waste conversion, the real beauty surrounding this niche movement is the creativity required to devise remarkable solutions for waste. Individuals in this space who take risks and tap into their appreciation for the arts have been phenomenally successful.

RISK À LA MODE

GQ's 2019 Chef of the Year, Matt Stone, infamously took risks to build his sustainable culinary empire.[125] At the mere age of twenty, he became sous chef of the Star Anise Restaurant in Perth, a reputable fine-dining establishment teaching him all about gastronomy and other advanced cooking techniques. A year into his work at Star Anise, Stone felt jaded

---

125 Brad Nash, "Matt Stone Wins Chef of the Year at GQ's 2019 Men of the Year Awards," *GQ*, November 28, 2019.

by the ordinary restaurant atmosphere and lack of liberating "pizzazz." Being pushed against the bars of this creative jail cell, he seriously debated ending his culinary career altogether.[126]

Do I really want the life of a chef confined to other people's recipe books and techniques? In that case, am I any different than a robot monotonously performing tasks in the likes of others?

These questions haunted Stone for many months, but magically he was approached by a Dutch artist with an ultimatum to eternally transform his career. With metallic blond hair, crystal blue eyes, and a face permanently entrenched with lines carved from years of laughs, Joost Bakker was mesmerizing. Even more mesmerizing was his proposal to build a restaurant made from 100 percent recycled or recyclable materials. This sustainable infrastructure could pioneer the sustainable hospitality industry in Australia—without a trace being left behind after its eventual close.[127]

Facing the path of uncertainty, with no footsteps to follow or insurance of a clearing on the other side, Stone declined the offer. As Bakker continued making progress on the proposed deal, Stone was left with the force of regret pounding on his doorstep every day. After a couple weeks of migraines, he finally caved into his creative desires and joined Bakker's mission. This leap of faith turned out to be one of the most crucial decisions he would ever make. Becoming the Head

---

126 *TED*, "Matt Stone: Beyond the Zero Waste Restaurant," September 17, 2014, video, 1:10.

127 *TED*, "Matt Stone," 1:28.

Chef of the new Greenhouse Perth, Australia's first all-recycled restaurant, Stone was able to work with his mentor and verse himself in zero-waste cooking, which he continues to thrive in today.[128]

Zero-waste cuisine in and of itself is a puzzling peculiarity. As one of the most wasteful industries in the world, hospitality heavily relies on disposable materials, diverse menus, and luxury escapades which are very resource intensive. As such, it has also bred a lot of social injustice throughout the world. For example, since the era of European colonialism India has been exploited for its spices. Even today, complex supply chains in the spice trade conceal the horrific treatment and abusive payments of Indian farmers who labor year-round to meet corporate demands. Not only has this indigenous neglect led to lower quality, "dusty" spices, but it also undermines the culture and beauty of Indian spices as a symbol of delectable cuisine. Luckily, companies such as Diaspora Co. have started to address this cultural annihilation, defining their mission as:

> Beyond highlighting gorgeous, indigenous spice varieties, it's also about creating a business for us, by us. Complicating and deepening what "Made in India" means, and how we tell our own stories of freedom, struggle, and diaspora through food.[129]

Even beyond their high wages, healthcare insurance, and cultural appreciation, Diaspora Co. has begun a surge toward

---

128 *TED*, "Matt Stone," 1:54.
129 "About," Diaspora Co., accessed February 4, 2021.

zero-waste, shipping all their spices plastic-free. Aspiring toward a similar mission of sustainable, locally-sourced cuisine, Stone began to learn and implement practical tricks to actively fight the many sources of waste in his restaurant. One such tactic included relying on seasonal ingredients. As Stone explains:

"If you eat seasonally, then generally the food is more localized, so it will be more delicious and it will create less waste."[130]

This is, of course, easier said than done. With a rotational supply of ingredients based on the time of year, the menu must constantly evolve as well. Some may view the continuous change of pace as a hurdle to a financially stable business. For Stone, though, the flexibility and experimental nature of this model energized him to become a serial restauranteur. Beyond his time at Greenhouse Perth, Stone opened a broth cafe, BROTHL, utilizing scraps from other local restaurants— including discarded seafood shells, chicken bones, and vegetable trimmings—to cook up nutrient-dense, delicious broth for customers.[131]

He also operated a zero-waste cafe, Silo, which recycled waste from all facets, from decor to ingredients. At this

130 Jordan Mooney, "Chef Matt Stone Is on a Mission to Make Australia More Sustainable," *Food & Wine,* accessed December 24, 2020.

131 Laura Price, "Top Australian Chef Champions Kangaroo Meat, Zero Waste and Eating Bark," *50 Best*, May 25, 2017.

establishment, Stone refused disposable to-go cups for coffee and other drinks, utilized furniture made from old irrigation pipes, and served meat from head to tail. While his meat methodology unsettled customers at first, Stone says, "It's taken us five years to get people's heads around the fact that they are going to get a delicious meal and it will be lamb, but I can't really say what cut it will be."[132]

The frustrating misconception that unconventional pieces of meat or other ingredients are inedible required much effort to quell. Over time, however, the restaurant staff built a reputation for culinary genius. For Chef Stone, Silo catapulted his career in tackling the zero-waste frontier. Thus, he made the decision to open a pop-up version of his Greenhouse restaurant built from shipping containers. The design was expertly engineered in such a way that all resource loops were completely closed to achieve complete biomimicry. Before its sudden closing, inhabitants served as participants in nature by contributing to the function of the restaurant. A bio-digester was used to turn human waste into cooking and heating fuel. Solar panels were utilized to store energy in the walls. Beehives, aquaponics, and cricket farming constituted alternative, regenerative growing systems. Rainwater runoff was caught and recycled for gardening.[133]

Unlike other restaurants attempting to make sustainable changes by simply purchasing composters (which

132 Jordan Mooney, "Chef Matt Stone Is on a Mission to Make Australia More Sustainable," *Food & Wine*, accessed December 24, 2020.

133 Hugo McCafferty, "Matt Stone: The Future of Sustainable Living," *Fine Dining Lovers*, April 22, 2020.

their restaurants also have), Stone and Bakker completely reimagined the meaning of the word "restaurant" as an ecosystem that is living, breathing, and cyclical. The pure originality in their ventures is striking, not only in their infrastructure but also in the waste-free dishes themselves. Plucked from one of his many menus, the dish listed on the menu as "Shiraz lees, grapefruit, and coriander" transforms inedible grapefruit skin, dead yeast from the bottom of a wine production tank, leftover egg whites, and stems of cilantro into a delectable dessert.[134]

"Shiraz lees, grapefruit, egg whites, and coriander" may be a final course, but the impact Chef Matt Stone's creativity made on Australia is just beginning. Even beyond the walls of Greenhouse, Silo, and BROTHL, Stone burst his zero-waste bubble to permeate the rest of society with delicious food and inspiration. Anyone visiting his restaurants will surely appreciate and share his mission of "maximum taste with zero waste."[135]

REIMAGINING THE DOUGHNUT

For Stone's restaurants, the marketing potential of his niche concept made his model trendy. Many other zero-waste businesses mirror this exciting aptitude. A brilliant example is bio-tech company Ecovative Design: "a startup that turns mushrooms into IKEA packaging." Most of us may not immediately think of shipping containers when faced with fungi, but with a bit of creativity and brainpower,

---

134 Laura Price, "Top Australian Chef."
135 Jordan Mooney, "Chef Matt Stone."

anything is possible. This company making plant-based meat and turning mycelium (fungi) into packaging has made headlines with *Forbes, New York Times,* and *Business Insider.* Since their spike in publicity, Ecovative has been recognized by their partners Dell and IKEA, with whom they now have formal partnerships.[136] Especially as sustainability becomes a growing priority among young business leaders, Ecovative and similar innovative companies, like Yanko Design (making plastic packaging alternatives from brewers' spent grain), have the opportunity to distinguish themselves. Thinking of waste as a medium for crafting can allow us to hydrate the sustainable needs of society.

Despite these opportunities for massive upheaval, we are restrained by the stigma of growth limitation associated with a fully circular economy.

Circular economist Kate Raworth counters this perception as she attributes the property of constraint to extract "creativity, participation, belonging, and meaning" from some of the most ingenious people, including Jimi Hendrix, Serena Williams, and Mozart. Jimi Hendrix had only six strings. Serena Williams is restricted to bounds on a tennis court. Mozart's sheet music had a fixed number of lines and notes.[137] All of these illustrious individuals weren't distinguished by completely unheard-of, inaccessible inventions or tools. Their remarkable contributions of talent were unleashed

---

136 "Partner with Us," Ecovative Design, accessed December 24, 2020.

137 *TED,* "Kate Raworth: A Healthy Economy Should Be Designed to Thrive, Not Grow," June 4, 2018, video, 15:10.

using the same instruments that you and I played as youngsters and the same tennis courts we stomped around on as tots. They utilized these bounded, mundane conditions to achieve greatness. Having guidelines and goals in place can push artists and leaders out of their comfort zone into an entirely new (constrained) ballpark. Using the precedent of these celebrated icons, we can mimic their formula to shift toward zero-waste.

Raworth's praise of boundaries led her to advocate for a shift in our global economic paradigm, from one oriented on a line to one stuffed inside a doughnut.

Perhaps the best starting place for understanding Raworth's ideology is the birthplace of the field of economics, dreamt up during the knowledge revolution of ancient Greece. Education and scholarship were foundational values of this civilization, and new philosophies were manufactured left and right. As a way of organizing trade, the theory of economics was formally invented.[138]

Originally, this concept of exchange was interpreted at the household level. Neighbors might trade a goat for some textiles, for example. It wasn't until the Industrial Revolution that economist Adam Smith applied this theory to entire nations, leading to the invention of metrics like unemployment and interest rates. But now, nearly three hundred years later, we have yet to apply these ideas to a global, earthly context.

---

138 *Doughnut Economics Action Lab,* "And Now... It's Time for Planetary Economics," June 4, 2017, video, 0:21.

We need to hold nature as a stakeholder needing replenishment as we extract her resources.[139]

Globalization has coalesced our nations, but in the process we failed to connect to the foundation of our existence: Mother Earth. It's high time we undo our current understanding of economics, which Raworth describes as "drawn up in the textbooks of 1950 … based on ideas drawn up in 1850."[140]

Imagine being a prodigy in any other discipline—be it computer science, fashion, or even education—and basing your knowledge off of methods developed in the 1850s. A majority of majors studied today didn't exist in the 1850s, or even the 1950s for that matter. The effects of this fixated perspective are exemplified by an encounter Raworth had with an advanced engineering student, Prakash, at a university in Germany. She recalls,

> When I asked whether he had opted to learn about ecologically smart technologies, he replied, "No, India has other priorities—we are not rich enough to worry about that yet." Surprised, I pointed out that almost half of India's land is degraded, the nation's groundwater levels are falling fast, and air pollution is the worst in the world. A flicker of recognition crossed his face, but he just smiled and repeated his words, "We still have other priorities."[141]

---

139 Ibid.
140 *Meaning Conference*, "Kate Raworth | Doughnut Economics | Meaning 2017," November 30, 2017, video, 7:15.
141 Kate Raworth, "Why We Need to Move toward an Economy That Can Regenerate Itself," *Business* (blog), *Ideas. TED.com*, April 11, 2018.

Raworth has criticized this 1850s "take, make, and waste" approach which commends traditional, outdated models, such as the Kuznets Curve.[142] As previously discussed, this model describes the hump-shaped trajectory of environmental impact along economic development. Contrastly, Raworth thrust her thinking beyond the hedge of our modern economic model to impose her theory of "Doughnut Economics." Detailed in her book, *Doughnut Economics: Seven Ways to Think Like a 21st-Century Economist,* she instills the need for industry to mend its design failure, which has led to massive amounts of waste. Her solution lies in new entrepreneurial strategies such as "design to distribute" and "create to regenerate."

To define this hefty theory, her thesis begins with a description of the linear economy as an industrial caterpillar. The hairy, sneaky vermin ingests resources at one end and excretes them out the other, leaving behind a valueless heap of material. Directly responding to this mindset of traditional (linear) economists, Kate Raworth presents an inventive solution in the form of a doughnut.[143]

Let's visualize it.

If you were to draw out a doughnut on a piece of paper, you would inevitably draw two circles, one inside the other. According to Raworth's model, the inner circle represents

---

142 Prateek Agarwal, "The Environmental Kuznets Curve," *Intelligent Economist*, March 1, 2018.

143 Kate Raworth, *Doughnut Economics: Seven Ways to Think Like a 21st-Century Economist* (Hartford: Chelsea Green Publishing, 2017), 9.

the minimum societal goals needed to sustain a functioning economy; these include health, equity, housing, food, and education. The outer circle represents the bounds of the environment, the limits of which we cannot exceed if we want centuries or even decades-long prosperity. Environmental limits specifically include chemical pollution, biodiversity loss, climate change, and ozone depletion. Accommodating both limits through a structure of resource reuse and renewal by markets, households, and the state, the needs of society can be met without taking an unnecessary toll on the planet. Rather than accepting the traditional notion that:

"Economies [...] need to grow, whether or not they make us thrive; what we need are economies that make us thrive, whether or not they make us grow."[144]

This evolution is a bit unsettling for many individuals as they feel restricted in terms of wealth. It directly contradicts the status quo of increasing economic exchange and resource extraction for economic growth. Long term, though, these boundaries are necessary to ensure success for future generations relying on our Earth's natural resources.

Is it really worth it to drown in cash today just for our children to drown in trash, debt, and rising sea levels?

---

144 Kate Raworth, *Doughnut Economics: Seven Ways to Think Like a 21st-Century Economist* (Hartford: Chelsea Green Publishing, 2017), 207.

We should not view limitations and moderations as demotions of our economy and world. As previously mentioned with her analysis of Jimi Hendrix and Serena Williams, Kate Raworth attributes all great successes to the existence of boundaries. If we can make this change in our thinking collectively, our "Doughnut Economy" will circulate health and prosperity for generations to come.

The restrictive conditions so fundamental to Raworth's theory are reminiscent of my own childhood rainy day pastimes. I vividly remember one night in fourth grade. I was at my best friend's house for a sleepover. The stars had been out for many hours and were soon to retire to the pinkish dawn. Eager to stay up yet bored and uninspired, my friend and I came up with the idea to build a cardboard house from scraps in her garage. We compiled an obscene amount of boxes of all sizes from her recycling bin and got to work. Instantly, our faces lit up and our hands starting crafting faster than we could have imagined in the wee hours of the morning.

The house we constructed was not to be shuffled into the mix of typical cardboard houses toddlers construct. Those clichés end with a functional four walls, door, and possible excuse of a roof. On the contrary, our house was an immaculate manor with a kitchen island, fireplace, and even a cardboard toaster with cardboard toast to go in it. Needless to say, by the end of our project, my fingers were cramped to the core from wielding scissors and my eyes were bloodshot.

As regretful as my body may have been the next morning, reflecting on this experience gives me pure joy and accomplishment to this day. Our youthful artistic capabilities not only gave us a few hours of uninterrupted delight, but we also revived a new, extravagant purpose for one of the most mundane physical objects in existence: a cardboard box.

CONCOCTING WITH CITRUS

Surely, not everyone has the time or willpower to spend hours on tedious cardboard house construction or desktop murals from old newspapers and birthday cards. The beauty in creativity, though, is that it can take on infinite forms. Evidenced by Matt Stone's completely closed loop dining establishments, Raworth's doughnut-shaped model was given life. To ensure the success of her theory, though, it is important to understand some of its idiosyncrasies. Notably:

> Nature doesn't turn a daffodil into a daffodil and a peacock into a peacock… so if we are going to create a circular economy, we can't be sending everything back to the people that bought them… it's got to be an ecosystem of resource use.[145]

In other words, while my cardboard house building was well-intentioned, it is not a scalable practice for many reasons, besides the fact that the market for cardboard houses is non-existent.

In the end, a cardboard house is still essentially a cardboard box. There isn't much transformation there. What we need is for industries to work together to utilize resources

---

145 *Meaning Conference*, "Kate Raworth | Doughnut Economics | Meaning 2017," November 30, 2017, video, 7:15.

in their highest value reuse and keep them in the loop as long as possible. Entrepreneurs and economists are already on the hunt to advance these connections. For example, Maayke-Aimée Damen's Excess Materials Exchange, the industrial matchmaking site, allows businesses to work cross-sector to revive waste. Another such creative mastermind is Adriana Santanocito, founder of Italian textile brand Orange Fiber.

Though she was born in Cantania, Italy, Santanocito's creative compulsions lead her to attend fashion design school in Milan. There, she met her roommate Enrica Arena, who was studying social entrepreneurship and sustainable development. In 2011, the two were brewing ideas for how they could combine their unique strengths for a successful business model after graduation.[146] Eventually, inspiration struck from an unsettling statistic Santanocito learned while proposing her thesis.

One-half the weight of a fresh orange is disposed of during the juicing process.[147]

What a shame it was that the bright, colorful sweetness of an orange was trashed after being mangled for its liquid. After

146 "What Makes Adriana Santanocito & Enrica Arena Global Shakers?" Global Shakers, updated October 21, 2019, accessed December 24, 2020.
147 "Innovation Goes Orange," *Face2Face* (blog), Fibre2Fashion.com, August 18, 2017.

pondering the misfortune, Santanocito came home with her thesis proposal to transform citrus surplus into a textile medium. In the likes of Coco Chanel, the iconic duo conspired that this novel concept could amplify far beyond the confines of their university. Infatuated by the idea of uniting two of Italy's most prized delicacies, citrus and luxurious fashion, they set off on a path of circular entrepreneurship. With Santanocito's fashion know-how and her co-founder Arena's distinctive business outlook, the pair imagined a company which would generate "a new life for [orange waste], transforming [it] into refined, ethereal fabric perfectly suited to Italian tradition of high-quality fabrics and high fashion."[148]

Beginning with the citrus waste, also called *pastazzo* in Italian, the team uses nanotechnology after soaking the peels to extract cellulose. The outcome of this extraction is a polymer which can be spun into yarn, similar to any other fiber. This fiber is also enriched with essential oils to give it a nourishing feel on the skin. That yarn is then transformed for textile manufacturing.[149]

In 2014, Santanocito and Arena presented their first prototype using this process at the Expo Gate of Milan at Vogue Fashion's Night Out, which benchmarked the founding of their company, Orange Fiber. Since then, the company has been used by top luxury fashion brands, such as Salvatore Ferragamo, in collections mixing the silky, lightweight fiber

---

148 "Who We Are," Orange Fiber, accessed December 24, 2020.
149 "Innovation Goes Orange," *Face2Face* (blog), Fibre2Fashion.com, August 18, 2017.

with other yarns and materials to fabricate unique blends supporting citrus waste reduction.[150]

Incredibly, the Orange Fiber team has managed to turn a fruit bowl casualty into a desirable commodity in the fashion industry through their artful assets. Although they are a widely recognized and respected textile manufacturer, they unarguably owe their success to their humble origins in the Italian countryside, which prepared them to cross two national treasures tainted with waste into a phoenix of sustainability.

Regardless of their beginning, the founders of Orange Fiber, like many of the other formidable leaders highlighted in this chapter, found their calling in the beauty of waste. Zero-waste lifestyles seem to automatically nurture this mental adjustment, as demonstrated by many of the other thought leaders in this book. During a *Harper's Bazaar* interview, for instance, environmental activist, entrepreneur, and blogger Lauren Singer revealed her unconventional use of stale bread to make croutons, breadcrumbs with garlic and herbs, and even fresh loaves with a bit of water and a trip to the oven.[151] Maayke-Aimée Damen notoriously refunctionalized her coffee pot covered in recyclable aluminum foil to cook her morning pancakes. The list goes on and on from personal to professional.[152]

---

150 "Who We Are," Orange Fiber.

151 *Harper's BAZAAR*, "Everything Zero Waste Expert Lauren Singer Eats in a Day," November 20, 2019, video, 6:30.

152 *TED*, "Maayke-Aimée Damen: Saving the Planet by Running a Dating Site," January 2, 2020, video, 2:50.

Reducing waste favors invention and creative expression. Whether that inspiration comes from the reciprocity of our global economy or the comfort of our own local villages, waste-reducing alternatives can be sought far and wide. By busting out our inner Andy Warhols and Michaelangelos we can find the beauty in trash to design a waste-free future.

"The enemy of art is the absence of limitations."

~ORSON WELLES

CHAPTER 6

ENGAGE

COMMUNITY MATTERS

—

"Think globally, act locally."

~PAUL MCCARTNEY

It was 5:50 p.m. when I was walking down Michigan Avenue on New Year's Eve 2020. The coronavirus pandemic was in full swing, leaving the streets bare as bone. Rotting and splintering sheets of wood were plastered to store windows as a weak fence against looters. In search of a warm beverage to shield against the Windy City chill, I opened Google Maps and searched: "coffee shops near me." Over thirty contenders popped up within walking distance; 90 percent of which were blatantly labeled in bold red font *temporarily closed* or *permanently closed.*[153] The most gut-wrenching part was

---

153 Google Maps (search item "coffee shops near me"; accessed December 31, 2020).

the majority of these scarlet-lettered shops were not international chains like Starbucks or Dunkin' Donuts. They were stores like Café Marie-Jeanne or Finom Coffee; shops with character and culture, defined by the diverse populations traversing through the downtown; shops that put care and love into their creations, with shopowners who did a little dance whenever they got a new regular or released an updated menu item; shops that were local.

If nothing else, the pandemic has shown us how important our surroundings are. During this time where most (responsible) people are unlikely to be caught more than ten miles from their home, it was the people in our communities who keep us sane and hopeful. It was the local farmer who supplied us produce when supply chains were destroyed by sanitation concerns. It was the local UPS driver who transported us puzzles, books, video games, or cooking gadgets when we were bored at home looking for a creative outlet. It was the local restaurant who gave us a taste of what life used to be like before we were all locked up inside, when we could go out and enjoy an evening meal with loved ones.

The magic of community is indisputable.

We need the people around us to give and take, to relate to, and seek hope from. Whether that be in the middle of a pandemic or an average Tuesday afternoon, recent demonstrations have revealed the value of support and recognition of our local communities. I only recently explored the power these neighborhoods and societies impart during my early years at university.

Freshman year of college was a foreign experience. Even in the midst of dull cornrows in Illinois, the diverse, lively atmosphere was much different than my suburban upbringing in a town where the majority of the population surpassed their midlife crisis. Wanting to understand this new culture (especially its views on sustainability), I probed their values through the infamous trash booth project—which, as discussed earlier, housed piles of recyclable and nonrecyclable items that participants severely struggled to sort correctly.

By engaging first-hand with the local population, I gained a comprehensive understanding of campus lifestyle and some of its obstacles. Students seemed eager about sustainability but incompetent in actually executing pro-environmental behaviors. The upsetting insights I discovered helped me advocate for more clearly labeled recycling bins with sufficient sorting containments including "plastic bottles," "paper," and "aluminum cans."

Most people may praise single-stream recycling as the ideal path forward with less work required by the tosser, but these systems tend to be problematic. Individuals may be unsure about what they can properly recycle (as we know is the case at my school) so they will either toss nonrecyclable items into the recycling bin, reducing the efficiency of processing facilities, or throw those items in the trash out of fear. Either way, less items are returned to the closed resource loop. On the other hand, multiple stream recycling increases the likelihood that materials collected (so long as they are properly sorted) will be revived back to a useful material.

Due to advocacy for these bins in public buildings such as the student Union, students and other visitors can have this state of mind. My classmates and I wrote a research paper detailing our findings of recycling confusion and submitted ideas to our Institute for Sustainability, Energy, and Environment, requesting action. Less than a year later, our facilities exponentially increased usage of these bins and access to recycling infrastructure has been on a promising incline. We now host over three-thousand bins for our thirty-thousand undergraduates. There are still other gaps in recycling knowledge that we clearly need to address, such as the benefits of rinsing dirty containers and understanding the numbers on plastic (displayed inside the recycling logo on plastic containers) accepted in our given municipality. Nonetheless, this preliminary step of new bins is a benchmark which may not have been instated had it not been for our student demands and contributions.

ADDRESSING TEXTILE TORTURE

Community engagement and local advocacy are indispensable coups needed to drive forth a circular economy. As my classmates and I proved with our recycling project, the educational system can be a potent megaphone for these campaigns. Rachel Faller, founder and CEO of fashion brand Tonlé, also used her education as a stepping stone to form a sustainable, socially conscious brand which continues to thrive today.

Faller's legacy took flight in 2008 on a trip to Cambodia with a friend, who had a vision of starting a clothing business in the socially distraught country recognized for its tarnished reputation in the textile industry. On this endeavor, Faller encountered numerous artisan organizations demanding a change in the manufacturing sector. Instating Fair Trade conditions was at the top of their docket. Upon hearing these protests, she decided to visit some industrial facilities. The treatment of the workers, especially women, was indescribably horrific. Witnessing these inhumane conditions in Cambodian textile manufacturing lit a match under her. Rather than starting a reckless wildfire, though, she directed her fury toward the creation of Cambodia's first zero-waste apparel brand.[154]

Amidst Faller's Cambodian deep dive, she also discovered the ungodly amount of waste generated through this industry. From inefficiencies in milling, spinning, dyeing, and cutting (not to mention consumer-facing waste), Faller felt disheartened by just how "trashy" fashion truly was. To combat both societal inequities, she employed her educational privileges to make change. She applied for a Fulbright Scholarship to continue her research on artisan groups in Cambodia, which led her to create her first ethical, zero-waste fashion label in 2008.[155] In 2013, this company was rebranded as Tonlé, translating to "river" in Cambodian. Faller's vision was to establish a company embodying John Elkington's "triple bottom line" ("People, Planet, and Profit"), which acclaims workers and inputs as sacred resources rather than disposable trash.

---

154 Ayesha Barenblat, Allison Griffin and Eleanor Amari, "Meet the Designer: Rachel Faller of Tonlé," *Stories* (blog), *Remake*, April 1, 2017.

155 Ibid.

Notably, her thirty-person strong team works half the number of hours of typical Cambodian textile factories, who push the limits of their employees' wellbeing with sixteen hours of treacherous work every single day. Considering the fact that much of Tonlé's workforce consists of HIV-positive women who have trouble finding employment elsewhere in the country, these conscientious conditions are especially important.[156] Although the rates of HIV/AIDS are now on the decline, a 2010 governmental report scapegoating the virus as a drain on Cambodia's economy has had reverberating effects on discrimination of the affected population.[157]

Tonlé provides this mistreated populace with the opportunity to create exclusive, handmade pieces, all while minimizing waste. All fabric scraps are cut into strips and re-woven back into yarn. The yarn can then be transformed back into fabric or utilized in jewelry collections, thereby closing the loop. Even excess thread is used for tags for garments or labels for packages. Belt buckles, pendants, and buttons are sourced from reclaimed wood from local handicraft organizations.[158]

Tonlé's commitment to the local community ushered massive waste reduction and workplace condition improvements in Phnom Penh, Cambodia, and beyond. A similar company called SOKO arose around the same time to support these ethical objectives through their sustainable jewelry and

156 Ibid.

157 Chun Bora et al., *Guidelines on HIV/AIDS in the Workplace* (Phnom Penh, Cambodia: Kingdom of Cambodia: Ministry of Labour and Vocational Training, June 2010), 9.

158 "Team," Tonlé, accessed December 25, 2020.

accessories lines supporting female artisans in Kenya.[159] These collective projects, and so many others like them, aim to integrate Fair Trade conditions and provide opportunities for marginalized populations around the world. From Tonlé specifically, more than thirty-five thousand pounds of fabric have been diverted from the one-million tons of textile waste globally generated each year.[160] Faller's mission and metrics demonstrate the influence of a passionate, locally driven individual to transform an industry innately intertwined with the term "waste."

GENERATION UP

Locally focused action, such as Tonlé's and SOKO's, has proven to be a universally practical business solution to addressing waste-management issues and social injustice. This sort of ingenuity can take a variety of forms. Whether that be framing companies to address global issues utilizing local quirks or directly tackling waste dilemmas unique to a particular region, honing the scales can be a useful device to simplify zero-waste.

For example, in my hometown, a local beekeeper instated a purchasing regime where customers can return and reuse honey jars. On one trip to the Sunday French Market one summer, I came across this particular booth, where the wholesome beekeeper enthusiastically pitched his waste-free alternative to supplying honey. Not only is this beneficial for supporting his small business by prompting loyal customers

---

159 "Our Impact," SOKO, accessed February 17, 2021.

160 "Team," Tonlé, accessed December 25, 2020.

and decreasing packaging costs, but it also lightens our local landfill. Seeing his face light up as he discussed his idea gave me even more reason to support by purchasing a four-pound jar of the stuff that I have yet to make even a sliver of a dent in. While the amount of honey I devoured in the five months since purchasing was miniscule at best, these small steps, like honey jar recycling, can add up to make substantial and targeted progress.

Similar to my own local beekeeping stand, a black-owned market called the Village Market in Atlanta empowers visitors who may have been unaware of the implications of their product usage through a conscious, black-owned marketplace selling apparel, food and other natural products. The Village and other comparable events, which can be scouted far and wide, condition visitors to vote with their dollar to support businesses providing active solutions to declutter our environment and society.

Beginning this process can be quite an undertaking. As with any environmental problem, looking at the big picture can often be counterproductive and overwhelming. Rescoping to focus on one small step at a time, on the other hand, can lead to gradual changemaking.

Take climate change as a comparison. If a group of engineers, policymakers, and activists were to ideate universal solutions that were implementable globally, they would spiral into a manic state of helplessness and defeat. To conceive actionable remedies more efficiently, one might propose opportunities tailored to their own individual corner of the universe. For example, maybe they live in a town known for its car manufacturing and therefore advise solutions related to emissions standards or electric vehicle requirements. Alternatively, maybe another stakeholder lives in a rural agricultural town and brings sustainable farming practices to the table.

Simply put, stick to what you know. Not only will an individual acting locally be more knowledgeable on the solutions they identify, but they can also track the progress and reap the benefits firsthand. Especially when reflecting on the resources local actors have access to, keeping the scope condensed can embolden some of the most synergistic remodeling in the field of waste management.

A discussion I had with Vanina Howan, host of the *Ecopreneur Show* podcast, exposed the strong zero-waste culture in her home of Portland, Oregon. With resources such as the "Zero-Waste Portland" Facebook group and conventions for zero-waste businesses, the progression has thrived. Likely, this is because of the shared understanding these businesses have of local consumer values. When local businessowners collaborate, they can share tailored insights, and at the end of the day everyone benefits when less waste ends up in landfill.

The founder of a biodegradable container company, Anastasia Mikhalochkina applied this capability of local cycles to normalize sustainable plastics in her hometown of Miami. From a young age, Mikhalochkina's Russian grandmother propagated stories of the cyclical nature of our planet. The lakes surrounding their summer home were characters in her tales of the holistic effect of the environment on health and well-being.[161] Blossoming into adulthood, Mikhalochkina's bond with these aquatic habitats inaugurated her concern with waste management, reflecting her grandmother's frequent sermon:

"The waste we create today is a health condition we deal with tomorrow."[162]

Understanding the direct local impacts of industrial and household waste, parallel to William McDonough's "Cradle to Cradle" ideology, Mikhalochkina had a reason to idolize sustainable change. Enter her company, Lean Orb. She founded this company in 2017 to distribute "sustainable disposables," including alternatives to plastic tableware and food-packaging made from plant roots, grass fibers, and highly sustainable wood. Their biodegradable flatware uses agricultural waste of sugarcane, palm leaf, wheat straw, bamboo, and birch wood to provide non-toxic, completely compostable options to hotels and restaurant groups in the Miami region. Lean Orb's designs fully disintegrate in under ninety days, a substantially shorter life cycle compared to parasitic plastic.[163]

---

161 "Meet Anastasia Mikhalochkina of Lean Orb in Wynwood," *VoyageMIA*, June 28, 2018.

162 Lizzie Bell, "5 Q's With Anastasia Mikhalochkina, Founder of Lean Orb," *Blog, Babson WIN Lab*, March 20, 2018.

163 Steve MacLaughlin and Chris Clark, "Miami-Based Company Produces Biodegradable Tableware," *NBC 6 South Florida*, September 13, 2019.

Mikhalochkina's application of local linkages was not confined to biological and environmental processes. Her brand's mission states:

> "Most days we focus 100 percent of our energy to delivering intelligent, sustainable, and empowering alternatives to plastic. The other 100 percent is spent to build awareness and activism around plastic pollution."[164]

In other words, besides intentional product design, local social networks were an additional circuit Lean Orb chose to electrify. Fortunately, this interlinking came easily due to her brand's business-to-business (B2B) structure. The "consumers" of her line are restaurants and local hotels, which requires solid relationships with the wasteful hospitality industry in Miami. Especially in a coastal city, awareness-building relationships with the corporate sector have the capability of making a world of difference in the physical state of beaches grappling with plastic pollution.

Lean Orb's attempts to beautify beaches extend far beyond board rooms and private meetings with hotel executives. Mikhalochkina also co-founded the #MiamiIsNotPlastic movement attempting to counteract dependence on

---

164 "Our Pursuit of Sustainability Is Rooted in Optimism," Lean Orb, accessed December 25, 2020.

single-use items in the Miami area. Her operation also advocated saving marine life as a part of the larger global agenda. The follower count for #MiamiIsNotPlastic has increased week to week, spreading awareness for the city's proliferation of plastic. This advocacy group posts photos of beach cleanups and local zero-waste solutions to rouse individuals to get involved, making it an educational haven for reducing disposable plastic in the beautiful city.

Mikhalochkina's personal outreach also entails face-to-face interventions. For example, she partnered with South Pointe Elementary to distribute paper straws and wooden cutlery while educating students on the harm caused by single-use plastics. Similar to the Drug Abuse Resistance Education (DARE) program model, Mikhalochkina hopes this early intervention will embolden elementary-aged students to grow up with concern for the environment and chase careers in sustainability.[165] Already, the partnership has illustrated hope. Many children subsumed practices into their own family units to facilitate behavior change. One woman in an NBC interview revealed:

> My kids absolutely talk about this at home... They do not like to use plastic straws. They will decline them at restaurants. They really don't want anything to do with plastic bottles. They both have their reusable waters they fill up on their own, independently.[166]

---

165 Steve MacLaughlin and Chris Clark, "Miami-Based Company Produces Biodegradable Tableware," *NBC 6 South Florida*, September 13, 2019.
166 Ibid.

The ricochet effect coming from personal engagement with the local area, as Lean Orb has demonstrated, is an astoundingly vigorous tool that enhances brand recognition and awareness for the problem of waste overall. While Miami and Portland have been successful mobilizing their citizens, nowhere is the importance of locale more apparent than on islands. The Sierra Club deemed islands as breeding grounds for sustainability due to their isolated nature and tight cultural ties.[167] These characteristics force local cooperation between their inhabitants and businesses, let alone their environment, which is becoming an asset for sustainable adaptation. To foster this further, an organization called Island Innovation brings together the private sector, governments, and universities to share sustainable solutions on particular islands. The circular economy is one major course of action being addressed. Over ten-thousand islanders attended their 2020 Virtual Summit, connecting progressive individuals to pioneer solutions to these issues using local assets.

From this, Aruba declared a 2050 Circular Economy Vision statement announcing they would minimize imports and exports from the island.[168] Even in its early stages, this bold commitment had noteworthy benefits on their resiliency during the COVID-19 pandemic. While international manufacturing and trade were severely injured, blows to multi-national exchange minutely affected the self-sustaining

167 Callum Beals, "4 of the World's Most Sustainable Islands," *Sierra*, accessed December 25, 2020.

168 Kevin de Cuba, "Making Aruba Future-Proof through Sustainable Circular Economy," *Blog, Circular Economy Platform*, 2020.

island. By and large, the independent island demographic has been a useful starting point for the circular economy to prosper. Many communities throughout the world could target and copy their devotion to nationalism and self-reliance.

REVERSING THE VACUUM

Amazing as these strongly-linked communities are, how is an individual to get involved in a locale not outspokenly concerned with waste? This was a question I faced myself in the process of learning and writing about the circular economy. I felt cognitively dissonant as I was prescribing individuals to make personal change and incite their communities, but I had no group of "zero-wasters" myself with whom I could relate and share. Unbeknownst to me, opportunity was hidden in plain sight, which I discovered one Wednesday afternoon at my favorite coffee shop.

Beelining to the register, I ordered my usual iced latte with almond milk. I then trudged toward an open table where I could unload my belongings and begin an hours-long affair of research and online textbook reading. Savoring each step as if it were the last chocolate in a Valentine's Day assortment, I slowly meandered the seating area. I allowed my eyes to wander a few seconds longer than normal, hoping for some sort of stall from my hectic work ahead. To my luck, I spotted the bulletin board, where people posted events, meetings, and the like for anyone interested. I was a frequenter of this board, but most times nothing really struck a chord with me. On this occasion, I happened to see an advertisement for a clothing swap at our local YMCA. Needless to say, my attention was immediately caught, and a few days later I swapped my old emerald flannel for a beautiful vintage-style silk dress shirt.

At the event, I interacted with other students and community members zealous about thrifting and reducing their fashion waste impact. I even learned about a local brand called Offbeat Apparel directly tackling the issue of fashion waste and selling sustainable clothes. Exploring the local style affirmed my own zero-waste transfiguration by providing me a group of accountable individuals from whom I could seek inspiration.

My local coffee shop's cork board was my personal oasis for sustainable fashion agendas. The *New York Times* ad campaign by a little-known brand called Patagonia, however, enlarged that sanctuary for millions of readers across the country. The Patagonia segment included a sleek, cerulean fleece pullover with the signature label on the breast pocket. Smeared over top in bold, all-caps, black letters read the claim, "DON'T BUY THIS JACKET."[169]

This successful marketing scheme reflected the company's impetus raising awareness for environmental issues. Patagonia boasts a long history of sustainability campaigns, beginning with their founding by environmentalist Yvon Chouinard. Advocacy for sustainability in active wear is esteemed the heart and blood of the company. Long-lasting garments and quality sportswear

---

169 Alana Semuels, "'Rampant Consumerism Is Not Attractive.' Patagonia Is Climbing to the Top—and Reimagining Capitalism along the Way," *Time,* September 23, 2019.

have been their signature all along, and they have offered free repair services for their customer's clothes since the 1970s.

Patagonia's outreach leapt lightyears with the release of their Worn Wear campaign in 2005, an incredible project sending employees to college campuses and climbing centers throughout the country. Their intent was to teach participants how to repair tattered garments.[170] As virtuous of a mission as it was, the local impacts never quite permeated beyond their point of interaction, as was the case with some of our other local leaders. This is not necessarily a bad thing because, as we discussed earlier, small scale projects are often most operative in waste engagement.

However, Rose Marcario, as executive of this prestigious brand, enriched the legacy of the Worn Wear campaign with a cross-country tour to repair garments out of a wagon. In total, *Delia* the Worn Wear wagon traveled 5,430 miles and repaired 562 items. Her journey became the focal point of Patagonia's documentary, *Worn Wear: A Film About the Stories We Wear*. After the completion of this mission, it became clear the mileage and garments covered on the tour would simply be scratches on the surface of Marcario's collaborative feats.[171] As CEO, she vehemently disputed the synapse between business and overarching society, stating:

---

170 Ibid.

171 Donnia Hedden, "On the Road with Worn Wear – 2015 Spring Tour Recap," *Stories* (blog), *Patagonia*, accessed December 25, 2020.

"Business doesn't live in a vacuum, but in an interconnected world."[172]

Marcario's belief nudged her to take action outside the scope of her company. Acting upon this newfound interconnectedness, Marcario edged in on particular communities to take Patagonia's advocacy to an entirely new level. Yvon Chouinard, Patagonia's founder, himself declared that:

> With Rose at the helm, we are leading an overdue revolution in agriculture, challenging [the Trump] administration's evil environmental rollbacks, growing a movement to increase voter participation in our elections, and raising the bar on building our product in the most responsible manner possible.[173]

To go after these lofty goals, Marcario launched a cooperative platform called Patagonia Action Works for individuals to learn more about the projects of local grassroots environmental organizations. She maintained her commitments by withdrawing Patagonia from the annual Outdoor Retailer trade show in Utah in 2017 to rebuke the governor's attempt to withdraw the protective status of Bears Ears National Monument.[174] In response to lobbying

---

172 Rose Marcario, "Rose Marcario: Business Doesn't Live in a Vacuum, but in an Interconnected World," *Stories* (blog), *Patagonia*, accessed December 25, 2020.

173 Jeff Beer, "Exclusive: Patagonia CEO Rose Marcario Is Stepping Down," *Fast Company*, June 20, 2020.

174 Ibid.

by nuclear power companies to mine the region's uranium deposits, the government succumbed to destruction of this natural beauty and rich cultural site. Many citizens of Utah (and even more so indigenous people who lived and performed ceremonies in the park) ardently protested the policy.

Despite Patagonia's bold statements and the local cries for help, the Trump administration successfully reduced the monument's size by 85 percent, according to the Washington Post.[175] Nonetheless, Marcario's efforts were valiant to unify a group of patrons with environmentalist values to work together for an important cultural cause.

Who knew that a company selling fleece pullovers could be so deeply rooted in the political and social spectra?

Marcario's concentrated commissions blossomed Patagonia into the sustainable fashion role model it is today. Her work also quadrupled Patagonia's sales since beginning her career there, making it worth over $1 billion.[176]

As described in the Recipe for Sustainability chapter, other large companies have started to take note of these benefits, which has led to a recent fad of greenwashing. "Greenwashing" is the use of misleading information to portray a business as more environmentally friendly than it is.[177]

---

175 Joe Fox et al., "What Remains of Bears Ears," *Washington Post,* April 2, 2019.

176 Beer, "Exclusive: Patagonia," June 20, 2020.

177 *Merriam-Webster,* s.v. "greenwashing (n.)," accessed February 12, 2021.

Previously, Tide and the Body Shop were honorably mentioned as greenwashing culprits. Exploiting the footsteps of Patagonia's sustainable fashion empire, however, Jack Wolfskin's fallacy of "recycled ocean plastic textiles" comes to surface. Jack Wolfskin is a European company boasting the reuse of plastic in its outdoor wear and equipment. Genuinely, though, only 10 percent of the material comes from recycled ocean plastic.[178] "Responsibly Sourced. Ethically Produced... We believe in complete transparency..." state the ads on their website.[179] "We are dedicated to making outdoor gear and clothing that doesn't harm the planet," says the snippet that appears beneath the first Google search result when you look up their website.[180] Dishearteningly, customers purchasing from companies like Jack Wolfskin think they are doing amazing things for the planet. The stark reality is nothing short of continued resource exploitation which has defined the fashion space for decades.

This slew of misinformation is made worse off by the fact that companies who often receive the most attention in sustainable fashion are often the worst greenwashing plunderers. Both Rose Marcario and Rachel Faller have expressed their disgust for these false allegations, and Faller has been quoted saying:

178 Azra Sudetic, "Fashion Made From Ocean Plastic Might Not Be What You Think It Is," *EcoCult,* June 17, 2020.

179 "Responsibly Sourced. Ethically Produced," Jack Wolfskin, accessed February 12, 2021.

180 Jack Wolfskin, *Google Search Results:"Jack Wolfskin's,"* accessed February 12, 2021.

"Unfortunately, the trend for the industry at large is that people and companies who have very little to do with sustainability now control the message about it."[181]

The advertising dollars and corporate recognition of these greenwashing fiends often outpaces smaller sustainable brands. Luckily, local engagement bestows an avenue for truly conscious companies to distinguish themselves from laundering corporate giants. These connections magnify waste reduction through action rather than idyllic, unfulfilled mission statements.

Although these initiatives may seem too microscopic to be impactful, the reality is that without passionate, concentrated might, change will never happen.

At some point, there is nowhere left to hang responsibility but on oneself, which is why we need community-oriented entrepreneurs and businesspeople to instigate domino effects. Time and time again this arrangement has proven effective, from the hospitality industry of Miami to artisan groups in Cambodia. As the saying goes, home is where the heart is—and where the heart is, there is a clear solution.

---

181 "Founder's Story With Rachel Faller: Tonlé, a Zero Waste, Ethical Fashion Brand on a Big Mission," *Travel Under the Radar*, accessed December 25, 2020.

"The greatness of a community is most accurately measured by the compassionate actions of its members."

~CORETTA SCOTT KING

CHAPTER 7

ENGAGE

PASSION FOR TRASH

"Success is not only in the hand. It's in the heart."

~BRIAN MCGILL

Cook. Paint. Puzzle. Movie. Repeat.

This was my quarantine mantra for the months of March through July. Any bit of spare time not spent hunched over my desk illuminated by my blue-light machine was likely spent on one of these activities. One dull Saturday afternoon, I decided to indulge in the mind-numbing venture of film. After thirty minutes of weary browsing through the Netflix recommended page, I uncovered a beacon of childhood bliss. This classic film ushered a grin to my face although I had no recollection of its plot. All I knew was that *The Lorax* projected an ethereal aura that brought me to a place of pure happiness and optimism. Hoping to assimilate some of that aura into my dingy dining room and transport back to a world I couldn't quite remember, I clicked "play."

Immediately, I was struck by Danny DeVito's raspy and embracing voice as the vibrantly orange Lorax strutted out onto an animated theater stage. His opening line, "I am the Lorax. I speak for the trees," was followed by a pan to an eerily familiar metropolitan oasis of plastic, construction, and disregard for nature. A town the Lorax calls "Thneedville."[182]

Hearing the name of this fictional city made me shift in my chair with discomfort as I recalled my first time viewing the movie in my seventh-grade biology class. It was right before Christmas break, and my teacher treated us to a film fest right before we went off for the holidays. Attempting to feather our brains with something somewhat science-related, my teacher, Mrs. Franklin, selected *The Lorax*. Little did she know, nor did I until my most recent viewing, the Truffula seed would be planted in my brain and blossom into a passion for trash not more than a decade later.

So many aspects of this film had a profound impact on my beliefs and values. The song "Let it Grow" (which I somehow knew all the lyrics to) is an anthem dissuading fast fashion's exploitation of trees and other natural resources. The exposé of decaying tree stumps on once lush Truffula forestland left a hole in my heart still tender to this day. The menacing laugh of Thneedville's mayor as he pitched O'Hare plastic-bottled

---

182 Chris Renaud and Kyle Balda, dir, *The Lorax*, 2012 (Santa Monica, California: Illumination Company, 2012) Blu-ray Disc, 1080p HD; Dr. Suess, *The Lorax* (New York: Penguin Random House LLC., 1971), 10.

air haunts my nightmares.[183] All of these bits of imagery seemed a reflection of my own ignorant suburbia.

Unlike other thought leaders in this book, I did not grow up in a scrapyard surrounded by the consequences of consumerism. I am not a beach baby enraged by surfing excursions soiled by Coca-Cola bottles and various plastic shreds. Until the end of my second decade on Earth, I was completely shielded from the waste epidemic despite the fact I lived three miles from a landfill. However, my second viewing of this heartfelt film unmasked my intolerance for plastic, resource degradation, and evil corporate instigators like Mayor O'Hare. Reminiscing on this shockingly progressive G-rated moving picture refilled my emotional gas to fuel my zero-waste shift.

Since viewing *The Lorax*, I have invested in reusable bags, bulk containers, shampoo bars, and waste-free toothpaste (yes, that exists). My inner drive for sticking it to the man far transcends temporary desires for take-out or trinkets from the drug store. Like the engraving in the prophetic stone from the movie states, I have found my "unless." Even in a world tormented by deforestation and biodiversity loss depicted in the story, the Lorax still expressed a glimmer of hope in spirit, which he deemed the "unless." Stepping onto his soapbox, he wisely professed,

---

183 Chris Renaud and Kyle Balda, dir, *The Lorax*, 2012 (Santa Monica, California: Illumination Company, 2012) Blu-ray Disc, 1080p HD; Ray Anderson and Robin White, *Confessions of a Radical Industrialist: Profits, People, Purpose: Doing Business by Respecting the Earth* (New York: St. Martin's Press, 2009), 4.

"Unless someone like you cares a whole awful lot, nothing is going to get better. It's not."[184]

Similar to the fuzzy orange fellow, I have activated this passion. Doing so, I unleashed positivity to live a more lively, valuable life unified with both nature and our economy. Because of my emotional bond, I started to transform my life into one that is sustainable and, to me, worth living. This bond is not only an asset to waste reduction, but it is absolutely imperative to establish a long-term commitment both personally and professionally.

IN THE FACE OF HYPOCRISY

Nobody better embodies the might of sentimental bonds with waste than activist and *Forbes* "30 Under 30" nominee Lauren Singer, who served as a guide through my own waste reduction journey. Before delivering her wildly successful TED Talk and blog *Trash is for Tossers*, she was an environmental studies student at New York University. It was at this point in her life that her temper caused her to start talking trash.

Singer's successes can be indirectly attributed to a nameless, faceless acquaintance in her environmental studies capstone course. The routine went like this: Every day, Singer, the willed environmentalist she was, would come to class and sit across from this particular student. Every

---

184 Ibid.

day, said student would jam-pack their plastic lunch bag with plastic clamshells containing food, a plastic water bottle, and, to top it off, plastic utensils. Then, at the end of every class period, they would throw it into the garbage can. This felt like blasphemy to Singer as a prodigy in sustainability.[185]

One particularly rough day, Singer was desperate to take out her frustrations caused by this insensible peer by cooking a nice meal for herself. Horrifically, as she opened the refrigerator, she was met by the face of hypocrisy. Every single thing in her fridge was wrapped or packaged in plastic. Her cheese, sauces, even vegetables—all blanketed by cold, hard plastic. As she would later profess in a TED Talk, the weight of trash she generated following this typical American lifestyle was equivalent to:

"Taking 8.5 of [her] friends and throwing them in the trash [every year]."[186]

Singer was completely beside herself. How could she be so critical of her classmate's food habits when she herself had been warped into the lull of plastic packaging? This dilemma began to eat away at her core, and in an instantaneous, meaningful decision, she decided to start eliminating waste.

---

185 *TED*, "Lauren Singer: Why I Live a Zero Waste Life," May 27, 2015, video, 0:10.
186 Ibid.

Her devastating discovery gave her an inner motivation which sent her on a journey to apply trash-reducing strategies into her own life and spread her discoveries with a spirited blog landscape. While other zero-waste bloggers lived out their idyllic lives in the spacious, accommodating comforts of California suburbs, Singer was trapped by the high-rises and corporate mindset of New York City. The Big Apple is the very essence of disposability and short-sightedness, as the population is in a constant state of reconfiguration and the Wall Street mentality infiltrates every inch of the culture. Not to mention, Singer was a college student with a limited budget of money and time.

Despite this, the obligation she had toward trash led her to modify some of the practices and ideas she learned online into her own crazy life.[187]

First, she began rejecting packaged goods and purchasing secondhand. Her kitchen slowly accumulated bulk jars and netted reusable bags while her closet inherited unique, thrifted items. Employing the tips of organizing consultant Marie Kondo, she purged and tidied her space by removing kitchenware and clothing lacking long-term value. Eliminating all of this extra "stuff" may seem to be the opposite of sustainable, but in the process of decluttering, Singer established a strong relationship with the items she decided to keep while remaining cognizant of those she got rid of. To document her commitment, she started her now well-known blog, posting tips for any soul who stumbled

---

187 Leah Rodriguez, "Meet Lauren Singer, the Environmental Activist Making It Easy to Go Waste-Free," *Global Citizen*, April 30, 2020.

upon her story. Her entries include articles on zero-waste gift ideas, zero-waste traveling tips, and articles like "How to Cook and Bake with Common Kitchen Waste Items."[188]

As time went on, Singer continued to be successful financially, but she had an itch to activate a wider audience on the issue of waste—which was her true calling. So, in 2015 she gave a TEDxTeen talk entitled "Why I Live a Zero Waste Life," which as of September 2020 has almost 3.2 million views on YouTube. Her discussion birthed the symbol of her mason jar of trash while discussing the multiple benefits of zero-waste, both spiritually and financially.[189] Singer's intentional lifestyle changes and awe-striking speeches sparked a devout following. Many of her readers and viewers, including me, were supportive of her fervent journey and eager to endorse it themselves, but they simply did not have the time or resources to make everything—from their skincare products to their whole food—themselves.

Empathizing with their struggle and given the heightened recognition for her movement, Singer founded her company, Package Free, as an outlet to fulfill her followers' spiritual values. Package Free offers easily-accessible alternatives for people wanting to go plastic and waste-free, including everything from bamboo toothbrushes to shampoo bars to reusable coffee cups.[190] Each product description outlines directions for how to properly dispose of any excess material reverberating from use, promoting an entirely closed loop.

188 "DIY and Guides," Trash is for Tossers, accessed December 25, 2020.
189 *TED*, "Lauren Singer," video, 0:10.
190 Rodriguez, "Meet Lauren Singer."

The website also offers soap-making, cooking, and sewing classes to teach people skills needed to obstruct waste once and for all.

Alongside her own relentless activism for zero-waste household and personal care products, similar black-owned companies, including BLK + GRN and OUI the People, have amplified a more inclusive waste-free future by specializing in zero-waste natural skincare, detergents, and other goods. BLK + GRN, for example, was founded by Dr. Kristian Edwards to deliver waste-free home, hair, bath, body, and menstrual care alternatives crafted by black artisan women while also supplying these women with access to "tools, resources, knowledge, and products [needed] to lead happier and healthier lives."[191] OUI the People also helped define Singer's zero-waste agenda with their gentle yet durable stainless steel razors, revolting against the two billion disposable plastic shavers ending up in landfill each year.[192] Both of these companies, among multiple others, have committed not only to offering circular alternatives for a broad spectrum of buyers, but also educating them on the issues associated with default consumerism.

Through validating her new fanbase, Singer has attracted over 385,000 Instagram followers, who she invites to develop their own emotional attachments with waste. Without Singer's drive and sentimental relationship with trash, her $4.5 million company—and her activism as a whole—would

---

191 "Behind the Brand," BLK + GRN, accessed February 4, 2021.
192 "The Reconstitution of Beauty," OUI the People, accessed February 4, 2021.

not be the insightful refuge it is today.[193] Her tenacious advocacy and business measures come from her deep commitment to managing waste in our capitalistic society. Therefore, it's safe to say that her legacy will always be understood by:

"The things [she] did while [she] was on this planet, not for what [she] left behind."[194]

In order to successfully replicate this zero-footprint legacy, individuals must embrace their relationship with waste as Lauren Singer did following her environmental studies class catastrophe. Given our current state, this is an extremely rare quality. As we have mentioned before, our modern society has become so accustomed to cleansing itself of plastic packaging, food wrap, and old garments by dashing them away to the ominous "garbage bin." Former CEO of environmental non-profit Green Seal, Arthur Weissman, attributes this waste detachment to the lack of financial incentive to reduce it and the ease of access to landfills.[195] Others may blame the blinding effect of materialism in our western world. Regardless of the cause of this synapse, it is non-negotiable that industrialized society does not depict landfills fondly or empathetically.

---

193 *TED,* "Lauren Singer," video, 0:10.

194 Jordan Crook, "Package Free Picks up $4.5 Million to Scale Sustainable CPG Products," *Tech Crunch,* September 26, 2019.

195 Arthur Weissman, "What Is It About Humans and Waste?" *Green Biz,* May 18, 2019.

We even demonize hoarding, whereby strong bonds prevent hoarders from throwing away their waste. Now, I am certainly not advocating a lifestyle of hoarding, but by combining the sentiment hoarders have for waste with a reduction in expenditures overall, there is certainly opportunity for change.

FUEL FROM OUR ROOTS

Marie Kondo's KonMari method extracts this potential. Generally, hoarders stash their items far beyond their prime or usability while continuing to accumulate new items. In a traditional intervention setting, a full-on power washing program may be administered where almost everything is deemed worthless and landfill worthy. Opposingly, the KonMari method introduces the stethoscopic approach. Individuals are asked to listen to their hearts and only keep items that spark intense joy.[196] Some may see this as an excuse to hoard items with any sliver of reminiscence. While this approach may unintentionally reinforce stashing of sentimental objects, the thought process is a spectacular parallel to the "passion for trash" mentality.

Being sympathetically spliced to the goods we own, purchase, and throw away is a magnificent tool.

The unique modified-hoarder mindset can manifest itself in unexpected ways. For Nicole Bassett, a peruse through

---

196 Marie Kondo, *The Life-Changing Magic of Tidying up: The Japanese Art of Decluttering and Organizing* (Berkeley: Ten Speed Press, 2014), 39.

her kitchen will reveal everything you need to know about her views on sustainability. On her counter lies a tattered, duct-taped, several-times-repaired KitchenAid mixer, which was gifted to her by her aunt at her wedding. This beat-up machine, which Bassett names her most prized possession, represents not only her deep aptitude for cooking, but also her affection for reuse.[197] Her mindset was bred as a youngster where she grew up in British Colombia on the land of the Wet'suwet'en First Nations, who taught her about the precious value of nature. While my youthful viewing of *The Lorax* energized my own eco-friendly behavior, Bassett's environmentalist parents fostered this same mentality in an upbringing where:

"The outdoors was [her] background and [her] dog was [her] babysitter."[198]

After learning compassion for nature in her youth, Bassett put it to use in a job working for the Discovery Channel. Her job as a video editor led her to an unanticipated crossroads. One project she developed highlighted the Ford Motor Company's newest site buildings containing green roofs. Staring at the lush infrastructure for hours on end galvanized her outlook that business is not always a destructive, pollution-oozing

---

197 "Interview with Nicole Bassett, the Renewal Workshop," Once, October 9, 2019.

198 *TED*, "Nicole Bassett: The Future of Business Is Circular," August 27, 2019, video, 13:27.

entity.[199] It can really be an accelerator of social and environmental benefit.

This "a-ha moment" transformed Bassett's career into a garden of social entrepreneurship; in other words, business as a force for good.

Bassett established her personal commitment to apparel waste specifically during a visit to a textile factory. As she stepped foot into the facility producing pink T-shirts the cogs in her mind started turning, and she realized that the manufacturing process typical of the fashion industry was "broken."[200] The monotonous factory equipment was leaking thousands of garments, leaving Bassett frustrated and curious as to where they all ended up. She began to question:

How did the industry come so far from its roots in homestead looms and knitting needles? And what were the consequences of that massive transition?

To answer these questions, Bassett began to explore fashion waste in all its forms, from returns to overproduction to warranty commitments. Through research, she realized, the numerous units annually wasted by the fashion industry had become an acceptable cost of business. Companies had become careless when it came to waste awareness and

199 Hélène Stelian, "Nicole Bassett, Co-Founder, the Renewal Workshop," *Purpose Stories* (blog), *Hélène Stelian Coaching*, November 21, 2017.
200 *Solve-MIT*, "Watch Solver Nicole Bassett Pitch the Renewal Workshop," October 8, 2019, video, 3:01.

instead relied on the "out of sight, out of mind" phenomena. Consequently, they had been notoriously,

> ## "Bad at tracking it, good at masking how big the problem is, and blind to opportunities for change."[201]

In our current climate, several conscious brands are actively countering the wasteful fast fashion industry, among other ethical concerns in textile production. For example, PROCLAIM, an underwear brand producing nude garments for a variety of skin tones, includes collections made from 100 percent recycled plastic water bottles and a highly efficient cellulosic fiber derived from wood pulp called TENCEL.[202] Additionally, Wasi Clothing is a woman-owned Bolivian-American clothing brand producing very little waste by turning their fabric scraps into recycled accessories, masks, and more while using recycled and compostable shipping packaging.[203] These new age operations are clearly necessary to reshape a zero-waste fashion future, but they are also small in scale. As disheartening as it may be, small businesses do not regulate our capitalistic society, but instead dominating corporations do. Recognizing this, Bassett set off to throw a wrench directly in the chain of big business.

---

201 Nicole Bassett, "Is Your Business Wasting Money on Waste?" *Green Biz,* November 16, 2018.

202 "Who We Are," PROCLAIM, accessed February 4, 2021.

203 "How Is Wasi Clothing Sustainable?" Wasi, accessed February 4, 2021.

As she reflected on her childhood perception of oneness with nature nurtured by her indigenous fellows, she hoped to reverse this disheartened craze by starting her own company embodying the circular economy.

Her platform, the Renewal Workshop, enables apparel and textile brands to become circular by providing them the operations to do so. They close the resource loop by taking textile waste, whether that be garments that were overproduced, returned, or scrapped from production processes and revamping them into new items. These unique pieces are also extremely affordable and originate from a variety of brands from Carhartt to prAna. The first factory opened in 2016 with five brand partners, and today that number has dilated to include partners such as the North Face and Pottery Barn.[204]

Bassett's raging success is driven by her frustrations which she outlines in her effective TED Talk:

"Today, all of you are forced into a system where you as a consumer are stuck buying things that are disposable and create waste, and you are forced to subsidize that system to manage all the waste that linear business creates."[205]

---

204 *Solve-MIT*, "Watch Solver Nicole," video, 3:01.
205 *TED*,"Nicole Bassett," video, 13:27.

Her demand for businesses to take responsibility for their process from cradle to grave has amounted to a resounding campaign and profitable business, serving as a model for the rest of corporate society. Bassett's yearning for change stems from her childhood exposure to preservationist customs and close convergence with the environment, which prepared her as an ambassador for the circular economy.

Luckily, in our current state, relationships with nature such as Bassett's are possible because of the sparsely untouched regions of nature and the continuance of cultures that value it. Ventures into state parks and forest preserves can be magical escapes from the consequences of corporate behavior. Even in our daily lives, because we are able to bury our waste underground and contain it sanitarily in most cases, we live without immediate concern of trash contamination. These projects, though, are not foolproof. Many parts of the country still endure dirty mounds of plastic bags and aluminum cans on top of toxic industrial pollution. Rather than having streets lined with white-picket fences or pristine skyscrapers, less privileged demographics are left to clear the hurdles of human health detriments and environmental contamination.

Just a couple decades ago, families in Love Canal, New York, were burdened with long-lasting health ailments like leukemia due to their unnotified residence on an abandoned toxic dump site. Their government refused to address the issue in a timely manner, leaving 56 percent of their children with birth defects.[206] Even today the number of superfunds,

206 *A Fierce Green Fire*, "Lois Gibbs—the Love Canal Story," April 18, 2011, video, 0:51.

or hazardous clean-up sites, are astounding. Unwaveringly these impacts have fallen onto communities of color, which ignited a demand for environmental justice fathered by Dr. Robert Bullard of Texas Southern University.[207] Since then, on the South Side of Chicago (along with numerous other areas around the country), environmental justice groups such as People for Community Recover have been advocating for responsible practices for waste disposal and manufacturing—along with compensation for the damages they directly suffered.[208] Decades in the process, there has been little recognition from the government to address the respiratory health concerns (or any of the other raised wrong-doings) plaguing the community. These emotional tragedies, while clearly devastating, have been huge motivations for proper waste management to preserve citizen health and environmental well-being.

THICKER THAN WATER

Becoming aware of health concerns presented by trash provides a unique and socially optimizing path for entre-preneurial intervention. This path was partially explored by the founder of Bee's Wrap, a compostable plastic wrap alternative. Sarah Kaeck was on a hunt for more ambi-tious business opportunities when she and her husband made the move to New Haven, Vermont. Living in a new house meant more than just a new set of neighbors to interact with and a new rate of property tax. Kaeck

---

207 "Biography," Dr. Robert Bullard, accessed February 12, 2021.
208 "History," People for Community Recover, accessed February 12, 2021.

and her husband made the commitment upon arriving to grow all their own food to protect their children and their health.[209]

The couple were well-rounded horticulturists with a formerly flourishing fungi business, so they were quite familiar with the ambiguity of agriculture in our country. From alleged uncertainty regarding pesticides and other chemicals to absurd plastic wrapping, Kaeck and her husband were skeptical the effects our current food network has on the human body. As a cure, they vowed to grow everything themselves. Lessons from their struggle justified a new venture to start their own business. She recounts:

"Recognizing how little we threw away through that process was really a turning point for me."[210]

Because all their fruits and vegetables were home-grown and unpackaged and their meat and dairy supply consisted of food they hunted or crafted themselves, the plastic index of their food supply was edging zero.[211] Once she became aware of this feat, Kaeck began to look more into the potential dangers of plastic and its impact on the lives of her and her family. The Center of International

---

209 Joyce Marcel, "The Big Buzz: Sarah Kaeck, Bee's Wrap," *Vermont Biz*, September 22, 2019.

210 Ibid.

211 Ibid.

Environmental Law has identified checkpoints along the life cycle of plastic and the health ailments attributed to each. For example, some cumulative impacts of microplastics in the environment include cancer, inflammatory bowel disease, neuro-degenerative disorders, and many other chronic diagnoses.[212] Declaring this diabolical material as the enemy, Kaeck became fixated on expelling plastic from her life all together "for the health of [her] family and the environment."[213]

Her desire to kick plastic to the curb only heightened as she learned from a UN Environment Programme report that only 9 percent of plastic ever manufactured has been recycled in its sixty years of production.[214] Furthermore, she came to recognize the average use time of a plastic bag is a mere twelve minutes, which is nearly non-existent compared to the thousands of years it takes to decompose. As seen with the *Majestic Plastic Bag* mockumentary, with its stalking of a plastic bag's journey to the Great Pacific Garbage Patch, this plastic pollution problem is persistent and extensive.[215]

Therefore, Kaeck wanted to devise a way to lessen this hefty burden.

---

212 "Plastic and Human Health: A Lifecycle Approach to Plastic Pollution," Center for International Environmental Law, accessed December 26, 2020.

213 Joyce Marcel, "The Big Buzz."

214 "Our Planet Is Drowning in Plastic Pollution," United Nations Environment Programme, accessed December 26, 2020.

215 *HealtheBay*, "The Majestic Plastic Bag—a Mockumentary," August 14, 2010, video, 0:21.

Aside from the earth-shattering plastic problem, a much pettier worry of Kaeck's was the aging of her baked creations. She would spend hours laboring over doughs and batters, precisely incorporating yeast, flour, and eggs, just to end up with an inedible baked good the following day. The warm, tantalizing pastry would turn hard as rock by the force of oxygen without a plastic barricade.[216] Engrossed with concern for her family's health and frustration for food waste, Sarah Kaeck vied for a solution.

Fantastically, her cousins approached her with a dual-purpose solution when they pitched the concept of waxed fabric to preserve her baked goods. Thereby, one package could exterminate two of her life's most persistent obstacles, hardened loaves and Ziploc bags.

She immediately started to refine this new business idea. After establishing the brand's logo, she recruited a local artist to develop the classic honeycomb design imprinted on many of Bee's Wrap's products. She seamlessly encapsulated the graces of nature, such as clovers, black raspberries, and maple buds—which became the very basis of the brand. With an artistic concept in mind, it was time to put the idea to the test and devise the first actualized model.[217]

Intrigued by the original prototype, Kaeck fine-tuned the design of her new business idea. She stood nervously in front of her well-trusted stove with a skillet in hand to tackle the mission. Haphazardly tossing beeswax, jojoba oil,

---

216 Joyce Marcel, "The Big Buzz."
217 Ibid.

and tree resin into the pan was an invigorating experience. As she hesitantly dipped her organic cotton fabric into the mixture and patiently awaited its dryness, she unveiled a washable, reusable, and compostable alternative to plastic wrap.

Realizing her success, Kaeck knew it was only a matter of time before her provision would spread to the masses. To inflate her outreach, Kaeck recruited neighborhood friends and fellow concerned mothers. Little by little her network grew, until eight months later her little at-home studio space was filled with matrons of Vermont who were eager to rid the area of plastic waste.[218]

After founding her business in 2011, Kaeck and her "hive" started to craft an online presence through their blog to rally community members to "bee" plastic-free. Establishing this presence was evidently a raving business plan which expounded when *BuzzFeed* released an article and video displaying what they referred to as "eco-wrap" in 2018.[219] Since then, support has flooded the company.

Even through all the buzz that Bee's Wrap has received, the core association to communal health will safeguard its plastic-reducing mission for many years to come. Kaeck's genuine sympathy for the health of her family and fellow peers allowed her to ditch the status quo and invent a circular ensemble with beaming triumph.

---

218 Ibid.

219 Gyan Yankovich, "People Are Obsessed with These $18 Reusable Beeswax Food Wraps," *BuzzFeed,* June 6, 2018.

Accustoming ourselves with the emotional undercurrent of garbage and the impact it can have on local communities can be an unmatched incentive. By activating that subjectivity rather than relying on purely scientific knowledge, CEO of design consulting firm IDEO Tim Brown conceives that we can "head toward the future with energy and enthusiasm and determination."[220]

As utopian as it may seem, without a clear, purpose-driven mission, these heroic intents will likely tank.

Conversations I had with founders of Lifebook, a personal development company inducing individuals to design their own "twelve category smart" life, revealed the importance of purpose when it comes to setting career goals. A clear motivation can not only incite employees and business stakeholders themselves, but customers will also draw in. As mentioned earlier with the rise of B corporations, the public has recently gravitated toward intention-driven businesses, which can in turn enhance revenue. The stronger the attachment with waste, the stronger this value will be in a business organization and the stronger the consumer base will be.

Former CEO of sustainable fashion pioneer Patagonia, Rose Marcario, is another brilliant demonstration of this. During a "moment of reckoning" at her corporate job, she made the snap decision to escape to India and Nepal on a soul-searching expedition. Weeks were spent in a stable state of meditation at temples in Rishikesh, India. Her committed studies of Buddhism served to clarify her personal beliefs

---

220 *GreenBiz*, "How to Design for the Future," September 8, 2020, video, 0:51.

and aspirations, bringing her home with more than just the brown Buddhist prayer beads which she still sports on her wrist. She unlocked a newfound obligation for holism when it came to her work. So, when an old friend approached her with the news that Patagonia was seeking a new CFO she jumped at the opportunity, which she accepted in 2008. The rest is history as she conducted Patagonia down the track of environmental responsibility and activism, a true leader in sustainability until she stepped down in 2020.[221]

Once someone gains clarity on their purpose and understands why veering toward circularity is beneficial, it becomes much easier to accomplish. Whether personal hypocrisy, deep-rooted childhood values, or filial devotion are the source of fiery emotion, sentimental attachment is a driving force of inspiration and a necessary boost through adversities of zero-waste living. This "spear in the chest" phenomenon, which prompted Ray Anderson to give Interface a 360-degree change in direction, can transform the way we see not only business, but the world.

> *"The most successful business leaders*
> *are often experts in emotions."*
>
> ~CHIP CONLEY

221 Jeff Beer, "Exclusive: Patagonia CEO Rose Marcario Is Stepping Down," *Fast Company,* June 20, 2020.

CHAPTER 8

ENGAGE

SEEING IS BELIEVING

"Some will open your heart, others
will open your eyes."

~C.C. AUREL

During the sweltering month of July, I treated myself to a dreamlike trip to the mystical destination of Molokai, Hawaii. Unlike any other Hawaiian island notoriously populated by tourists, Molokai is an isolated gem with a rich, local culture and open landscape to reflect and heal. As gorgeous as the scenery may be, it conceals some hidden blemishes. One day, my friends and I decided to go down to the shoreline of jagged volcanic rocks and crystal blue waters to pick up litter. Assuming the small, eco-conscious population of Molokai, I braced myself with a small bag to store the scraps that had washed up on the rocks.

Once I ventured a few feet inland, a world of waste was exposed among the kiawe trees protecting the shoreline. Old Sprite and A&W cans with distinctly 1950s design stuck out like a sore thumb. We even spotted a "plastic shrine" made of fishing nets and broken buoys ironically set up by one of the residents as a reminder of the immortality of plastic. Given the remoteness of this island, the amount of trash was quite staggering.

Consequently, I began to ponder my own accountability to prevent this tragedy. Now when I pick up a bottled coffee or can of La Croix, I visualize its afterlife and eventual journey to the washed-up shores of a forgotten island.

Is it really worth a few moments of blissful caffeination from a Dunkin' Donuts bottled coffee for thousands of years of environmental havoc?

My epiphany illustrates the capability of the senses, in this case a horrific anti-ecological sight, to awaken a concern for plastic waste. By visually intaking the effects of our purchasing habits, inspiration for zero-waste solutions can strike in a multitude of ways.

FROM LANDFILL TO LUXURY

Kresse Wesling's trash encounter is a stellar example of this feat. This British designer mogul is notable for her luxury accessories brand Elvis & Kresse, which sprung from her own first-hand clash with firehoses. Before beginning her audacious brand, Wesling's studies in Hong Kong at age seventeen caused her to despise waste. She attributes her seminal travels as the starting line of her environmental concerns. She stated in an interview with Cartier Women's Initiative:

> Had I stayed in Canada, I'm not sure I would have seen the scale of destruction that can exist in the world. I had never seen single use goods at such scale, or land reclamation with waste, or known that a significant amount of the world's sewage is pumped, untreated, into the sea.[222]

Her foreign ventures into the sea of waste only persisted when she moved into her new home in the UK. While attending a course on environmental management spurred by her time abroad, she met members of the London Fire Brigade and toured their Croydon base. Upon exploring the facility, Wesling eagerly requested to see the fire hose assessment site. Granting her wish, the firemen guided her to the site where she was presented with coils upon coils of "trashed" fire hoses. These hoses were tainted with tears and imperfections, making them unusable by the life-saving brigade. While they were at the end of their life in the firehouse, Wesling envisioned a gloriously revived life for these dust-covered, rubber heaps.

As she stroked the "lustrous red rubber," her brain circulated with possibilities for reuse.[223]

Running home with this project buzzing in her mind, she began to get her hands dirty and craft some prototypes. The

---

222 "Laureate 2011 Europe: Kresse Wesling," *Fellows* (blog), *Cartier Women's Initiative*, updated December 21, 2020.

223 Ibid.

first task was to slough off all the dirt and grime coating the hose. The next challenge was to find a way to cut through the industrial-grade fiber, which was no easy feat. Finally discovering the proper slicing technique, it was time to determine the hose's future use. After extensive materials research, proposals for roof tiles, furniture, and Christmas ornaments were shut down. Either too expensive, materialistically unsound, or unmarketable, these conceptions never made it off the chopping block. Serendipitously, Wesling came around to the idea of luxury accessories. While on a hunt for the best product, her partner "Elvis's leather belt split so [he] cut off a bit of hose, added his buckle, and hey, presto!"[224]

This happenstance prototype became the basis of the brand Elvis & Kresse, officially launched in 2007. The mission of the brand, defined in her speech at the Unreasonable Impact summit, is to redefine luxury through material inputs and commit to reclaiming resources by sustainably crafting their lining, packaging, business cards, workshop, and even their home.[225] Essentially, she and her partner built their brand to embrace the oxymoron of luxury pieces made of trash. Selling everything from bags to key rings to rugs, Elvis & Kresse constructed an entirely new neighborhood in department stores. Their durable luggage has a modern and industrial charm, with earth-toned bodies and geometric stitching— emitting hints of their sustainable design. The company's belts and bags also have brass buckles and fittings, adding a classic touch.

---

224 Ibid.

225 *Unreasonable*, "Turning Trash into Luxury Fashion Items | Kresse Wesling," December 22, 2017, video, 1:27.

Elvis & Kresse cite their inspiration for their wondrous designs as the Japanese art of kintsugi, the repair of broken pottery with gold.[226] Meticulous craftsmanship multiplies the value of a collection of ceramic shards into enviable art pieces. Respectfully honoring this cultural practice, Wesling decided to commemorate kintsugi in her designs.

Her admirable dedication to this mantra has attracted much attention from consumers, beginning with their first sale at the Live Earth Music Festival.[227] All five hundred belts supplied to their green-merchandising team were sold, and the revenue accumulated from this bashing success was invested into buying the company's first sewing machine. Wesling's instant graduation from entrepreneurial rookie to aspirational businesswoman was especially shocking given the prevalence of green marketing in today's society. Juxtaposed to greenwashing, which we explored through falsely eco-friendly companies like Jack Wolfskin, Wesling distinguishes her brand, saying:

"People aren't just buying green because it's green any more. They want design and craftsmanship too."[228]

Committing to these high-quality standards, Elvis & Kresse have been majorly successful. Simultaneously, keeping the

226 "Our Story," Elvis & Kresse, accessed December 27, 2020.
227 "Laureate 2011 Europe," *Cartier.*
228 Ibid.

visual of trash piles at her center through the expansion of her enterprise, Wesling managed to stay grounded to her values. To achieve long-term success, Wesling believes business must start with a problem rather than an idea. And what better way to get acquainted with a problem than to meet it head on with one's own eyes? In her case, the original problem was mountains of abandoned fire hoses in London eating away at landfill space. Her more recent stakeouts at waste transfer stations, supermarket depots, and industrial estates have also revealed the weight of old coffee sacks, tea sacks, and failed parachute silk, which are also incorporated into their collections as lining and tags.[229]

Wesling's accomplishments are not just measured by dollars and cents or number of press appearances. Her company's operations have accompanied a 100 percent diversion rate of London fire hoses from landfill for the past ten years, and this statistic will presumably ride out for the continuation of the brand.[230] Without her physical encounter with the London Fire Brigade in 2005, Wesling's attention to fire hoses would have likely been slim to none. Due to her close and personal exposure, she has directed her passion for eliminating trash to keep firehoses out of the landfill and at the forefront of her client's field of vision.

By default, the majority of us are tantalized by the "out of sight, out of mind" principle that naturally infects humankind.

---

229 Ibid.
230 "Our Story," Elvis.

This tendency has been requisite to anthropological survival. For example, if a bear is chasing you through the thick of a coniferous forest, you likely won't think about what you will eat for dinner that night. There are even biological causes for this laid out by the American Psychological Association. Our body's nervous system automatically responds to stress by activating our sympathetic nervous system, boosting our heart rate and hormone production.[231] When we encounter a fight-or-flight situation, all other concerns diminish to dust while our body supplies the heart and muscles with oxygen needed to perform optimally in the heat of the moment.

This natural response is logical and justified when we are being mauled by large mammals or being pulled over by a police officer (especially as a BIPOC), but what about when we are living out our comfortable everyday routines? For example, maybe we are placing our bell peppers into plastic produce bags at the grocery store or tossing our leftover rice and beans from our at-home Taco Tuesday. Not a thought is given to the waste created in these mundane situations. Analyzing these scenarios, is "out of sight, out of mind" justified?

In other words, is it acceptable to neglect the afterlife of the items we consume on a daily basis just because they don't end up in our front yards?

As you can probably guess by now, my answer to that question is a resounding "no." The challenges we face in waste

---

231 "Stress Effects on the Body," American Psychological Association, accessed December 27, 2020.

accumulation are so grand that we can no longer afford to plead complacency. Contesting the "not in my backyard" (NIMBY) philosophy, whereby individuals tend to neglect environmental concerns that are not affecting them personally, there must be a challenge to bring our interpretation of trash closer to home. Seeing and experiencing waste first-hand can secure this affinity. If we can physically assess the size of the problem, the motivation to contest it will amass. Even though it may be a traumatic undertaking, it may be necessary to stimulate change.

PLASTIC IN PARADISE

Alex Schulze and Andrew Cooper, founders of 4ocean, unintentionally sacrificed themselves in this way. After taking a disturbing dive into the paint of plastic pollution, their business-oriented discourse was eternally shifted. The two grew up in coastal Florida, and upon becoming best friends in college they went on a destiny-cementing journey they would never regret. Bonding over their love of saltwater, Schulze and Cooper wanted to test their talent on a surfing excursion in Bali in 2015.[232] For months they accumulated every last penny they could sacrifice until finally the piggy bank maxed out. Visions of cerulean seas decorated with stark white crests danced in their heads. The anticipation of toasted graham cracker sand beneath their heels built up trifling excitement for their vacation.[233]

---

232 Rachael Lobeck, "4ocean Co-founders Andrew Cooper and Alex Schulze Named Forbes 30 under 30 Social Entrepreneurs," *Cision PR Newswire,* November 14, 2018.

233 "About," 4Ocean, accessed December 27, 2020.

To their misfortune upon arrival, the stark white waves were tarnished with plastic blemishes and the toasted graham cracker sand was contaminated with rubbish. Appalled by the scenery in this world-renown destination, the duo asked a local why the beach resembled a dumping ground with bits of trash strewn about. The answer to this inquiry was a lot more discouraging than financial instability to address the garbage epidemic. Much to their demise, the response was:

"The beach had just been cleaned [that] morning."[234]

Those distressful words meant that the massive trash piles dispersed about the beach had mounted within just a few hours. The cause of this issue became abundantly clear upon analyzing the visitation statistics of the island. According to the Bali Province Tourism Development Statistics, 6.3 million tourists visited the country in 2019 for various reasons.[235] Because visitors see this destination as a temporary paradise resilient to the brunt of their flagrant vacationized consumerism, Bali's beaches have certainly seen better days. Clearly, tourists employ the "out of sight" mentality as their stays typically only span a couple of weeks maximum, which causes them to exasperate their purchasing and disposing habits commanded by the hospitality industry. Because of

---

234 "'We Are in This for the Long Haul': Florida's 4ocean Founders Work to Save the Seas from Trash," *CBS Miami*, May 31, 2019.

235 Ross Woods, "A Brief Review of Bali Tourism in 2019," *Hotel Investment Strategies, LLC*, February 4, 2020.

this, the indigenous populations are left to deal with the trash of vacationers past, which cuts gaping gashes into their time and industry.

Schulze and Cooper, in utter despair, started to propose solutions to fix this overwhelming issue. They eventually formulated the idea to hire local boat captains and workers, who were familiar with cleaning the oceans and coastlines, full time. These fishermen had to deal with bottles, six-pack rings, and bags pinching off their commercial fishing artery day by day, so they were already experts in the cleanup process.[236] The hope of 4ocean was to financially and technologically assist these local toils to mitigate the tide of plastic pollution coming primarily from westernized nations.

In 2017, 4ocean was officially cofounded to assist this mission. They employ three clean-up methods to eliminate plastic:

1. Daily offshore cleanups using handheld fishing nets
2. Beach cleanups where volunteers slough the stuff by hand
3. Partnerships with cleanup organizations

The offshore vessel 4ocean primarily uses has the capacity to mechanically gather 310,000 pounds of plastic in a single trip through its wide-armed design. Supplemental ships can carry additional 1,500-pound loads.[237]

The collected plastic is then sorted, weighed, and documented through a TrashTracker system, after which it is washed and

---

236 "'We Are in This," *CBS Miami.*
237 Ibid.

pelletized to create jewelry.[238] Their stylish bracelets, with clear beads and a plastic fiber thread, are a minimalist's dream and environmentalist's sublime. Additionally, they sell reusable cutlery, apparel, and stickers to heighten their cause of keeping our oceans clean. For every one of their twenty-dollar bracelets purchased, one pound of trash is pulled from the ocean. The revenue accumulated from these sales is fed directly back into cleanup operations and donations to marine conservation groups. Ultimately, this model brings plastic pollution from the unimaginable stretches of the salty seas to convenient wrist-wear as a reminder of our disruptive habits.

After starting 4ocean, Schulze's waste-witnessing persisted on a visit to Haiti. As the plane was preparing to touch base, the view of gorgeous seaweed colonies spotted off the coast through his window stunned him. He later found out the green bands were actually plastic tidal pools.[239] On the grounds, this deceptive problem was only magnified, where a local river mouth contained a ten-foot-deep, three-hundred-foot-wide reservoir of plastic.[240] Similar to Bali, the local fishermen were literally swimming in the problem. They were forced to use their nets and tools to construct barricades to block the plastic from entering the marine ecosystem. Reaffirming the expansive nature of the issue in less-privileged nations throughout the world, 4ocean defined their mission as complete only when:

---

238 "About Us," 4ocean, accessed December 27, 2020.
239 "Innovator: Andrew Cooper and Alex Schulze," *Newsweek*, January 16, 2019.
240 4ocean, "What's 4ocean Doing to Stop Plastic from Entering the Ocean?" February 14, 2019, video, 0:22.

"We can walk along our beaches—in Bali, in Haiti, in Florida, and around the world— and see nothing but warm sand and rolling waves."[241]

A more definitive and urgent goal, in my opinion, would be a future where local citizens of Bali, Haiti, and Miami are no longer burdened with the consequences of the westernized obsession with single-use.

Large strides have already been made toward this goal, with plastic pollution being reduced around the world one pound at a time. Beyond selling physical goods, the company has also administered a donation service called "Pull a Pound+" which allows customers to purchase plastic pulling from the ocean. Singular donations or monthly subscriptions allow users to subsidize the cleanup of one, five, or ten pounds of trash at a price of ten dollars per pound. As of October 2020, donors have paid to pull over eleven million pounds to support their mission.[242]

Witnessing the monumental issue of ocean plastics was an eye-opening observation for Alex Schulze and the 4ocean team, who now identify themselves as "the happiest garbage men in the world." Of course, the first step in the eye-opening "seeing is believing" protocol 4ocean and Elvis & Kresse effectively took advantage of is *seeing*. Ironically, this is also the

---

241 "About Us," 4ocean.
242 Ibid.

first obstacle typically endured by individuals trailing waste reduction.

Many people fail to actually look at what they are throwing away, let alone understand where it ends up. The Shelton Group, a sustainability consulting firm, has revealed through its surveys that only 22 percent of Americans admit to looking at an item's recycling label before disposing of it.[243] So how can we responsibly dispose of waste if we don't even take the time to look at the things we throw away every day? And if we can't face the existence of trash in our own homes, how can we begin to comprehend it on a global scale?

SOURCED BY SCARCITY

As an environmentalist, I previously viewed myself as aware of the scope of scrap and many of the various implications it has globally. That is, until I read *Junkyard Planet*.[244] This book details author Adam Minter's background growing up in a metal scrapyard run by his absent father and the "scrapyard tour" he took around select regions of America and China. Part of his venture included a visit to a Chinese Christmas light recycling facility. The workers would strip and melt down the massive bales of lights, comparable in size to a semi-truck, into a somewhat-homogenized goop to parse out the precious copper. Seeing the facility, especially

---

243 Suzanne Shelton, "Engaging Middle America in Recycling Solutions: The Challenges & Opportunities," *Shelton Group*, September 2, 2020.

244 Adam Minter, *Junkyard Planet: Travels in the Billion-Dollar Trash Trade* (London: Bloomsbury Press, 2013), 1.

a recycling facility, send enormous amounts of plastic to a landfill seethed Minter to his core. This frustrating realization not only gave him a reason to continue his tour exploring the corruption of the recycling industry, but it simultaneously renewed his understanding of recycling and waste as a whole.

Examining the repercussions of our consumption is unequivocally important for circularity. On the other end of the spectrum, though, comes the value in visualizing resource scarcity. Thus far, seeing end-of-life materials in excess has been the basis of entrepreneurial action, but equally as convincing is the perspective of natural resource limitations. Through this realization, Dame Ellen MacArthur, founder of the Ellen MacArthur Foundation, was subtly impelled to elevate the circular economy.

As a ten-year-old, she was on a quest to become a professional sailor. To make headway toward this goal, MacArthur sacrificed her taste buds at school lunch, where she succumbed to the economical pull of mashed potatoes and baked beans costing a grand total of eight cents per day. Her hope was to save up money to purchase an eight-foot dinghy as a virtuous vessel to kickstart her sailing career. This endearing determination slowly became more than a pipe dream as she continued the practice for an entire three years of schooling. MacArthur's frugal, carb-loaded lunches were just the beginning of her respect for diligent conservation. After finally purchasing her first vessel, which she called Threp'ny Bit, she gained the confidence to hoist even larger sails on larger ships. This advancement in equipment also gave her a face-to-face encounter with scarcity.[245]

When she turned seventeen, after her teacher slashed her dreams of becoming a veterinarian, MacArthur impulsively dropped out of school to start an apprenticeship in sailing. Although MacArthur likely veered from the veterinary practice to pursue sailing as a last-ditch effort, what she made out of this dissent was absolutely extraordinary. At the ripe age of nineteen, in 1995, she completed her first circumnavigation of the globe, and in 1998 she was named "Yachtsman of the Year" in the UK. A mere seven years later, she broke the record for the fastest solo sailing trip around the world.[246]

Spiting the fact that a French woman swiped her title soon after, MacArthur reinterpreted her sailing as a valuable endeavor which allowed her to seek meaning elsewhere in her life. Meditation and reflection on her sailing surfaced her intention to build her current career vested in the circular economy. She recalls her enlightenment as follows:

> If I said to you all now, "Go off into Vancouver and find everything you will need for your survival for the next three months," that's quite a task. That's food, fuel, clothes, even toilet roll and toothpaste. That's what [sailors] do, and when we leave we manage it down to the last drop of diesel and the last packet of food. No experience in my life could have given me a better

245 *TED*, "Dame Ellen MacArthur: The Surprising Thing I Learned Sailing Solo Around the World," June 29, 2015, video, 1:15.

246 Ibid.

understanding of the definition of the word "finite."
What we have out there is all we have. There is no
more.[247]

Cognizant of the scarcity of resources, MacArthur interpreted the lessons she learned from sailing to the economy
by and large. Currently, the global ecological footprint of
humanity equates to about 1.6 Earths according to the World
Wildlife Fund. This footprint tabulates the carbon dioxide
associated with our use of resources such as food, timber,
and livestock. That demand is then weighed against the
biocapacity of our planet to sequester that carbon through
productive land such as forest, grazing, and croplands, which
calculates the 1.6 Earths.[248] When these two numbers are
exactly equal (in other words a footprint of 1.0 Earths), our
world is living within our planet's means. Unfortunately, the
ratio has been obscenely off-kilter for many years. Humanity
is burning through resources at a rate over one and a half
times the rate the planet can replenish itself, which will
create significant impacts on climate resilience and resource
scarcity.[249]

Related to this concept is Earth Overshoot Day, the day of the
year when humans have used up the equivalent of resources
that the Earth can annually supply. After this point, resources
used are "overshoot," which goes to deplete resource capacity
for the future. Averaging global resource use, this day has

---

247 Ibid.
248 "Ecological Footprint," World Wildlife Fund, accessed December 27,
    2020.
249 Ibid.

fallen around mid-to-late August in recent years, leaving a full four to five months of overshoot. In countries like the United States, our westernized lifestyles use up our annual quota of resources around mid-March.

This, of course, is unsustainable long-term and needs to be addressed to ensure security for our children and grand-children. Complex, exciting, and extremely challenging as it would be, MacArthur's vision was to draw back those reigns within the capabilities of our earth by sparking a global advance toward conservation and resource reuse. In 2010, she launched the Ellen MacArthur Foundation to get her mission started.

This organization works with cities, multinational corpo-rations, and nationwide governments to commission the circular economy. From cases in Asia to Latin America, her team has studied and actualized schools of thought such as "Cradle to Cradle" design and sharing economy to sever the leash between economic growth and resource exploitation. Essentially, the foundation promotes the use of industrial waste, recycling programs, and purposeful design to escape the toxic linear progression of our economy.[250] Due to her foundation's relentless affairs, the number of private market funds with a circular economy focus has grown ten-fold in the past four years. The number of signatories on the New Plastics Economy, an initiative to concoct a circular market for plastics, increased from one in 2017 to over two hundred

250 "Mission and Vision," Ellen MacArthur Foundation, accessed February 12, 2021.

in less than three years. These partners include big brand names such as L'Oréal, Walmart, and PepsiCo.[251]

MacArthur's effort to bend our economy into a circular model began with her youthful understanding of frugality and the finity of resources. Incredibly, she has applied these values to the pillaging economy that currently exists and has worked tirelessly to bring forth this same awakening for others. In her words, to resolve this dilemma we will need to address the question:

"What if we could build an economy that uses things, rather than uses them up?"[252]

For all of these zero-waste and circularity advocates, the sense of sight was a reliable muse for economic over-throw and fear for failure to change our customs. From their first-hand encounters, these leaders delved themselves into research of business models, source materials, and financially viable reuse strategies. For Wesling, it was heaps of firehoses; for Schulze, plastic-laden beaches; and for MacArthur the scarcity of sailing sparked her resource conservation.

---

251 "Financing the Circular Economy," Ellen MacArthur Foundation, accessed December 27, 2020.

252 Ellen MacArthur (@ellenmacarthur), "What if we could build an economy that uses things, rather than uses them up?," Twitter, June 4, 2020, 5:00 a.m.

So although the reliability of sight may be contested in religious and spiritual contexts, its capacity to increase awareness of environmental issues is irrefutable. By increasing personal relevance and providing relative scale, our eyes give us the clarity necessary to reverse the trend of trash.

"We are only as blind as we want to be."

~MAYA ANGELOU

CHAPTER 9

CONNECT

RIDING TRENDS

———

*"It's no longer the big beating the small,
but the fast beating the slow."*

~ERIC PEARSON

From my perspective as a junior in college, most students seem to have their future path at least somewhat carved out. I, on the other hand, am just laying my foundation in the field of purposeful business. As a crucial addition to that path, I made the decision to apply for a social entrepreneurship club which is part of a wider international organization called Enactus, which I attributed earlier as an extremely valuable educational undertaking.

As a part of my local chapter, one of the nine projects currently developing is called "CreAlgae." This team is researching a way to manufacture bioplastics from harmful algal blooms in our local waterways to mediate both plastic pollution and repercussions of toxic algae. Another project called "Grounds for Growth" takes used coffee grounds and vegetable oil from local establishments to make handmade soaps and scrubs while employing financially insecure individuals in the Campustown area.

The projects of this organization are truly remarkable, and the opportunity to be a part of them has been a real honor. The most surprising thing I heard upon joining this group was by one of the project managers who said during the recruitment process:

"You don't always need to reinvent the wheel."

I was originally a bit astonished hearing this mantra from the same person legitimately trying to make plastic out of plants. Upon further reflection, I recognized that while these ideas were extraordinarily creative in their own respects, they utilized existing frameworks and trends as inspiration. Plastic alternatives are a wildly popular item of discussion in the scientific arena, with bioplastics being a front-running candidate. Applying this existing current, the CreAlgae team embarked on a noteworthy project tailored to our local area. Ultimately, by taking advantage of academic conversations and current events, sustainable solutions on my campus have flourished.

#FINDYOURVEGAN

Thankfully, the communication of sustainable solutions has not only existed within the scientific and professional community; they have also exploded on trendy social media platforms in recent years. Between Earth Day 2019 and Earth Day 2020, the discussion on "innovation" and "action" in sustainability grew 285 percent on Twitter.[253] Businesses have even taken to these social platforms to advocate for environmentalism, including recycling company TerraCycle. Their #KeepOnRecycling campaign urged individuals to hang onto their recyclable goods until their programs were restored following the pandemic.

Besides TerraCycle's campaigns, promotion of sustainable behaviors on such platforms is multi-faceted. As an accessible oasis of information, these websites helped to formulate an enthusiastic consumer base for waste-free products larger than it has ever been. Social media is an impressive display case concurring sustainable brands with suitable customers all over the world.

For me, daily Instagram checks normally consist of hyper speed cooking videos, unwarranted revealing shots of millennial celebrities, and, if I'm lucky, a video compilation of baby goats. Feed content is completely unique and tailored to every individual person, but there is one quirk of Instagram that every single user has come across: advertisements. Though I normally scroll past these nuggets of inconvenience, which look different for everyone based on the ominous

---

253 F. Ashraf, "Earth Day 2020: Celebrities Take to Twitter to Join the Conversation on the Environment," *Indulge*, April 22, 2020.

"algorithm," the subliminal messaging persists, and I am left with unconscious memories of Instagram ads past. While my personal knowledge bank of ads is enormous and varied, one campaign sticks out in my mind: Pela phone cases.

Pela, founded in 2010 by Jeremy Lang, has flourished as a wing under an online marketing company into a symbol of waste-reduced living. The muse behind the brand came from an archetypal tale about the founder's life-altering trip to Hawaii's trash-laden beaches, just as I had on my trip to Molokai. After this traumatic encounter, he began experimenting with biodegradable and compostable plastic alternatives to a slew of everyday items. Eventually, the Pela team came upon flax shive, an agricultural byproduct that was 100 percent compostable and durable enough to produce phone cases, which is exactly what they did.[254]

Phone cases are an ideal alcove because cellular users replace their phone on a regular basis. While old phones may be reconfigured or recycled, their defunct cases last thousands of years in the environment. Therefore, finding a way to reduce their uninvited residence in our planet's forests, waterways, and rolling meadows was a natural yearning. Besides Pela's appeal to sustainably focused demographics, the brand has also tapped into the exploding market of smartphone accessories. A website named Wildflower Cases pioneered the smartphone accessory movement after a chance encounter with Miley Cyrus, who fell in love with the founders' unique homemade designs. Since

---

254 Brad Anderson, "How Are Sustainable Startups Like Pela Fighting Plastic Waste?" *Lead* (blog), *ReadWrite*, March 12, 2020.

then, Wildflower has partnered with celebrities and social media icons to design their own cases available for purchase.[255] Other companies such as CASETiFY have also ridden the wave of smartphone accessories—where they have been equally successful.[256]

Not just any phone case start-up is guaranteed a golden ticket though. Since the up-and-coming generation is surgically attached to their cellular devices, it is only reasonable they sport cases they are proud to share. For Pela's solutions, that sense of pride comes from advocating sustainability. Recognizing this capacity, CEO Matt Bertulli used the Pela brand to appeal to customers resonating with his philosophy:

"Retail shouldn't really have a legacy. It should have zero impact on the planet."[257]

His successful campaigns and customer retention diverted one billion pounds of plastic waste from the landfill globally. Pela also had the financial and environmental capacity to certify as a B corporation, Climate Neutral Certified business, and a member of One Percent for the Planet.[258]

---

255 "How Wildflower Cases Blossomed," Wildflower Cases, accessed February 13, 2021.

256 "Welcome to the New CASETiFY," CASETiFY, accessed February 13, 2021.

257 Matthew Bertulli, "The Legacy of Retail in One Number: Zero," *Matthew Bertulli* (blog), *Medium*, July 19, 2017.

258 Grow Ensemble, "Fueling a Circular Economy Through Sustainable Everyday Products," *B The Change* (blog), *Medium*, June 9, 2020

Much of this accomplishment is attributable to CEO Matt Bertulli's ability to "find their vegan."[259] Vegans are a fascinating population to draw inspiration from because as the running joke goes: if you're a vegan, everyone will know about it. Usually people who choose to be vegan are very devoted to their commitment and invite conversations to inspirit others to consider a plant-based lifestyle.

What better audience is there to activate than one that enthusiastically advertises one's service out of the goodness of their values?

Reminiscent of vegans, Pela's target group was the zero-waste community. The online base of "zero-wasters" is small but gaining traction day by day. These waste warriors are making zero-waste more and more prevalent through their messaging on plastic pollution and other trashy subjects, further feeding Pela's success. As more people are exposed to the zero-wasters' revolution against consumption, they are also primed to support Pela's mission.

This devoted group proved a compelling marketing tactic. In April of 2020, as the COVID-19 pandemic was eroding the world's economy, the company had over 350,000 total viewers on their website. Facebook, YouTube, and Reddit make up the majority of their social media sales, and their online presence as a whole is quite impressive.[260] Not to mention,

---

259 *INspired Insider*, "Matthew Bertulli of Pelacase & Demacmedia on Inspiredinsider with Dr. Jeremy Weisz," March 12, 2020, video, 24:20.

260 "Pelacase.com January 2021 Overview," SimilarWeb, accessed December 29, 2020.

the Canadian Business' Fastest Growth List of 2020 ranked them in ninth place.[261] Non-arguably, the brand's tenacity in "finding their vegans" and mobilizing zero-waste activists fed this success. By engaging this emerging community through social media, Pela transformed wasted flax into a durable global solution to the plastic pandemic.

THINKING SECONDHAND FIRST

As Gen Z becomes more and more concerned with the environment, Pela's success spreading zero-waste has greater likelihood for wide-scale acceptance. Even though 92 percent of Gen-Zers allegedly care about sustainability issues and 89 percent express worry for the overall state of our planet, there is still a shortcoming putting these beliefs into universal practice.[262]

Otherwise put, this hypothetical "concern" younger generations have for the environment needs to tie to relevant action to really drive progress forward.

Social media is a perfect unifying ground for this insurrection to occur. Software company Conversocial shared a report that indicated about one-third of millennials use Twitter over email as a way to contact customer service.[263] Since social networking is becoming a primary source of communication between these two points of the business

---

261 "Growth List 2020," Canadian Business, accessed December 29, 2020.
262 "Cone Communications Gives Companies a Lesson on How to Speak Gen Z," *Sustainable Brands*, September 12, 2017.
263 Conversocial Report: The State of Social Customer Service (New York, NY: Conversocial), 3.

supply chain, capitalizing on fads prominent through these networks can be a great way to endorse successful circular solutions while enhancing brand recognition. The first step in this methodology requires identifying trends to respond to purchaser interests in a timely manner. According to a report by Sprout Social, a social media management and optimization platform, nearly two-thirds of marketers surveyed felt this technique of "social listening" would be a constitutive strategy in 2020.[264]

Social listening, though, is not only a science but an art. It requires patient, conscientious awareness and an enthusiasm to learn. With that being said, market research itself can take on multiple personas, from analytical software to face-to-face conversation. James Reinhart, a bold master's business student keen on chasing trends, demonstrated one such scheme as he meandered the campus of Harvard University, approaching fellow students with a clipboard in hand and a tenacity for answers. For reasons not entirely clear, Reinhart's clothes had just been rejected from a local consignment shop despite his haul of intact J.Crew and Banana Republic attire. After this troubling rejection, he set out to investigate the science of fashion resale by interrogating friends, colleagues, and just about anyone he happened to pass on campus, asking them about the story behind their closets.[265] He began by pressing individuals on how often they used their garments. To his astonishment:

264 Brent Barnhart, "The Most Important Social Media Trends to Know for 2020," *Social Media Trends* (blog), Sprout Social, August 4, 2020.

265 Justin Biel, "ThredUP's Founder Shares His Formula for Developing a World-Changing Business," *Grow Wire,* January 9, 2020.

"Not a single person said they wore over half their clothes."[266]

The average participant admitted that only one-third of their wardrobe was "active," leaving the remaining 70 percent a complete waste of space. This utility ratio in any other entity or service would be ridiculed as wasteful and subject to re-tooling. Armed with research confirming this unfortunate propensity, Reinhart cofounded his online platform thredUP to give fashion a sustainable makeover.

As an online thrift store, thredUP allows users to buy and sell certified preowned garments at the convenience of their smartphone or computer. At the time of his start-up, eBay and Craigslist had been the only comparable platforms. However, the logistics and user-friendly nature of thredUP's exclusively-apparel marketplace was a one-of-a-kind conception. Reinhart forewent the reinvention of the wheel and utilized the tenors of his local community plus existing online thrifting platforms to conceive a unique circular business model.[267]

His mission is to "inspire a new generation to think second-hand first," with a Clean Out Bag in every American closet devoted to thredUP's marketplace.[268] While donating clothes may be a common household practice, the bleak reality is that the majority of donated clothes don't end up in the hands

---

266 Ibid.
267 Samantha McDonald, "Why Both Macy's and JCPenney Teamed up with thredUP—in Less Than 24 Hours," *Footwear News*, August 15, 2019.
268 Biel, "ThredUP's Founder."

of those who need them; they end up outside of the reuse cycle. An article by Green America reveals that Goodwill stores typically landfill about 5 percent of their immediate inflow due to mildew contamination, and after four weeks of shelf life a lot of the donated goods are shredded into construction insulation material (ending the closed loop), or shipped overseas as a donation to impoverished areas.[269] While some of these alternatives may seem beneficial, these "repurposed" textiles constitute less than 20 percent of the textile waste stream with the rest being immediately incinerated or landfilled. Plus, the recycled and exported clothing still takes a heavy toll on local economies by suppressing their own unique clothing brands. Not to mention the excessive processing and transport associated with these solutions undermine the environmental benefits of reuse.[270] Given the fashion industry has revenues valued over fifty billion dollars annually, there is definitely a need to maintain the life of these garments.[271] By joining thredUP, traditionally trashed garments are posed as hot commodities on a global platform promoting transparency and quality-assurance. Users actually become participants in the circular economy, which allows them to see out the entire life of their clothes, giving homage to the "seeing is believing" concept.

Of course, there are limitations. After sixty to ninety days, unsold garments are either shipped back to the seller or

---

269 Beth Porter, "What Really Happens to Unwanted Clothes?" *Green America,* Winter 2019.

270 Ibid.

271 "Financing the Circular Economy," Ellen MacArthur Foundation, accessed December 27, 2020.

"responsibly recycled."[272] Because there is no absolute way to eliminate trashed textiles so long as we rely on fast fashion, collectively reaching zero-waste is currently impossible. Taking thrift store benefits to an online, easily accessible, and widespread model is nonetheless a step in the right direction.

As we have seen, the fashion industry is incredibly resource-intensive. Over 85 percent of the industry's waste is land-filled each year, amounting to ten billion pounds annually in the United States alone.[273] As my high school environmental science teacher told me back in Tipping the Scales, a single pair of jeans requires a daunting two thousand gallons of water to manufacture. On the other hand, according to thredUP, twenty-five billion gallons of water, 5.2 billion pounds of CO_2 emissions, and 449 million pounds of waste could be curtailed if everyone simply bought *one* used clothing item instead of a new one this year.[274] The company is well on its way to making this fantasy a reality, as they have taken in one hundred thousand individual items each day and are moving in an upward trajectory. Moreover, thred-UP's Resale-as-a-Service program partners with JCPenny, Macy's, and America's largest physical retailer, Walmart, to offer accessible in-person locations for resale exchange.

Much of thredUP's success can be attributed to the popularity of thrifting and digital fashion, which was

---

272 Mara Leighton, "ThredUP Rewards You for Cleaning Out Your Closet While Donating to Those in Need—Here's What It's like to Use," *Business Insider,* September 11, 2020.

273 *TED,* "Amit Kalra: 3 Creative Ways to Fix Fashion's Waste Problem," March 9, 2018, video, 1:28.

274 Biel, "ThredUP's Founder."

a major template for the brand itself. As social media influencers display their golden vintage finds and even sell their own unique garments second-hand, the culture of waste-free fashion has become much more preeminent. According to retail analytics firm GlobalData, the twenty-four-billion-dollar resale market is expected to grow twenty-one times faster than traditional retail, reaching a whopping fifty-one billion dollars by 2023.[275]

This trend is not only high trajectory, but it also appears relatively stable, ensuring the prolonged success of thredUP and similar platforms. For example, the 2020 Tokyo Olympics Nike apparel was set to be made of completely recycled polyester and yarn, a decision which required international cooperation and buy-in. Specifically, their Space Hippie sneakers were made from factory yarn scraps, recycled plastic water bottles, and T-shirts.[276] Even though this Olympics did not occur due to the COVID-19 pandemic, the collaborative emphasis on sustainability and circularity associated with this event was a major progress marker.

Reinhart holds hope for this collaboration in sustainable fashion. From his researched perspective, during the pandemic secondhand apparel has been a "bright spot" outperforming traditional clothing. He firmly believes,

---

275 Ibid.
276 Edgar Alvarez, "Nike's Chief Design Officer on Why the Company Is Going All in on Sustainability," *Input,* February 2, 2020.

"It's an exciting time for resale even though it's an uncertain time for the rest of us."[277]

With the unprecedented path of his brand, James Reinhart relied heavily on riding trends throughout the birth and lifecycle of thredUP. He started by diving into his acquaintances' history with resale and, like Sherlock Holmes, scouted adjacent societal dynamics to institute a circular solution. With conscientious market research and timeliness, Reinhart paved a path for zero-waste to become the new norm.

REBOUNDING FROM "CANCEL CULTURE"

Not only does surfing the wave help identify a nesting place for one's business, it can also be used to troubleshoot shortcomings and catastrophic missteps. For example, one waste reduction initiative conducted by health giant CVS Pharmacy was goaded by buzz in the Twitter meme community. One of my mentors is a consultant under a branch of this corporation, and he has noticed some tangible change in the receipt department. These changes came partially as a reaction to the influx of memes criticizing the length of receipts from the store, such as, "Insane fact: The sun is approximately eight CVS receipts from Earth."

In response, the corporation took steps to reduce their amount of paper utilized for receipts, and they have since offered paperless alternatives throughout their nationwide

---

277 *CNBC Television*, "ThredUP CEO James Reinhart on the Company's New Partnership with Walmart," June 23, 2020, video, 1:55.

stores. Albeit it may have started off as a comical and petty critique, CVS really took this feedback to heart to upholster a more sustainable future. This debacle gave the already dominating brand an additional hoist in popularity and admiration in the sustainability space.

Not all brands come out the other end of media-induced scrutiny unscathed. "Cancel culture" on social media, which is distantly rooted in practices of public shaming and Chinese *renrou sousuo* ("human flesh search"), occurs when heavy bouts of criticism toward previously accepted people or concepts come in momentary doses. Often times, the intent of this angry retortion is to call attention to unjust systems and power dynamics, but through the process of criticism it has occasionally birthed more resilient and sympathetic brands.[278] In September 2019, Rent the Runway, a fashion app that allows users to rent designer pieces and return them whenever they so choose, accomplished just this.

Gone are the days where event-goers need to spend two thousand dollars on a designer dress. Instead, this virtual rental service allows subscribers to adorn decadent pieces for a night (or otherwise specified period) before returning them. Multiple subscription services exist, which can allow users to rent as many items as they would like in a month for a flat rate. Alternatively, customers can rent single pieces or purchase if they are truly in love with the item. Between users, the garments are inspected, dry-cleaned, repaired, and reassembled at their Dream Fulfillment Center to ensure quality.

---

278 Ligaya Mishan, "The Long and Tortured History of Cancel Culture," *New York Times,* December 3, 2020.

Deemed "the closet in the cloud" and "Netflix model of haute couture," Rent the Runway's vision has become widely recognized and praised. Diane von Fürstenberg, a designer fashion icon, blessed their journey with good luck charms for CEO Jennifer Hyman and a stamp of approval.[279] A fertile societal landscape also nurtured the fast spread of the app. The increasingly popular Marie Kondo mindset encouraged closet purging, and the rise of environmentalism and smaller urban apartments gave people a reason to own less.[280] Combining these undercurrents with the economy of access model, reminiscent of Netflix, Hyman's brand brought in a diverse audience committed to her vision, which is for:

> People [to] think of their closets like they think about a stock portfolio. There are things you want to invest in, you make those investments and those are your blue chips... but for everything else you should just have that on rotation.[281]

She advocates for a constantly evolving closet where users can test out new fads, embrace newfound ingenuity, and do so while bypassing traditional retail. With the average subscriber using Rent the Runway 150 days of the year, it's safe to admit:

279 "Our Story," Rent the Runway, accessed December 25, 2020.
280 Claire Ballentine, "Rent the Runway CEO Says Access, Not Ownership, Is Fashion's Future," *Bloomberg*, November 21, 2019.
281 *CNBC*, "Rent the Runway CEO: Closet in the Cloud | Mad Money | CNBC," May 23, 2018, video, 2:00.

"The pride of ownership is dead, and the pride of access is the new luxury."[282]

Hyman recognized and embraced this trend early in the game and built a successful business from it. Suddenly, the brand's social media praise, similar to CVS, went awry as a wave of torrent came down through Twitter. Rent the Runway's Dream Fulfillment Center underwent a major redesign in September 2019 intended to improve the customer experience by making the turnover of garments more efficient. The modulation immediately had the opposite effect, causing delayed orders and a massive backlash from subscribers. An influx of tweets and magazine articles came out, attacking Rent the Runway for being inconsiderate of their customer's needs, exemplifying the recent tendency identified by Conversocial to indirectly express dissatisfaction with a company.

During this crisis, it was dire to the Rent the Runway team to reverse the demolition of the brand. To mediate concern, Hyman tweeted:

> Currently I'm doing customer service instead of playing with my two young babies on a Saturday so I appreciate your vocalness to improve things, but please understand that we are all working hard and giving 110 percent.[283]

---

282 Ballentine, "Rent the Runway."

283 Jennifer Hyman (@Jenn_RTR), "I am present and doing all I can. Currently I'm doing customer service instead of playing with my 2 young babies on a Saturday so I appreciate your vocalness to improve things but please understand that we are all working hard and giving 110 percent," Twitter, September 14, 2019, 1:59 p.m.

In addition, they sent out individual apology emails and coupons to their devoted customers to mend this mishap. Since that entanglement, Rent the Runway has shown their resilience and drive to honor their mission, which is still going strong to this day. Besides maintaining customers' direct needs, they have strengthened their mission by paying attention to relevant waste reduction conversations. The company now utilizes reusable plastic garment bags which are sanitized between orders to use over and over, unlike traditional disposable plastic clothing wrap. Although their "environmentally-friendly" packaging still contains plastic, it has saved over nine hundred tons of shipping waste.[284]

In spite of their imperfect efforts, it would be naive to expect business to be wholesome and unproblematic 100 percent of the time. Comparatively, Rent the Runway's reusable bag scheme and fashion renting model overall is heads and heels ahead of other apparel distributors, who collectively exploit 180 billion plastic garment bags annually. For that, Hyman and her team deserve a standing ovation.[285]

In October 2020, Rent the Runway also decided to partner with thredUP in a sustainable fashion duo raising the industrial bar. Through their collaboration, Rent the Runway will feature reused items from thredUP's inventory to display a more affordable and individualized virtual closet. Their core visions to create a world with a single fluid closet has been given life. Through the convergence of other tendencies,

284 "Our Story," Rent the Runway, accessed December 25, 2020.
285 James Murray, "Hundreds of Companies Crack down on Plastic from Fast Fashion to Supermarkets and Beyond," *Green Biz*, March 6, 2020.

Hyman and Reinhart manifested platforms where users can indulge in both their love for fashion and affection for the environment.

Through the good, the bad, and the ugly, it is clear social media is an ominous bystander in modern business. Rather than avoiding its inherent ramifications, these brands have found a way to use these communicative sites as tools to optimize their operations. Social networks have the capacity to rapport consumers and breed societal crazes. Identifying and capitalizing on these trends can leave a lasting impact for circularity. While Pela, thredUP, and Rent the Runway have distinguished themselves through creativity and logistical advances, the basis for their models emerged from already apparent developments, concepts, and values.

By responding quickly to current crazes and working together to form solutions, the circular economy can become equally as widespread.

"As long as existing structures and cultures are left intact, responding to these complex and accelerating challenges in isolation will only create more overload, intensification, guilt, uncertainty, cynicism, and burnout."

~ANDY HARGREAVES

CHAPTER 10

CONNECT

SIX DEGREES OF CIRCULARITY

"If you want to go fast, go alone. If you want to go far, go with others."

~AFRICAN PROVERB

"The Silent Pandemic."[286]

"The Behavioral Pandemic."[287]

---

286 "Social Isolation and Loneliness: The Silent Pandemic," *Harris Regional Hospital*, August 31, 2020.

287 Tzung-Jeng Hwang et al., "Loneliness and Social Isolation During the COVID-19 Pandemic," *International Psychogeriatrics* 32, no. 1 (October 2020): 1217–1220.

"The Double Pandemic."[288]

All of these refer to the insurgence of mental health issues during our time of isolation and social distancing the COVID-19 pandemic has caused. Some have turned to unique personal hobbies, like whizzing up barista-worthy coffee creations or banana bread, as coping mechanisms. Others have relied on their own family units by starting board game marathons or family art projects. Most notably, with our world's dependence on social media, was the insane usage of electronic media platforms such as Zoom and TikTok, which have united people across the globe to help them feel less lonely during such an unprecedented time. The benefits of connection even go beyond mental health, with reduced carbon emissions attributed to the "work from home" domain permitted by these platforms.[289] In our current circumstances, globalized communication through online platforms has become commonplace in the corporate world, with everything from meetings to general networking to conferences.

Circularity 20 is one such prestigious conference, sponsored by GreenBiz, which brought together over ten thousand professionals in the circular industry in 2020 through the power of Zoom. To my good fortune, I was personally counted among those esteemed participants. As an attendee,

288 Julianne Holt-Lunstad, "The Double Pandemic of Social Isolation and COVID-19: Cross-Sector Policy Must Address Both," *Health Affairs Blog, Health Affairs*, June 22, 2020.

289 Daniel Crow and Ariane Millot, "Working from Home Can Save Energy and Reduce Emissions. But How Much?" *Commentary* (Blog), *International Energy Agency*, June 12, 2020.

I was able to learn about current conversations in the circular space. The event featured interactive breakout sessions, networking opportunities, and cutting-edge presentations on topics from "Reusable Packaging: Scaling Past a Pandemic" to "Habits and Hooks: Changing Consumer Behavior."[290] This collaborative seminar was immensely valuable to my research inventory, but it was equally important at recruiting professional consorts.

After the event, I posted on LinkedIn about my experience with the #Circularity20 and gained more than ten new followers within the first couple days. Considering my profile had a network the size of my small family before the event, this about doubled my following. Since posting and herding a new group of peers, I even sought some collaboration. For example, I connected with Raj Daniels, host of a green exploration podcast called Bigger Than Us, to discuss current conversations in the circular economic space. Other colleagues from this conference were some of my greatest supporters for this book, giving me the courage to press forward on my journey.

By mimicking binding networks in the circular economy shift, businesses can reduce waste in an industrial setting.

Doing so celebrates a mantra fundamental to sustainable business: sustainability cannot be achieved by individual

---

290 John Hocevar et al., "Reusable Packaging: Scaling Past a Pandemic," (panel, 2020 Circularity20 Conference, August 27, 2020); Karen Winterich et al., "Habits and Hooks: Changing Consumer Behaviors," (panel, 2020 Circularity20 Conference, August 27, 2020).

action. It requires the work of a system, synergizing individual parts to culminate an effective outcome. Earlier, we explored analyzing waste issues through a scientific, systems-oriented lens to address this complexity with respect to materials themselves. Recall John Hoke reusing Nike Grind material or Carl Hodges inventing a farm in Eritrea producing absolutely no waste. Enabling networks highlights the benefits of human connectivity, forming sustainable relationships beyond the purely inanimate resource cycles themselves. By welcoming the perspectives of multiple stakeholders and enhancing fluent communication, we can expedite circular solutions. Without this asset, segregation will surely inhibit change.

Contemplate this: one solar-powered home in an isolated area traditionally electrified by coal is completely offset by the fossil fuel usage of others. With no access to a unified solar grid, the benefits of this technology are hampered. Of course, the power of one should never be underestimated; change ultimately begins with the small and passionate few (which I hope you understand by this point). However, during these early stages of adopting sustainable solutions with little support and collaboration, failure most often occurs. Obstacles seem to be hurling from every direction and cheering from fellow supporters seems scant. Analogously, one circular enthusiast in the context of a capitalistic society will struggle to stay afloat. With that in mind, we all need to participate for the circular switch to proceed. Online platforms can be efficient mechanisms to make this connection between both waste materials and people to warrant prosperous solutions—often in the form of social media.

ALL THE LITTLE "OHS"

Clearly, the meaning of "social media" has extended far beyond the confines of square-shaped Instagram photos and 280 Twitter characters. These personal applications have provoked the formation of academic and career-oriented networks, prompting collaboration by diverse groups of people from around the world. Maayke-Aimée Damen is an innovator who, by testing network potential, has led a continent-wide movement toward circularity. Through her use of artificial intelligence, she fundamentally challenged the way industry functions from all corners of the European Union.

As an undergraduate, Damen devised a tool called the "Resources Passport" to commit to this legacy. Think of her tool as an ingredients list for any given unit, tediously describing all the inputs going into its manufacturing and the waste that consummates. Damen's website eloquently describes the concept as:

"An information management system that collects static and dynamic resources data on products (think of origin, composition, load, and maintenance data)."[291]

Like a traditional passport, it demarcates all the locations parts of a product have been. It also details identification

---

291 "Our Resources Passport Is Not Just Another Way of Storing More Data," Resources Passport, accessed December 29, 2020.

information of inputs and outputs of the design, production, use, and recycling phases of a good, similar to "Life-Cycle Analysis." Unlike a real passport, this information is universally accessible by industry and individuals to forge circular associations. As expressed in her Eco17 Amsterdam speech, this tool directly addresses three of the major hurdles in manifesting a circular system:

- Lack of transparency
- Lack of reliability
- No central location[292]

Damen's thorough idea and well-threaded network caught the European Union's attention in 2011 when they assimilated her framework as a model for sustainability. She had sown these relationships which ultimately spread her proposal through her attendance of Singularity University: an accelerated, interdisciplinary program bringing together the world's brightest minds in sustainability, economics, computer science, and many other fields. Spurred by a Dutch Innovation Contest which granted access to the reputable community, Damen was convinced to submit her Resources Passport idea. Much to her surprise, her model led to an invitation to attend the program, where she learned about the role of artificial intelligence as a force of positive improvement rather than a catalyst toward a "slave zombie world." Equipped with the relationships she personally formed at Singularity University, and the backing of the European

---

292 *ecosummitTV*, "Eco17 Amsterdam: Maayke-Aimée Damen Excess Materials Exchange," July 10, 2017, video, 1:22.

Union, Damen went on to found her claim to fame: Excess Materials Exchange (EME).

EME, as mentioned earlier, is a unified marketplace for secondary industrial materials ranging from steel plates to textiles to coffee grounds. Building upon her Resources Passport template, Damen established a virtual network for industrial relationships seeking to turn trash into cash.[293]

William McDonough, founder of the "Cradle to Cradle" concept, describes the necessity of a closed loop for technical waste where it can be reused and recycled over and over again until the end of time. Before Excess Materials Exchange, a centralized residence for this loop never existed. Much of the business supply chain was (and still is) clouded with environmental negligence. McDonough exposed this haze when he reached out to corporate partners asking where their inputs came from. Respondents shrouded McDonough's sliver of hope as they simply answered: "suppliers." Equally as mundane was their answer to their products' destination after their time in the factory: "customers."[294] Maayke-Aimée Damen's Excess Materials Exchange directly seeks to mend this unfortunate short-sightedness in the corporate world.

According to the Ellen MacArthur Foundation, by building a circular economy around just five materials (steel, plastic,

293 TED, "Maayke-Aimée Damen: Saving the Planet by Running a Dating Site," January 2, 2020, video, 2:50.

294 TED, "William McDonough: Cradle to Cradle Design," May 17, 2007, video, 14:41.

aluminum, cement, and food), we can prevent the release of 9.3 billion tons of greenhouse gas emissions, which is the equivalent of emissions from all transportation worldwide. A complete adjustment to a fully circular economy could also generate about 2.5 trillion dollars in savings.[295]

While this model is undeniably beneficial for "People, Planet, and Profit," misunderstandings surrounding it have presented a bit of a challenge. For example, on numerous occasions, Dutch companies claiming to be "circular" revert to incinerating their waste for biofuel to heat their facilities. Their intention using biofuel heating is not to convert to a (debatably) more sustainable fuel source; lured by greenwashing, they want to catch the investor's eye which is keen for environmentally-friendly goods and services. Not only does this process fail to fully banish waste due to the formation of ash, but it is still immensely carbon positive and violates the fundamental reuse principles of the circular economy. Luckily, due to the strong transparency and identification processes required for Excess Materials Exchange partners, these "greenwashers" cannot access the service.

In order to truly actualize the benefits previously explained, businesses need to reuse waste in its highest value form rather than turn it into ash. These manipulative companies, if they truly want to be sustainable, should turn to alternative fuel sources such as solar or wind power and begin to question what circularity could actually look like for their business. Damen has incited this thought process and path for action through the creation of her network. Members of EME are

---

295 *TED,* "Maayke-Aimée," video, 2:50.

devoted to abiding to the guidelines of the circular economy as it is lawfully intended.

The company's economy-wide influence has even trickled down into the mindsets of individual consumers. For example, in the Netherlands, a Zero Plastic Challenge urged citizens to completely avoid single-use plastics for an entire month. Initially, there was a shocking bout of discouragement among participants, as it seemed that everything, from lotions and toothpaste to individual cheese slices, were packaged in plastic. But over time, all these frustrations turned into little "oh" moments:

"Oh, I never thought about waste like that."

"Oh, I've never seen it like that."

"Oh, I didn't even know it was possible."

All these little "ohs," Damen says, have led to fundamental consumption and production changes. Through her launch, a carbon reduction equivalent to 843 car rides from Amsterdam to Copenhagen was achieved. Enough energy was reduced to light Amsterdam, Rotterdam, and the Hague for five straight years. Total water use was reduced by 64 percent.[296] These benefits amounted to $1.9 million in savings.

---

296 "Exclusive Interview with Maayke-Aimée Damen—Co-founder at Excess Materials Exchange," *Blog, London Speakers Bureau*, accessed December 29, 2020.

Metrics such as these only begin to describe EME's virtual, cross-industry, waste-based marketplace.

The impact and trajectory of platforms such as EME is explained precisely in Malcolm Gladwell's eye-opening bestseller, *The Tipping Point: How Little Things Can Make A Big Difference*. In his book, Gladwell explains that to provoke widespread change, there are three types of essential people: salesmen, mavens, and connectors. Salesmen, as the name implies, are extremely persuasive, and despite their lack of expertise have the enticing ability to nudge people into action. Mavens use their obscene amount of knowledge to pressure others to do things, like a spewing library of information. Lastly, and most relevantly to these platforms, are the connectors. Connectors form links between individuals to escalate little-known concepts into societal crazes.[297]

In the day and age before social media, this was an astonishingly unique skill to have. Having a diverse and widespread network was a blue-moon attribute that needed to be cautiously crafted and constantly tended. Nowadays, though, it is deceivingly simple to be a connector. Logging onto Instagram and following a handful of popular pages will give you a platform of at least a few hundred followers. Alternatively, willfully following strategic pages can allow just about anyone to form a group of devoted individuals with a common goal or interest. For example, on my own social media, I follow pages such as CNN Climate, the Ellen MacArthur

297 Malcolm Gladwell, *The Tipping Point: How Little Things Can Make a Big Difference* (Boston: Little, Brown and Company, 2000), 30-89.

Foundation, and Circularity Blog, which developed my page into an oasis for zero-waste advocates like myself.

Regardless of the logistical approach, these tactics can heave the building blocks of a strong network. Leveraging connection-style platforms can be vital to reduce waste in our modern economy. With a supportive atmosphere of businesses and patrons actively engaged in circular linkages worldwide, human capital investment skyrockets, thereby increasing profits. As seen with the B Corporation movement and "triple bottom line" ideology, investing in stakeholders and the well-being of people associated with one's business is critical. Therefore, inflating the breadth and jointure of the targeted audience will breed financial success.

GROCERY POSITIONING SYSTEM (GPS)

Narrowing in on one's target population is not necessarily an intuitive feat. It requires meticulous planning and pointed involvement. European-based food waste app Too Good To Go has refined this target practice to an enviable yet societally beneficial level. The success of their company commenced at an intersection in the middle of New York City. As the traffic signal flashed red urging pedestrians to halt their journey, the city-dwellers abided their social expectations. One in particular, Mette Lykke, was on a journey to her hotel room when a mysterious woman inched toward her and presented a postcard before mysteriously vanishing.

Out of both fear and curiosity, Lykke peeked at the card and scrutinized it word for word: "Whatever our wildest dreams may be, they only scratch the surface of what's possible."[298]

Lykke took this ethereal message as an excuse to quit her job at a consulting firm and make her own entrepreneurial dent in the universe. Soon after, she founded Endomondo, a GPS-enabled fitness app that tracks and reports the running and cycling habits of users to motivate collective physical activity. This one-of-a-kind platform came far before the explosion of GPS technology on mobile devices, so her idea steadily and heftily gained attention for over a decade.[299] Unsurprisingly, her creative use of technology paid the bills and then some, but after ten years she recognized the debt this project left in her desire for societal change. At this point, she wanted to apply her network management skills to a broader community scheme.

Promptly, she sold her business to Under Armor for $85 million, after which she was left to reflect on her life's aim and next steps.[300] Lykke's time seeking significance was expedited, as another serendipitous escort guided her to her current company, Too Good To Go. On a bus-hopping excursion in Copenhagen, she met a fellow passenger who opened her eyes to the issue of food waste by introducing her to the company's app. Connecting the dots with her location-based app Endomondo and researching deeper into the gargantuan food waste issue in Europe, she felt

298 James Clasper, "Meet Startup Queen Mette Lykke," *Scandinavian Traveler,* August 31, 2017.
299 Ibid.
300 Ibid.

provoked to jump aboard this venture and stretch it to new heights.[301]

Too Good To Go's mission is to unite individuals on the hunt for a low-cost munch with grocery stores, restaurants, and other suppliers with a hand to lend. Since the food posted through this application is generally on the docket for the dumpster, it is discounted, saving money on both sides of the equation. Food-insecure customers have access to discounted meals. Restaurants gain a prospective base for the food they would otherwise toss.[302]

In 2020, as Europe's largest food waste app, Too Good To Go has more than 450 employees and twenty-nine thousand partnerships with supermarkets, restaurants, bakeries, hotels, and other food retailers. The excitable customer base consists of seventeen million users who have recovered over twenty-five million meals.[303] In just three years, this app has spread like wildfire, sparking a mesocosmic food waste fight. As of 2020, they even expanded their reach to the United States. Providing a platform such as this allows both buyers and businesses to reach their goals of saving money by saving waste. Demonstratively, the strength of connection reigns supreme in achieving a circular system.

As a global society, we are so fortunate to have achieved such efficient international communication. Using this to our advantage in business has already proven to be a

301 Adrienne Murray, "The Entrepreneur Stopping Food Waste," *BBC News*, January 6, 2020.

302 Ibid.

303 "Mette Lykke ~ Denmark," Inspiring Fifty: Nordics, accessed December 29, 2020.

monumental maneuver. Besides specialized applications like EME and Too Good To Go, LinkedIn is an apparent example. As I view my suggested posts, many of them appear in other languages such as Dutch or French. While I don't personally speak either of these languages proficiently, I can tell by the images attached and English-translated comments that these foreign posts closely align with my own interests in circular economic models and corporate sustainability. Based off this fact, there is enormous international excitement to scale circularity. Many entrepreneurs and economists have already taken note and dedicated themselves to designing solutions.

STAYING IN THE LOOP

A Princeton dropout by the name of Tom Szaky donated his two cents to the power of user-friendly platforms through several waste-reducing enterprises. Before manifesting these platforms, Szaky's appreciation for waste began with a casual visit to his friend's cannabis garden. Several phone call conversations were spent attempting to remedy his weeping plants in the confines of a congested, concrete basement. To Szaky's surprise, several weeks later, when he took the steps down into the bunker to bestow a prognosis, he was presented with lush, thriving leaves stolen straight from a Miracle-Gro commercial. Flabbergasted by the evolution, his friend explained he was using worm poop, a fertile compost medium, to feed the plants. This process, also used by the Compost Kitchen, is called vermicomposting.[304]

---

304 The "I Am" Q&A," *CNBC*, accessed December 29, 2020.

Moved by his personal acquaintance, Szaky capitalized on the idea and founded his company, TerraCycle, in 2002. Besides selling vermicompost, TerraCycle was also the first company to source pre-used packaging for their operation. His company was crested on the intuitive equation:

"Consumption + Complex Materials = Garbage."[305]

This irrefutable scripture laid the basis for his company's expansion. It also caused him to further interrogate the preposterous linkage between consumption and the production of garbage. At the time of TerraCycle's founding, being a consumer and being sustainable were mutually exclusive. To explain this dilemma more thoroughly, Szaky devised a pyramid of the post-consumer destination for any given object. The scale ranged from least useful at the bottom of the pyramid, where used products are sent to landfill, to most useful at the top of the pyramid, where they are reused in their unadulterated form. Between these two extremes lie incineration, recycling, and upcycling.[306]

Gaining this thorough understanding of the formulaic insurance of waste, Szaky ventured to design a universal solution. For that reason, he terminated the vermicompost branch of his company, and redirected his success

---

305 *Chicago Ideas*, "Tom Szaky: Eliminating the Idea of Waste," March 7, 2013, video, 0:55.
306 Ibid.

to transform TerraCycle into a state-of-the-art recycling company.

In 2007, TerraCycle became a cornucopia of recycling avenues for traditionally non-recyclable items like cigarette butts, soiled diapers, and, more recently personal, protective equipment (PPE). He forged relationships with schools and community organizations to centralize recycling of these formerly trashy items for individuals, who can collect and ship them back to TerraCycle for free processing. TerraCycle also hosts a Zero Waste Box program in which they supply purchasers with a bin to collect traditionally "non-recyclables," such as art supplies, small automotive parts, and beauty supply packaging.

Despite his accomplishment with recycling campaigns in schools and community groups, Szaky wanted to take his advocacy capacity to the next level by going virtual. Not only would this allow his company to tackle a broader spectrum of waste streams, but he also recognized the leading power of digital media in the waste space, with discussions of turtles pierced by plastic straws going viral.

Alongside the increasing weight of online waste coverage, the issue of trash itself shifted from "being a problem to a crisis."[307]

Realizing the corruption of our current conventions, Szaky saw a path forward through the very vessel that caused this problem in the first place: the consumer dollar. Nowadays,

---

307 *Impakter*, "Tom Szaky—Full Interview," September 24, 2019, video, 2:10.

you are hard-pressed to find a person who hasn't purchased an item off Amazon or other single-use promoting sites. Of course, the convenience of Amazon and other similar delivery services has been incredibly useful and even life-saving in some scenarios. Medicine and supplements are easily accessible whereas they might be unavailable in a patient's local area. The issue, however, lies in the compulsive, mindless purchasing that occurs on the site—like when we purchase fruitless items from the homepage we didn't even know existed. By amending online stores to provide durable, reusable items, we can flip this backward economic setup back onto its feet.

Like Maayke-Aimée Damen and Mette Lykke, many entre-preneurs have recognized the promise of virtual partner-ship. Zero Grocery, for example, was founded in 2019 as an online platform to distribute affordable groceries in Los Angeles and the Bay Area completely devoid of plastic waste. Within just two years, they have made over 1,300 unique products in returnable jars and recyclable packaging, which is available on their website for environmentally and financially-conscious consumers.[308] Around the same time, Szaky announced a TerraCycle initiative called Loop at the World Economic Forum in May 2019, a global reuse platform for food and personal and household care items utilizing a fleet of reusable containers. Loop currently links over one hundred thousand buyers with eighty companies, including Tropicana, Seventh Generation, and Häagen-Dazs, testing durable, reusable packaging through an online and in-store platform. Over four hundred items are available for purchase

---

308 "Zero-Waste Groceries, Delivered Fast," Zero, accessed February 19, 2021.

in stainless steel containers from nut butter to shampoo.[309] Once the customer has used up all their product, they simply bring the empty containers back to the store or notify the logistics provider and ship the empty, dirty containers back in their accompanying tote bag where they can be repurposed in the Loop.

This novel idea is still in the early stages in limited areas around the globe, but the response so far has been astonishing. During Loop's first couple months since launch, over a hundred products were made available across the entire United States. Additional brands are currently confirmed across the UK, France, Canada, Australia, and Japan. Notable brand partners that have already committed to signing on to this zero-waste service include Unilever, Nature's Path, Tide, and Burger King, among others.[310] By giving customers a service through which they can support their favorite brands without manifesting waste, Loop is determined to end the permeation of plastic through virtual connection.

In our digital age, some of the greatest recastings have come from virtual, cross-industry collaboration. DoorDash, for example, weaves the relationship between hungry users and the food service industry through their online app without any physical interaction. Taking this model to the arena of waste has been masterfully efficient, as we have seen with Excess Materials Exchange, Too Good To Go, and Loop. In

309 Dan Ochwat, "Terracycle's Loop Platform Hits Milestone Reach across 48 States," *Store Brands*, September 22, 2020.

310 "Loop Expands Nationwide to Meet Consumer Demand," *Press Release* (blog), *Nosh*, September 22, 2020.

a time where individuals are more attached to their phones than their own family members, let alone the things they throw away, it is time for both businesses and consumers to take note and utilize their technological devices for good.

"Your network is your net worth."

~PORTER GALE

PHASE THREE

EMBRACING ETHEREAL CHANGE

*Ethereal: "lacking material substance…
marked by unusual refinement"*

MERRIAM-WEBSTER

CHAPTER 11

CONSUMER CONNECTION

———

The year was 1941 when the United States officially entered
World War II.

Sure, this is a significant year for American history, mark-
ing our prevention of a global Nazi dictatorship, but equally
as important was its demonstration of the aptitude of unity.
During the war, there was fascinating mobilization of all populations in America as industrial factories began producing war
paraphernalia and weapons, men were sent directly to war
without much notice for their families, and women were sent
to attend the working roles their husbands once played while
they were off fulfilling war duties. This backflip of societal and
economic norms may seem an anomaly in human history, and
it's safe to say that no one could have predicted the complete
metamorphosis that transpired in those few short months. As
rare and extraordinary as this era may seem, there are count-
less examples of accelerated change in American and world
history that closely mimic such a societal overthrow, and not

all of them were a direct outcome of states of emergency such as war, famine, or immediate natural disaster.

As mentioned earlier, the Industrial Revolution is an exquisite example. The invention of the steam engine during that period expedited technological advancement and a reorganization of our world's economy and social strata. Similarly, the Space Race between the United States and Soviet Union drew in an element of competition to incentivize collective and rapid invention. The list goes on and on.

Knowing that we have repeatedly defied the limits of what we ever imagined possible on a broad economic scale, why do we accept our cycle of defeat in adapting to a more sustainable economy? Why don't we have faith in ourselves as the resilient societies that we are? Our current economic compass is broken and leading us down a path of doom. Now is our time to shift gears onto a fast track toward zero-waste utilizing the virtue of diverse connection throughout the world.

From networking to systems-oriented thinking to local engagement opportunities, it is clear that interconnectedness is the key piece to the puzzle of product waste. Collaboration, while it is frowned upon by our capitalistic society, can speed up and enhance circular engrossment. To scale society-wide change, we cannot just focus our efforts on companies themselves and the goods and services they choose to offer. This needs to be an all-in affair.

Both businesses and individual consumers need to valiantly contribute to fight for sustainability, and combine their assets to bring waste elimination within our midst.

For the majority of our discussion, we have analyzed the inspiration and blueprints businesses have used to head toward zero-waste, which is just one (very important) half of the equation. Luckily, though, the strategies and principles for individuals to succeed in circularity are synonymous with those we have already explored

FORGE CONNECTIONS

Generally, the power of association is the most indispensable component of this revolution. Despite our global intellectual capacity and exceptionally advanced technology, without a way to share progress, the entire circular flow will be much more cumbersome for both producers and purchasers searching for solutions. To our great privilege, forming and maintaining these relationships is easier than ever before with our modern media landscape. Social media and other online refuges lay out common ground to ideate, collaborate, and educate fellow peers on the importance of zero-waste. Even activities as simple as watching a YouTube video can help you get started.

For example, a family named the Carters released a smashingly successful eight-minute short film produced by Happen Films with over one million views on YouTube.[311] Essentially, the documentary depicts the Carters' journey as a typical Tasmanian family blossoming into an emblem of the zero-waste movement. While undertaking a fourteen-day Sustainable Living challenge, they found themselves producing over two hundred items of waste in a single week span. This

---

311 *Happen Films*, "Tips for Zero Waste Living—How a Family of 5 Makes Almost No Waste! | Life with Less Waste," June 28, 2019, video, 1:15.

horrific discovery led them to declare a surprisingly simple, waste-free life their "new normal."

The Carters also wanted their enlightenment to serve as inspiration for others, indicating that:

"By osmosis, a lot of that will filter broadly across the population and then upward into the chains of power."[312]

The Carters' "osmosis theory" is similar to the concept of herd immunity for vaccines, where after a certain percentage of individuals are vaccinated, the entire population becomes protected. Analogously, if a certain percentage of the population starts to go zero-waste, not only will the benefits be widespread, but it will also encourage more citizens to participate in those behaviors and eventually lead to change higher up in the regulatory hierarchy. If only going zero-waste was as commonplace as getting a vaccine.

Practicing some of the Carters' tips and interacting with the viewers of this popular documentary through the comments can be an immersive step in the osmosis. Currently, the diffusive tendency surrounding waste management has been more of a top-down flood of regulation to shove recycling down the throats of irresponsible citizens in hopes of a sudden awakening. Not only does this perpetuate the fallacy of recycling sustainability, as items can typically only

---

312 Ibid.

reprocess two or three times, but it also neglects the powerful collaborative component of making change.[313] Without excitement on the consumer end surrounding the principle and proper procedures for waste reduction, the regulatory process is impeded.

Drastically transitioning to a zero-waste lifestyle can be understandably discouraging, and going at the grind as a lone soldier can make the journey seem even more insufferable. By sharing that vulnerability and inviting advice through such open platforms as the comments on a zero-waste documentary on YouTube, we can progress together more efficiently. My own zero-waste journey took off by perusing and interacting with several TED Talks and Lauren Singer videos on YouTube. Taking advantage of this online platform supplied me with necessary insight and troubleshooting in times of uncertainty throughout the process.

Beyond scattered and happenstance media correspondence, more centralized communities of zero-wasters also exist. The Carter family, for example, offers an online course for zero-waste prodigies wanting an outlet for meaningful support. Their website, Zero Waste Families, is an excellent resource for practical tips and tricks, and you can also conspire with other waste-reducing fellows maintaining an optimistic commitment to the lifestyle.[314]

---

313 Lilly Sedaghat, "7 Things You Didn't Know about Plastic (and Recycling)," *National Geographic Society Newsroom* (blog), *National Geographic*, April 4, 2018.

314 "About the Course," Zero Waste Families, accessed February 14, 2021.

This dedicated group and several others like it can offer guidance for personal waste reduction. Even more accessibly (and completely free), the Carters opened a booming Facebook group called "Zero Waste Tasmania" where users share inquiries on dealing with plastic-wrapped textbooks, inspirational photos of recycled-jar stocked shelves, promotions for locally made, unpackaged vegan soaps, and zero-waste short film recommendations. These sorts of groups exist for almost any imaginable city or country across the globe, including everywhere from Portland to Nigeria.

Actively joining virtual or in-person communities can also present professional opportunity. For instance, Vanina Howan, an enthusiastic zero-waste advocate, has secured interviews with sustainable business leaders through the pertinence of social media. Securing these interviews for her podcast, the *Ecopreneur Show*, she has been able to network with everyone from Tonlé's CEO Rachel Faller to Jocelyn Corral from Go Box, a reusable packaging subscription service for restaurants. Reaching out to these closed loop leaders via online platforms led to some amazing collaboration and conversation, allowing Howan to build her brand as a sustainability superstar.

INVEST IN ENGAGEMENT

The beauty of many of these functional connections is in their capacity for zero-waste education. Without an end goal or clear direction, sustainable action is futile. Therefore, in tackling zero-waste, education in all its forms is a vital component laying that intentional foundation. Because waste creation has become so inundated with our westernized daily routine, it can be difficult to break that cycle or even care enough to give it the time of day. To throw a wrench into that chain, dramatic relearning or, as CEO of luxury brand Elvis & Kresse describes it, "unlearning" needs to occur with respect to consumerism and the linear economy.

The addiction to personal, material gain in our modern world is ludicrous, and it violates the golden rule many of us were taught as kindergartners: "sharing is caring." As we grow older, many of us fall into the cult of egocentrism set out by our institutional mechanisms, where "an eye for an eye" is necessary to survive in our capitalistic world. Granted, it may seem like an impossibility to reverse this system and the unfortunate waste that comes along with it. But the evidence of our ancestors would suggest otherwise.

Kresse Wesling idolizes the lifestyles of her grandparents' generation, who (out of necessity) didn't grow up producing a ton of waste. Every morsel, scrap, and extra tidbit was savored and used to its fullest potential. Back then, the compulsive obsession with buying and disposing did not exist, and scarcity was a real detriment. Throughout that era, the cause of scarcity was a lack of technological solutions, but today our upheavals have led us to the point of overexploitation. Understanding this, we can educate ourselves on how to use technology to our advantage for a more sustainable future. For example, by bringing our food scraps to state-of-the-art composting facilities or purchasing products packed in bioplastics, we can promote a more sustainable future. In doing so, we can turn disposable, trashy items into the enemy and return to our roots devoid of these toxic practices.

In addition to relearning historical western practices, which tend to be much more sustainable than our current way of doing business, modern indigenous groups hold a reliable key to sustainability stemming from their close entanglement with the local environment. We have seen the excellence and resilience of Balinese and other islanders when it comes to embodying a circular economy, which many of their cultures have embraced for centuries. Teina Boasa-Dean, a Māori (indigenous Polynesian persons) environmental activist, outlined her culture's framework where "humans become relevant because of their connections to the natural world." A thriving reality of circular harmony with nature awaits in the Māori socio-political belief and associated practices.[315]

Contrary to popular thought, this value-based transition does not pay off in a dull and unexciting life. Kresse Wesling, whose "landfill to luxury" brand directly disputes this misconception, even describes her reality and relationships in her waste-reduced lifestyle as "decadent." By beginning the journey with a *tabula rasa*, or "blank slate," on the meaning of opulence and consumerism, a new interpretation can be built up to embrace this new way of living. As they say: beauty is in the eye of the beholder. If we choose to see waste reuse as beautiful, instantaneous shifts will occur.

Upon personally understanding the basis and practices driving the zero-waste mission, it is essential that we share this knowledge. The long-lasting effects of educating others have been clearly demonstrated by some of our waste

---

315 Nelson Meha, "Indigenous Worldviews and the Circular Economy," *Scion Connections*, June 2019.

warriors. Himkaar Singh, for example, was triggered to found his Compost Kitchen based off the speech of a keynote speaker in his third-grade science class on the shortcomings of modern recycling. Paying this education forward, Singh has continuously sermonized to civil engineering students to venture into social entrepreneurship. Additionally, he has initiated family interventions and school seminars to teach children about recycling and vermicomposting, prompting eco-friendly practices in their own homes. By devoting time and effort to zero-waste education, both in his own life and the lives of others, Singh sparked change-making in his neck of the woods in South Africa.

A parallel scenario played out for Anastasia Mikhalochkino, founder of Lean Orb, as she invested in the education of students at South Pointe Elementary School in Miami. After delivering her lessons on the detriment of plastic pollution, students left with a passion for eliminating trash and practical reduction habits which they happily adopted into their own routines. Creating that emotional attachment for young people, as demonstrated by the stories of Nicole Bassett's youth in Canada and Sarah Kaeck's concern for her family's health, are extremely influential.

All over the country, these revolutions are beginning to take place on educational grounds. The campaigns are not purely lecture style either, with some of the most effective commitments authorizing students to take charge ideating zero-waste solutions themselves. In Wheaton, Illinois, elementary students in an extracurricular program called Future Cities were challenged to utilize waste materials to craft a circular city model in the Philippines. The children literally used pill bottles and Styrofoam packaging to engineer real-world solutions to one of our planet's greatest environmental problems.

At the university level, my school has brought about a zero-waste behavior change campaign, and October is now deemed Waste Reduction Month, where students are encouraged to track the items they dispose of. Student engagement has even transcended to positions of authority, as groups like the Student Sustainability Committee have been given control over funding for sustainable programs proposed by other students. As a part of these decisive, hands-on opportunities, students themselves can teach their peers to address community-level environmental issues.

As motivating as these youth-oriented programs have been, our global circumstances are rigid and demanding. It is too late to mobilize *only* revolutionary young people (which, don't get me wrong, are extremely valuable people). While traditional educational settings are an ideal breeding ground for collaboration and enlightenment, we need to break that seal to instigate a cascading effect on populations other than students. Despite the fact that these populations will be the most heavily impacted in the future if we fail to take action, that shouldn't mean they need to bear the full brunt of fixing the system on their own. As empathized by one of the employees of sustainable pioneer Interface in his poem "Tomorrow's Child," the viewpoint of parents and grandparents should be as follows:

> "Begin I will to weigh the cost
> of what I squander; what is lost

If ever I forget that you
will someday come to live here too."[316]

Fortunately, non-traditional methods of learning such as demonstrations and campaigns can stimulate this mindset in older generations. Rose Marcario's cross-country Worn Wear crusade, for example, spanned a reach of over five thousand miles, touching individual patrons each and every step of the way while teaching them about trashy fashion.[317] Alex Schulze lengthened 4ocean's recognition through virtual awareness campaigns such as #CleanCutsForCleanOceans, which pulled a pound of plastic for every tweet using the hashtag on Facebook. Both these business-fueled endeavors triggered personal action in waste reduction by larger populations.

Environmental activist Rob Greenfield has also been monumental in providing spontaneous educational opportunities around the country. Donned the "Robin Hood of modern times" by France 2 TV, Greenfield has challenged various environmental concerns while posting about them on his blog, Instagram, and YouTube channel to promulgate change by less involved audiences.[318] For example, in 2013 he embarked on a national bike tour on which his exquisite menu featured 70 percent dumpster-derived ingredients and meals, amounting to about 280 pounds of food that would

---

316 John Anderson Lanier, "Tomorrow's Child," *Ecocentricity* (blog), *Ray C. Anderson Foundation*, August 1, 2016.

317 Donnia Hedden, "On the Road with Worn Wear – 2015 Spring Tour Recap," *Stories* (blog), *Patagonia*, accessed December 25, 2020.

318 Olivia Schaller, "Green Planet—Rob Greenfield, a 100 percent Green Life," France 2 TV, November 9, 2016, video, 0:05.

have otherwise been sent to landfill. Along the way he also set up public artistic displays in eight major US cities using food recovered from dumpsters. Taking the decomposing ingredients as a medium, he arranged them into visually appealing compilations exposing the heft of food waste for bystanders.[319]

The response from targeted communities was angry and intolerant as citizens woke up to the funnel of food wastage straight to their dumpsters. Many of them even took food from the display, demonstrating their newfound compassion for this urgent issue. Greenfield continued this insurgence with a thirty-day trash-wearing challenge in New York City. He vowed to live like an average American consumer while stashing all his waste inside his thirteen-pocket clear suit, which he wore around to dismantle the "out of sight, out of mind" mentality.

In response to his outlandish experiment, Greenfield received heavy social media traffic as passersby laughed and stopped for pictures, thus inflating his reach. His challenges directly tapped into the affective and logistical reasoning behind sustainable living, making them an ideal model to educate people on the consequences of their actions and the incremental changes they can make to mitigate them. As revealed by Kresse Wesling's encounter with fire hoses in London and Alex Schulze's brush with plastic pollution in Bali and Haiti, basking in the presence of capitalist byproduct can be

---

319 Rob Greenfield, "The Food Waste Fiasco: You Have to See It to Believe It," *Blog, Rob Greenfield*, October 6, 2014.

an illuminating educational experience, which was exactly what Greenfield sought out to do.[320]

Ultimately, it is as the saying goes: a man without education is like a building without foundation. Therefore, getting educated on circularity and waste reduction is a key primary undertaking to manifesting a sustainable future. Whether that be in a traditional institutional setting, through physical or virtual campaigns, or a transparent business model, awareness and activism are compulsory. Fortunately, inspiration and knowledge, like waste, are in endless, diverse supply. Seeking out resonating stories and statistics can instill a renewed sense of personal purpose.

DESIGN YOUR SUSTAINABLE FUTURE

Although education and connection are the backbone of the zero-waste movement which are never completely "checked off," there are certain actionable, clear-cut decisions that can greatly improve the chances of success. Many of these come in the form of conscious purchasing decisions. As Patty Lloyd, my amazing sustainability mentor, preaches, utilizing the following principle when making consumption choices can simplify the sometimes complex world of zero-waste:

> "Use it up, wear it out, make it work, or do without."

---

320 Mary Bowerman, "Man Pledges to Wear All the Trash He Produces for 1 Month," *USA Today*, September 30, 2016.

The Carter family uses a similar three-step interrogation for their grocery store finds:

1. Do I need this thing?
2. Is there an alternative that produces less waste?
3. If there is waste, where will that end up?[321]

While being disciplined is necessary to activate zero-waste living, designing a life and community conducive to waste reduction can abolish the taunt of consumerism altogether. Surrounding oneself with awakened people, waste-reducing infrastructure, and plentiful virtual opportunity can assist the switch.

As for people, Chef Matt Stone's story demonstrates the importance of a loyal zero-waste customer base through the success of his restaurant. While some customers were initially a bit skeptical of the unconventional, scrap-based menu items, their open-mindedness and general values of sustainability were intrinsic to Greenhouse's admirable reputation. The power of people is a two-way street though. It does not just benefit businesses seeking green customers, but it also helps the customers themselves—as like-minded individuals can affirm them. As explained by virtual connections discussed earlier, the more one can tap into these networks, the more well-versed they will be in everyday solutions and waste-free alternatives to invest in.

---

321 *Sustainable Living Tasmania*, "Reducing to Zero Waste! #Dontwastehobart (14/15)," November 22, 2015, video, 2:13.

Besides the effect of peers on personal habits, institutional mechanisms are another fundamental bit of context that can aid waste reduction. Oftentimes, this is the variable scapegoated for failure to comply with zero-waste. For example, if a particular city does not have a composting facility, food waste is much more difficult to address. If nearby grocery stores do not allow reusable grocery bags at check-out, plastic alternatives may seem like the only option. To avoid this issue, we can simply change our surroundings. Moving may not be realistic for all individuals hoping to espouse circularity, but the change of scenery need not be as drastic as a cross-country replanting. Zero-waste programs and solutions may actually be a lot closer than one might expect.

In the United States, there are over twenty-five thousand recorded consignment and thrift stores.[322] Even in fast-paced places like the Chicago O'Hare airport, zero-waste solutions can be scavenged. During my most recent visit there, I spotted a vending machine called "Farmer's Fridge" selling healthy to-go salads, sandwiches, and other munchies in reusable containers that I could return to any Farmer's Fridge machine dispersed throughout the city. This and other small-scale solutions can compound to large percentages of waste diversion.

Importantly, not all infrastructure is restricted to brick-and-mortar or other physical establishments. Our technological landscape has made it easier than ever to reduce waste through the tips of our fingers, not only through consumer ties but also

---

322 "Industry Statistics & Trends," NARTS: The Association of Resale Professionals, accessed December 30, 2020.

waste-reducing resources. We can slay food waste by downloading Too Good To Go or other food waste apps. We can kick fashion waste to the curb through digital platforms like thredUP and Rent the Runway. Websites like Lauren Singer's Package Free Shop fundamentally shift e-commerce and the incessant packaging so often accompanying it. By investing in the fruits of the labor of the front-running waste warriors described throughout this book, many of which can be accessed virtually, we can design our own circular bubbles.

Even if there truly seems to be no access to circular alternatives, there are numerous resources you can use to kickstart them in your own area. For example, recently I contacted the founder of a food waste app called Last Call to get a chapter started on my college campus. Because the individuals and companies involved in this progression tend to be sentimentally bonded to their mission, similar to Sarah Kaeck and Lauren Singer, starting these programs comes with continuous support. As we continue to grow this alliance, the lifestyle change will become even easier. No matter where you are, be it in the middle of a booming, disposable metropolis or a rural desolation, the growing affection and ingenuity of this community will be your savior.

In fact, neglecting to utilize this support to make changes is simply oblivious and irresponsible. In a TED Talk by William McDonough, creator of the "Cradle to Cradle" design, he states:

> If we come here and say, "Well, I didn't intend to cause global warming on the way here," and we say, "That's not part of my plan," then we realize it's part of our

de facto plan. Because, it's the thing that's happening because we have no other plan.[323]

In order to avoid the "de facto" mindset of environmental obliteration we must surround ourselves with an environment that is not only conducive to waste reduction, but conducive to growth. We can work to redefine waste by amassing this renewed sense of value.

Rather than being a rusted can or useless scrap, waste needs to be interpreted as a delicious Thanksgiving dinner; a source of fuel; a source of innovation; a source of passion and creativity.

While it may seem strange to be excited about something reaching the "end of its life," as we discussed earlier, this compassion is not necessarily a new precedent. It is a revamping of ancient and indigenous conservation practices, which directly contradict our current take-make-waste structure. Exchange has been a fundamental tradition in civilizations like China, where it was rude and unacceptable to leave someone's house without leaving a gift after dinner. The Hawaiian Islands have superstitions on bad karma for those who take things from the island, like beautiful rocks or seashells, without leaving something behind. The concept of moderation has been long contested as an enlightened trait in religious contexts. This balancing, yin-yang philosophy is an all-pervasive paragon, so it only makes sense that it serves as a template for our economy. So let us return the

323 *TED*, "William McDonough: Cradle to Cradle Design," May 17, 2007, video, 14:41.

favor to our Earth. Let us replenish her resources and repair her damage. Let us gift her not with digested, inorganic trash, but with a sense of ownership and responsibility, knowing that everything we have achieved as a species can and will be attributed to her gracious donations.

By and large, while personally going zero-waste and fully transitioning our economy may seem two separate and unrealistic endeavors, their complementary relationship is actually an instrumentality to a waste-free future.

By pondering the underlying values of these radical propositions, we can begin to take tangible steps forward. These introductory measures should include netting ourselves in relevant communities and educating ourselves on affective objectives and tactical plans needed to design lifestyles conducive to zero-waste. Doing so, we can bring that absolute, distant vision into focus. We can dethrone societally constructed barriers and overcome misconceptions through intentional action.

Our world is finally in a spot where circularity can ignite. Environmentalism is a raging inertia dipping its toes into several aspects of society. The pandemic has seen the fragility of product-based industries, which has set the stage for successful circular models. Political organizations such as the United Nations have released clear intentions to reduce environmental footprints through regulatory ambitions. Ideas of the activists, thought leaders, and corporate visionaries outlined in this book are catching sparks. These ethereal eclipses of our modern economy all culminate with the introspective question: when will you begin to take responsibility for your part in the war on waste?

CHAPTER 12

COMING FULL CIRCLE

In a world so tribulating and troubling, it can sometimes be hard to focus our attention directly on the things that are crumbling to bits. However, choosing to ignore the problems before us can lead into a cycle of hopelessness, which is a hard continuum to break. The answer to escaping it is not through further oblivion and avoidance. Instead, we must be aware of the hurdles our society is squaring up to, and rather than interpreting them as insurmountable barriers, we can see them as opportunities for innovation. Applying this tactic to our war on waste is a critical mindset shift that needs to occur to escape utter doom for our planet and our pocketbooks.

As previously acknowledged, one garbage truck full of textiles is burned every second.[324] By 2050, there will be more plastic in the ocean than fish.[325] Americans waste 40 percent

---

324 "One Garbage Truck of Textiles Wasted Every Second: Report Creates Vision for Change," Ellen MacArthur Foundation, November 28, 2017.

325 Anna Bruce-Lockhart, "More Plastic in the Sea Than Fish? Not If We Do These 3 Things," *World Economic Forum: Agenda*, January 16, 2017.

of the food grown nationwide and produce 4.9 pounds of trash every single day.[326]

These are massive issues—not issues we can pass off to our children or our children's children.

A RACE AGAINST TIME

At the writing of this book, 2050 is only thirty years away. Three decades. That's it. And that mile marker is an absolute last resort. We cannot afford to wait that whole grace period to start making change. I'm not sure about you, but I don't plan on waiting until plastic pollution is legitimately piling up on my doorsteps to make my move. This trash is already wreaking direct havoc on our health and wellbeing, especially in low-income neighborhoods and communities of color. Decades ago was the time to begin addressing this problem. Right now, it is our duty to recoup the failure of past generations and reverse the trends causing America to produce double the amount of trash per day than any other western country, which is an unacceptable amount in itself.[327]

Our current generalized projection does not seem to lead in this direction of intent. At the household level, we have lost touch with the meaning of trash. The "not in my backyard"

---

326 Dana Gunders et al., *Wasted: How America Is Losing up to 40 Percent of Its Food from Farm to Fork to Landfill* (New York City, NY: Natural Resources Defense Council, 2017), 4; US Department of the Interior, Environmental Protection Agency, *National Overview: Facts and Figures on Materials, Wastes and Recycling* (Washington D.C., 2018).

327 Ian Tiseo, "Volume of Household Waste Collected by Local Authorities per Capita in England from 2010 to 2018," *Statista*, June 29, 2020.

(NIMBY) mindset has taken over, causing the majority of us to shield our eyes to the existence of trash past the lid of our dumpster. We have leaned into the "out of sight, out of mind" principle for far too long. In many cases, our association with trash is worse than complete dissociation. It has become interchangeable with disgust and nuisance. Disposability has effectively crept its way to normalcy, leaving our earth scattered with valuable "waste" material from our landfills to our oceans and everything in between.

In the past few years, the omniscience of this problem has fortunately taken center stage of media outlets. Videos of turtles pierced with plastic straws and memes about Dunkin' Donuts dumpsters brimming with day-old pastries have become a part of our collective culture. Rather than taking necessary response, our culture (as it so often does) has mangled itself in a fit of finger-pointing.

Who is the victim of this shameful blaming? More often than not, it is the government. Regarding a poll I posted on my LinkedIn profile asking participants what they thought the largest obstacle was in preventing conversion to the circular economy, 67 percent voted for governmental regulation. To some extent, this is reasonable. The environment is a shared responsibility directly linked with land ownership and property rights, which is inherently a governmental concern. Additionally, many governmental actions, such as the Resources Conservation and Recovery Act and toxic site cleanups, set a precedent for their role in this issue. The fact is, though, the aforementioned moves have already been made. Certainly, our leaders can set more stringent standards and build waste-reducing infrastructure to improve recycling, but these measures will only go so far without education and activism from the people themselves.

THE POWER OF ONE

At some point, we as individuals need to accept responsibility for our actions.

It may feel discouraging being asked to tackle such a dynamic, multi-faceted issue. That is the inevitable case with any environmental problem. These problems are complex, dynamic, and interrelated, but that does not mean they are not worth solving. As daunting as that may sound, there exists clear, incremental remedies we can take as responsible contributors to society. As individual people, if we completely boycotted plastic-infested goods, those items would slowly run out of production. As manufacturers and business owners, assuming waste-free protocol would force changes in expenditure. Eating away at this problem from both ends can help us manifest our end goal of the United Nations' Sustainable Development Goal number twelve: responsible consumption and production. We have the ability and need to do "more and better with less."[328]

We have the ability and need to "decoupl[e] economic growth from environmental degradation, increas[e] resource efficiency and promot[e] sustainable lifestyles."[329]

---

328 "Goal 12: Ensure Sustainable Consumption and Production Patterns," United Nations, accessed December 31, 2020.
329 Ibid.

Rather than sitting back and banking our progress on the action of our unreliable and constantly revolving political administration, we need to take some initiative now.

I recognize this may seem blunt, but it is definitely not unwarranted nor is it impossible. Personally, I only recently became aware of this calling after watching Lauren Singer's Earth Day Presentation introducing her mason jar of trash.[330] Hearing about the benefits of living in alignment with her values and spending less with her minimalist purchasing habits made me want to transition myself, which I have already begun to do through my daily habits.

For example, I have completely shifted my grocery hauls to farmer's markets and bulk stores, where I have the option to secure food without the implication of plastic packaging. I have refrained from buying apparel from anywhere other than a thrift or secondhand store. I have always thrifted as a hobby, but now I choose to partake as part of a meaningful lifestyle modification. On the rare occasions I do eat take-out, I am sure to refuse bags and any additional plastics like cutlery and lids. If I can, I try to dine in or get my food in recyclable paper wrapping. Ultimately, I have tried to cut down to the bare bones of consumption, and rather than basking in fruitless materialism, I now relish the sentient connection I have with the few investments I do make.

This complete transformation really started with a little jar of trash.

---

330 *Future Coalition*, "Minimizing Your Environmental Footprint with Lauren Singer | Earth Day Live," May 5, 2020, video, 1:23.

COMBINING OUR ASSETS

Through my research and personal curiosity, I learned the role of that jar on a whole new table: the global economy. At a global virtual summit I attended called Circularity 20, the speakers distinguished between manufacturer-driven and consumer-driven circular systems. My interpretation of this distinction was a division between personal and industrial waste-reduction schemes. Upon reflection, my bifocal vision started to converge. Conjoining the zero-waste lifestyle with the circular economic model, I began to see a pragmatic association that could lead to a profitable societal transformation.

Environmentalism, entrepreneurship, and personal accountability were unique lenses of this kaleidoscope, merging together to form an integrated solution. By joining the principles for success in each component, we can expedite our path toward zero-waste.

EMBRACING THE ECLIPSE

This area of uncharted growth is not limited to any one particular field but rather mandates input and excellence along every step of the process, starting with the design phase. Traditionally trained designers, such as John Hoke, have turned the world on its head with their commitment to circularity. This has had reverberating effects on not only the fashion industry, but an overall societal remodeling in other sectors such as food and other single-use products. Determinately, the general population is gaining increasing access to these services and products, which has allowed the zero-waste populace to embrace decadent trash-free lifestyles.

Taking advantage of these meticulously-designed goods and systems is the first actionable step in eliminating waste.

Waste education is equally as important in the preparatory stages of circular obligation by forming sympathetic attachments with things that are thrown away. Rachel Faller explored this aptitude in her founding of Tonlé. Her first trip to Cambodia started as a shot-in-the-dark attempt to start a textile business, but once Faller dug into the social and environmental inequities of the region, her vision slowly manifested into her globally-recognized sustainable brand.[331] Enlightenments surrounding the movement, as we have seen, doesn't have to occur so far from home. Local elementary school programs, like "Future Cities," and at-home events, like clothing swaps, can be educational foundations obliging us to take action within our community and beyond.

Connection formation is the final phase of a successful waste-free revamp. No matter the scale of these relations or how they originate, having stakeholders and meaningful supporters in your corner is always a plus. Excess Materials Exchange and Too Good To Go are corporate networks that serve as accountability schemes for sustainable behavior. Users can physically commit to circularity through these measures. For individual zero-wasters, this looks slightly different and much less formal, with the value coming from warm affirmation and practical lifestyle advice to reduce waste. Collaborative online courses, like those released by

---

331 Ayesha Barenblat, Allison Griffin, and Eleanor Amari, "Meet the Designer: Rachel Faller of Tonle," *Stories* (blog), *Remake*, April 1, 2017.

Zero-Waste Families, and social media advocacy groups are fertile spaces to drive these kinships.

The cross-relevance of these principles on a personal and industrial basis is abundantly clear. Intentional design, emotional investment, and carefully-forged networks make up the toolkit sufficient to craft a zero-waste lifestyle and an entirely circular economy. Overarchingly, zero-waste may seem a completely value-laden, personal choice. The reality is that the implications are far spread and extremely relevant to the society at large. As a wise man named Neil Armstrong once said, "One small step for man, one giant leap for mankind."[332]

Taking a look at my own small steps, the footprints I have left behind have made a substantial effect on the lives of those around me. Since my reusable cup use at local coffee shops, for example, many of my friends and family have followed suit. They have sat back in awe, even making comments like, "Huh, I didn't know you could do that. I'm going to bring a cup next time."

In their personal recognitions, I can see a reflection of my own journey to a waste-reduced lifestyle prompted by Lauren Singer. Now, I am most definitely not comparing myself to Singer's well-deserved status, but nonetheless I am hopeful for the change I have personally sparked. My own reformation, I will say, was quite drastic. Even as an

---

332 Olivia B. Waxman, "Lots of People Have Theories about Neil Armstrong's 'One Small Step for Man' Quote. Here's What We Really Know," *Time*, July 15, 2019.

environmentalist, I lived a pretty resource-intensive life. I would frequent fast-fashion villains like Forever 21 and light up whenever I received a package from Amazon, ready to bust open the plastic covered "treat" I ordered for myself. Nowadays, I get a sense of uneasiness when I see a box arrive on my doorstep with my name on it, delegating the responsibility of associated trash to my own negligence—making me feel extremely guilty. To ease this personal and planetary guilt, there are tactical steps we as stakeholders can take.

Consumers: If you are looking for meaning in your life, are interested in sustainability, or even if you are looking for ways to save some change in your bank account, start making small changes to head toward a zero-waste lifestyle. Here are some steps to get you started:

- Seek out short films and documentaries that resonate with you to learn more about the zero-waste movement and circular economy and how that may pertain to your lifestyle.
- Join local zero-waste and sustainable living groups, whether through social media or in person.
- Take classes to learn practical skills that can assist you in moving toward zero-waste (i.e. sewing classes, cooking classes, soap-making, and the like).
- Search your area for thrift or secondhand shops.
- Purchase reusable containers and bags to cut back on plastic.
- Investigate food waste reduction and second-hand fashion apps active in your region.

The opportunities are endless and forthcoming. Most importantly, just be aware that your daily actions truly do impact on the state of our economy and the state of our planet.

Producers: If you are concerned with your profit margin, have sustainability as a core value, are looking for ways to reduce your reliance on volatile resource inputs, or care about an excitable consumer base, transition to a circular economic model. Even though this movement entails constrictions in resource use, the scientific and creative liberties involved are a source not soon to be drained. There is so much potential to unleash and so many current mechanisms in place to help you get there. Here are some tangible first steps to get going:

- Initiate conversations with your staff and suppliers on the importance of waste reduction in business.
- Recruit and engage an active customer base concerned and personally affected by trash's implications.
- Join circular think tanks like Kate Raworth's Doughnut Economics Action Lab or networks like Excess Materials Exchange to nip wastage at the bud.
- Learn about zero waste strategies and action plans from groups such as Blue Daisi Consulting, a Black-owned zero-waste consulting firm.
- Utilize online tools like Nike's Circularity Guide for ideas on how to reduce material waste in your own systems.
- Welcome creativity to invigorate out-of-the-box next-generation solutions to waste.
- Create campaigns to empower waste reduction.

In sum, if all of us were to commit to being open-minded in our sustainable decision-making, we could legitimately reinvent our entire consumption and production complex. Together, not by pointing the finger to forces outside of our control, we are capable of making massive change. For environmentalists and conscious decision makers, I hope you seek out ways to go zero-waste that fit your lifestyle. For business owners, I hope you advocate for ways to make your company more sustainable by reducing waste. For everyone, I hope you start to see waste not only as an asset, but a key to our future.

AFTERWORD

The Black Lives Matter and BIPOC (Black, indigenous, and people of color) justice movements, which are just now receiving a sliver of their deserved recognition in mainstream American media, are imperative societal upheavals not only with respect to basic human rights but also the zero-waste/circular economy movement. Being such a prominent topic of discussion, I felt it irresponsible not to include this reflection for my audience, who I can only hope is as diverse as our nation (and world) as a whole. I am a young, white, middle class, American female. Therefore, some of the personal stories and ideas I include in this book may not resonate with other demographics. My intent in sharing my own experiences is to expose my own philosophical journey learning about zero-waste practices in hopes that some aspect of my stories may strike a chord with you or inspire you to critique your own personal habits and the waste that may come from them.

Additionally, I wanted to call attention to diversity inclusion throughout the book. Whilst curating my book's content, my goal was to encompass economists, entrepreneurs, and thought leaders from various walks of life with different educational and professional backgrounds from distant parts of the world. I do understand that, as I was delving into research about this topic I was not previously well-versed in, my findings were biased (as is the case with all authors and researchers). The rationale behind choosing specific professionals came from the concept of the brands themselves and their unique proposals for reducing waste in the western world, which is largely responsible for the trash pandemic in the first place. These unique ideas were what drew me into this fantastic field, and they taught me so much as an aspiring sustainability professional. In delivering this message to you, I want to draw attention to diversity inclusion—so I have included this reflection to emphasize the contributions of BIPOC perspectives and the amazing work they have contributed to the zero-waste crusade. This is especially important considering many indigenous cultures are sustainable role models and minority groups tend to be most adversely affected by the externalities of waste. Additionally, as I hope you have come to recognize through reading my book, systems analysis is an important procedure for enacting circularity. These systems don't only include technical supply chains or product life cycles, but also the systems of oppression that are ingrained in our current "business as usual." In various parts of my book, I try to identify social injustice issues associated with traditional industrial practices and how particular businesses directly address them, but I do recognize that there are areas where diversity and inclusion are underrepresented. In an attempt to directly call attention to this societal inequity, I have included a directory of BIPOC zero-waste businesses and activists, which I sincerely hope you will support. The remarkable work by BIPOC zero-waste professionals and activists is by no means limited to the list I attached, so I also recommend searching diverse environmentalists in your own area. My genuine hope is that by raising awareness for this important cause, we can better represent and support this field beyond the white, privileged subset of society to reflect a more inclusive, progressive community as responsible producers and consumers.

BIPOC ZERO WASTE DIRECTORY[333]

ZERO-WASTE BUSINESSES

Check out these existing directories and collective resources for up-to-date indigenous and Black-owned businesses that may help you with your transition:

United States

- Official Black Wall Street
- Five Fifths
- BLK + GRN
- The Village Market
- Post Landfill Action Network

---

333 "Black & Indigenous Owned Sustainability Businesses to Support and BIPOC Zero Wasters To Follow," *Zero Waste Blogs, Stores & Apps* (blog), *Reusable Nation*, June 26, 2020; Kathryn Kellogg, "Why We Need an Intersectional, Anti-racist Zero Waste Movement," *Blog, Going Zero Waste*, November 16, 2020.

United Kingdom

- UK Black Owned Businesses
- Oona Black British Business Directory

Australia

- Supply Nation
- Blak Business
- Australian Indigenous Fashion

REUSABLE KITCHEN AND PERSONAL CARE PRODUCTS
United States

- Nappy Bunz
- The Honey Pot
- OUI the People

United Kingdom

- Mama Luna
- Illuminate Essentials Skincare
- Roop
- Bespoke Binny
- Green Soul Grace

Australia

- SisterWorks
- Kakadu Tiny Tots

South America

- Spaza Store
- Supa Wraps Shweshwe (reusable food wraps)

NATURAL BEAUTY PRODUCTS
United States

- Quw'utsun' Made
- Essentials by Temi
- Bohicket Apothecary
- Nailey's Naturals
- Melaku Aromatherapy
- Beelove
- Base Butter
- Dirt Don't Hurt
- Black Girl Sunscreen
- Lalin et La Sirèn
- Hanahana Beauty
- Eu'Genia Shea

United Kingdom

- Earth to Earth Organics
- Shimirose
- Liha Beauty

Australia

- Willow+Co
- Smoke and Ochre

- Bushbalm
- Bush Medijina

CLEANING PRODUCTS
United States

- PUR Home

Australia

- NOOD Australia

SUSTAINABLE FASHION
United States

- Grant Blvd
- Thando's
- PROCLAIM
- Wasi Clothing
- Taylor Jay
- Aliya Wanek
- Galerie.LA
- Omi Woods Jewelry

United Kingdom

- Sancho's
- KKG Goods
- Kemi Telford

Australia

- Yhi Collective
- The Koorie Circle
- Gillawarra Arts
- Collective Closets

FOOD AND OTHER
Australia

- Jarin Street

United States

- Rheaply
- Blue Daisi Consulting
- Zero Grocery
- Ivy's Tea
- Batiqua
- Diaspora Co.

United Kingdom

- It Is All About You
- La Basketry
- Ocean by the Sea
- Earth For All

ZERO-WASTE ACTIVISTS
@marandas_world
@reducereusesuze

@eco.styles
@jhanneu
@thediaryofagreengurl
@heyashleyrenne
@wastefreemarie
@zerowastehabesha
@queerbrownvegan
@the_mixedup_minimalist
@greengirlleah
@dominiquedrakeford
@ajabarber
@mikaelaloach
@browngirl_green
@cookiecat.herine
@thatcurlytop
@soulful_seeds
@kameachayne
@oldworldnew
@itsecogal

ACKNOWLEDGMENTS

———

The amount of people I could thank for making this book possible could be a book in and of itself. Without the warm, cheerful messages and consistent curiosity and challenge by my family, friends, mentors, colleagues, and loved ones, I'm not sure this vision would have left my head to make it on paper. Like waste, my gratitude and love for these people is in endless supply, and I could not ask for a more supportive group of people in my corner, encouraging me along every step of the way.

First and foremost, I would like to thank my family. To my dad, mom, godmother, and brothers, thank you for all your heartfelt affirmation, eagerness to learn, and passion to listen. Nothing in the world got me through this process more than the sturdy and grounding support you gave me, even through all the ranting phone calls and nervous breaks. From my most exciting moments of cover design and social media outreach to my most horrific moments of losing my entire manuscript, you were there. For that, I cannot thank you enough. Know that I recognize and praise the changes you have all made in your daily lives, which give me hope for a more circular future. Mom, I appreciate your switch to reusable grocery bags. Dad, your transition to brands like Patagonia and use of reusable cups and containers is truly inspiring. Auntie, the curiosity and frustration you have with recycling (which I continue to face myself) is all a normal part of this process, and I have faith that together we can cut down our waste day by day.

To the Butcher family, words cannot even begin to express how much of an impact you have had not only on my book-writing process, but my entire life. Your refusal of anything less than a purely bad-ass life empowered me to chase this path less traveled and unleash my creativity in ways I never even thought possible. From your art expertise to your tremendous Lifebook community to your sponsorship and motivation, you guys really helped me find and share my purpose. And to Jade, thank you for being there for me through the ups and downs. Through the weeks on end I would spend isolated away and hard at work, you helped me see the importance of a creative break, and you were always there for me when I needed one most. I love you and am so happy you decided to hop onto this project with me.

Thank you to my beta readers, who were unafraid to provide their honest feedback and remain devoted to uncovering my book's highest potential. To Tatiana, Justin, Karin, Patty, Teagen, Himkaar, Shashi, Joe, and Amy, your words of wisdom helped me beautify my book in a way that appeals to each of your unique perspectives so that hopefully our waste-free future is not just possible by sustainability professionals, college students, or upper middle class Mid-westerners, but for a much broader population.

Thank you to the professors and staff at the University of Illinois at Urbana-Champaign who built my foundation of knowledge to deliver this complex message. To Dr. Renata Endres, thank you for providing your unique perspective on natural resource economics and giving me a guiding light to follow for a more sustainable future. To Dr. Carena van Riper, thank you for directing me through the nuances and techniques of scientific communication and enforcing pro-environmental behavior. To Robert McKim, thank you for teaching me lessons on the publishing industry I never knew I needed and for seeing the significance of my message on a much larger scale. To MK, your work continues to astonish me, and having your support in every way possible was something I couldn't be more grateful for.

To the Creator Institute and New Degree Press teams, Eric Koester, Brian Bies, Gjorgji Pejkovski, and so many others, I have absolutely no idea where I would be without your guidance and support—almost certainly, I would not be here writing this book. I recall the first week of June 2020 when I had my introductory call with Eric Koester. Originally, I went into his program with the idea of creating an online course for living sustainably in dorm rooms. Eric, you challenged me to challenge myself, and commit to something that could pave my future and push me outside of my comfort zone. Now, nine months later, here we are. My comfort zone is at least double or triple the size before this journey, as a timid girl whose internship got cancelled last minute. To Cass Lauer, your warm encouragement and cheerleading made the endless hours of research all worth it. Your unique perspectives and expertise left me with a first draft manuscript I was proud to share, making my revisions a much more enjoyable and seamless process. Last but not least, Julie Colvin, my wonderful marketing and revisions editor. If compassion and positivity could be defined as a person, it would most certainly be you. During times when I felt like my writing was average and unimportant, you lifted me up and showed me just how much of an impact my book can have. Your hard work and excessive time spent devising opportunities for me and supporting my outreach for endorsements never went unnoticed. Single-handedly, you were the biggest boost my book ever received. You helped me see my vision beyond the pages of my book, in the complex and wounded world.

I couldn't conclude this round of acknowledgments without an astounding thank you to the thought leaders, entrepreneurs, economists, and activists I feature throughout my book, some of whom I had the pleasure of speaking with screen to screen. Without your stories and infinite wisdom, I could not have found my motivation to fight for a world without waste:

Lauren Singer
Ellen MacArthur
Maayke-Aimée Damen
Tom Szaky
Himkaar Singh
William McDonough
John Elkington
Ray Anderson
Rob Greenfield
Carl Hodges
John Hoke III
Matt Stone

Kate Raworth
Adriana Sanatanocito and Enrica Arena
Rachel Faller
Anastasia Mikhalochina
Rose Marcario
Nicole Bassett
Sarah Kaeck
Kresse Wesling
Alex Schulze and Andrew Cooper
James Reinhart
Ian Le Clair
Jennifer Hyman
Matthew Bertulli
Mette Lykke

Lastly, but certainly not least, I would like to give a massive thank you to those who supported my pre-sale campaign. Without you, I would not have been able to spread this very important message or see my hard work on paper in all of your hands. Even without insurance of the end result, you all had confidence in me enough to support my journey. For that, I commend a major shoutout:

Missy and Jon Butcher
Steven W. Smith
Michael J. Smith

Christine Smith
Karin Wittich
Carey Lewis
Kevin Gavin
Sandra Wittich

Justin Smith
Dotty Bens
Amy Bartucci
Patrick and Mary Curran
Bonnie Meltesen

Eric Koester
Cass Lauer
Jade Butcher
Patty Lloyd
Anne McPeak
Himkaar Singh
Shashikiran Duraisamy
Ryan Smith
Stephen Lewis
Kionna McCain
Abby Hanselman
Sapir Shanskhalil
Mark Smith
Albert White
Matthew Crandall
Simon Marinelli
AJ Parnell
Dario Bartucci
Garett Collins
Cambrie Lane
Maria Flach
Caroline Wuerl
Kailen Inouye
Colman P. Reiss
Sahil Patel
Oriya Falk

Nandini Kuntamukkula

Eddie Rajcevic

Randy Janson

Anya Ranjan

Lauren Komrska

Sydney Kwan

Chaya Lee-Isranukul

Elizabeth Larson

Justin Holding

Raffi Kaul

Tracey Kihnke

Maleek Ayoola Akeju

Nicole Hagemann

Adam Brock

Kristin DiTella

Bethany Herrera

Thanh-Thao (Sue) Do

Carolyn Skowron

Mary Wittich

Lauren Kilberg

Rose Carroll

Noelle Schultz

Sue Olson

Raju Patil

Tiana Aldora

Nia Rainer

Brittany Do

Joseph Oetter

Alex Guillen

Rick H. Peterson

David Downing

APPENDIX

INTRODUCTION

Bruce-Lockhart, Anna. "More Plastic in the Sea Than Fish? Not If We Do These 3 Things." *World Economic Forum: Agenda*, January 16, 2017. https://www.weforum.org/agenda/2017/01/more-plastic-in-sea-than-fish-3-strategies/.

Gibbens, Sarah. "Plastic Proliferates at the Bottom of World's Deepest Ocean Trench." *National Geographic*, May 13, 2019. https://www.nationalgeographic.com/news/2018/05/plastic-bag-mariana-trench-pollution-science-spd/.

Gunders, Dana, Jonathan Bloom, JoAnne Berkenkamp, Darby Hoover, Andrea Spacht, and Marie Mourad et al., *Wasted: How America Is Losing up to 40 Percent of Its Food from Farm to Fork to Landfill*. New York City, NY: Natural Resources Defense Council, 2017. 4. Accessed January 5, 2021. https://www.nrdc.org/sites/default/files/wasted-2017-report.pdf.

Lindwall, Courtney. "Single-Use Plastics 101." *Our Stories* (blog). *NRDC,* January 9, 2020. https://www.nrdc.org/stories/single-use-plastics-101.

"One Garbage Truck of Textiles Wasted Every Second: Report Creates Vision for Change." *Ellen MacArthur Foundation,* November 28, 2017. https://www.ellenmacarthurfoundation. org/news/one-garbage-truck-of-textiles-wasted-every-second-report-creates-vision-for-change.

TED. "Lauren Singer: Why I Live a Zero Waste Life." May 27, 2015. Video, 0:10. https://www.youtube.com/watch?v=pF72px2R3Hg.

TED. "Maayke-Aimée Damen: Saving the Planet by Running a Dating Site." January 2, 2020. Video, 2:50. https://www.youtube. com/watch?v=7A8x_cIjG10.

Thompson, Andrea. "From Fish to Humans, a Microplastic Invasion May Be Taking a Toll." *Scientific American,* September 4, 2018. https://www.scientificamerican.com/article/from-fish-to-humans-a-microplastic-invasion-may-be-taking-a-toll/.

US Department of the Interior. Environmental Protection Agency. *Inventory of US Greenhouse Gas Emissions and Sinks: 1990-2018.* Washington D.C., 2020. https://www.epa.gov/sites/production/ files/2020-04/documents/us-ghg-inventory-2020-main-text.pdf.

US Department of the Interior. Environmental Protection Agency. *National Overview: Facts and Figures on Materials, Wastes and Recycling.* Washington D.C., 2018. https://www.epa.gov/facts-and-figures-about-materials-waste-and-recycling/national-overview-facts-and-figures-materials.

Zero Waste International Alliance. "Zero Waste Definition." Last modified December 20, 2018. Accessed December 22, 2020. http://zwia.org/zero-waste-definition/.

PHASE ONE

TIPPING THE SCALES

CBS *This Morning*. "Device Developed by Young Entrepreneur Collecting Pacific Ocean Litter." September 10, 2018. Video, 1:12. https://www.youtube.com/watch?v=ofOeZNNWeUo.

Cirilli, Mark, Joan Briggs, Adam Rein, Kyle Tanger, Sarah Matheson, Blythe Chorn, Robert Bui, Sierra Bayles, JD Lindeberg, David Stead, Hunt Briggs, Nick Lange, Monica Walker, Michael Nieling, Abby Lindstrom, Amy Leibrock, Tom Beck, Melody Serafino et al., *A Roadmap to Reduce US Food Waste by 20 Percent*. Berkeley, CA: ReFED, 2016. 5. Accessed January 5, 2021. https://www.refed.com/downloads/ReFED_Report_2016.pdf.

De Smet, Michiel, Lenaïc Gravis, Sarah Churchill-Slough, Magali Outters, Lucille Guiheneuf, Alessandra Pomé et al. *The New Plastics Economy: Rethinking the Future of Plastics & Catalysing Action*. Cowes, United Kingdom: Ellen MacArthur Foundation, January 2016. 19. Accessed January 5, 2021. https://www. ellenmacarthurfoundation.org/assets/downloads/publications/ NPEC-Hybrid_English_22-11-17_Digital.pdf.

Eastern Illinois Food Bank. "Map the Meal Gap." Accessed December 22, 2020. https://www.eifoodbank.org/impact/challenge/ map-meal-gap.html#:~:text=Overall%20food%20insecurity

%20rates%20for,assistance%20under%20current%20program
%20requirements.

Food and Agriculture Organization of the United Nations. "Fao
Policy Series: Food Loss & Food Waste." June 30, 2016.
Video, 0:40. https://www.youtube.com/watch?list=PLz
p5NgJ2-dK6rvLoneIyknuTmM-3QKwBh&v=pxoz88-GXyk
&feature=youtu.be.

Gibbens, Sarah and Laura Parker. "Creatures in the Deepest
Trenches of the Sea Are Eating Plastic." *National Geographic*,
February 28, 2019. https://www.nationalgeographic.com/
environment/2019/02/deep-sea-creatures-mariana-trench-eat-
plastic/.

Gibbens, Sarah. "Plastic Proliferates at the Bottom of World's
Deepest Ocean Trench." *National Geographic*, May 13,
2019. https://www.nationalgeographic.com/news/2018/05/
plastic-bag-mariana-trench-pollution-science-spd/.

Hawken, Paul. *Drawdown: The Most Comprehensive Plan Ever
Proposed to Reverse Global Warming.* New York: Penguin
Publishing Group, 2017.

HealtheBay. "The Majestic Plastic Bag—a Mockumentary." August
14, 2010. Video, 0:21. https://www.youtube.com/watch?v=
GLgh9h2ePYw.

Hebblethwaite, Cordelia and Anbarasan Ethirajan. "Sandblasted Jeans: Should We Give up Distressed Denim?" *BBC
News*, September 30, 2011. https://www.bbc.com/news/mag-
azine-15017790.

Holland, Oscar. "Gucci Abandons 'Worn-Out Ritual' of Fashion Seasons as the Industry Looks Inward." *CNN*, Updated May 26, 2020. https://www.cnn.com/style/article/gucci-fashion-calendar/index.html.

Ingre, Serena. "New Report: California Communities Spend Nearly $500m Annually in Keeping Trash Out of Waterways." *Natural Resources Defense Council*, August 28, 2013. https://www.nrdc.org/media/2013/130828.

Institute for Sustainability, Energy and Environment. "Reduce Foodwaste." Accessed December 22, 2020. https://icap.sustainability.illinois.edu/project/reduce-foodwaste.

National Oceanic and Atmospheric Administration. "A Guide to Plastic in the Ocean." *Hazards* (blog). *National Ocean Service*, Updated August 14, 2020. https://oceanservice.noaa.gov/hazards/marinedebris/plastics-in-the-ocean.html#:~:text=While%20it's%20tough%20to%20say,the%20problem%20continues%20to%20grow.&text=That%20means%20plastic%20can%20stick,wreaking%20havoc%20on%20marine%20ecosystems.

"One Garbage Truck of Textiles Wasted Every Second: Report Creates Vision for Change." *Ellen MacArthur Foundation*, November 28, 2017. https://www.ellenmacarthurfoundation.org/news/one-garbage-truck-of-textiles-wasted-every-second-report-creates-vision-for-change.

Poots, Paula. "What Goes into a Keurig K Cup Pod?" *Expert Advice* (blog). *Office Barista*, December 7, 2017. https://www.officebarista.co.uk/blogs/better-office-coffee/keurig-k-cup-

whats-in-it#:~:text=Most%20K%20Cup%20pods%20are,food
%20packaging%20material%20used%20today.

Recycling Works Massachusetts. "Food Waste Estimation Guide."
Accessed January 21, 2021. https://recyclingworksma.com/
food-waste-estimation-guide/#Jump01.

Smithsonian Institution. "Laysan Albatrosses' Plastic Problem."
Accessed December 22, 2020. https://ocean.si.edu/ocean-life/
seabirds/laysan-albatrosses-plastic-problem#:~:text=Laysan
%20albatrosses%20(Phoebastria%20immutabilis%20
)%20are%20incredible%20birds.&text=Along%20the%20
way%2C%20they%20accidentally,it%20fills%20up%20their%20
stomachs.

TED. "Amit Kalra: 3 Creative Ways to Fix Fashion's Waste Problem." March 9, 2018. Video, 1:28. https://www.youtube.com/
watch?v=yeVU2Ff4ffc.

United States Environmental Protection Agency. "United States
2030 Food Loss and Waste Reduction Goal." Accessed January
21, 2021. https://www.epa.gov/sustainable-management-food/
united-states-2030-food-loss-and-waste-reduction-goal.

Vishnu Vardhaan. "What if every piece of trash you produced
this month was not taken away but was dumped back in your
front yard?" LinkedIn, June 16, 2020. https://www.linkedin.
com/in/vshvrdhn/.

RECIPE FOR SUSTAINABILITY

Agarwal, Prateek. "The Environmental Kuznets Curve." Intelligent Economist, March 1, 2018. https://www.intelligenteconomist. com/kuznets-curve/.

Anderson, Ray and Robin White. *Confessions of a Radical Industrialist: Profits, People, Purpose: Doing Business by Respecting the Earth.* New York: St. Martin's Press, 2009.

BLK + GRN. "Toxic Twenty List." Accessed February 4, 2021. https://blkgrn.com/.

Brundtland Commission. Our Common Future: Report of the World Commission on Environment and Development. Oxford: Oxford University Press, 1987.

"Cone Communications Gives Companies a Lesson on How to Speak Gen Z." *Sustainable Brands*, September 12, 2017. https:// sustainablebrands.com/read/marketing-and-comms/cone-communications-gives-companies-a-lesson-on-how-to-speak-gen-z.

Elkington, John. *Cannibals with Forks: Triple Bottom Line of 21st Century Business.* Oxford: Capstone Publishing Ltd, 1997.

Ellen MacArthur Foundation. "What Is a Circular Economy?" Accessed December 23, 2020. https://www.ellenmacarthurfoundation. org/circular-economy/concept.

Fleming, Sean. "Here's How One Company Is Championing the Circular Economy." World Economic Forum Agenda,

February 25, 2020. https://www.weforum.org/agenda/2020/02/
loop-milkman-reusable-packaging-groceries-retail/.

Georgiadis, Candice. "Angela Richardson of Pur Home: 5
Things I Wish Someone Told Me before I Became a CEO."
Authority Magazine, January 18, 2021. https://medium.com/
authority-magazine/angela-richardson-of-pur-home-5-things-
i-wish-someone-told-me-before-i-became-a-ceo-6e6460ffad39.

Grunders, Ray. "Zero Waste in Business : Documentary on
Business and Environmental Waste (Full Documentary)."
January 15, 2016. Video, 1:22:40. https://www.youtube.com/
watch?v=NXTLsRcSAQE.

Instagram. "#Plasticfree." Accessed February 15, 2021. https://www.
instagram.com/explore/tags/plasticfree/.

Instagram. "#Earthday." Accessed February 15, 2021. https://www.
instagram.com/explore/tags/earthday/.

Khan, Sana and Abdul Malik. "Environmental and Health Effects
of Textile Industry Wastewater." Environmental Deterioration and Human Health (December 8, 2013): 55-71. https://doi.
org/10.1007/978-94-007-7890-0_4.

Krupp, Fred. "Ceos Need to Fill the Leadership Void on Climate Policy." Fortune, February 21, 2019. https://fortune.
com/2019/02/21/climate-change-policy-corporate-sustainability/.

Mahoney, Charlie and Steffen Bixby. "Chart of the Week: America's
Most Just Companies Are Bouncing Back More Quickly during
the Current Recession." JUST Capital News, May 21, 2020.

https://justcapital.com/news/chart-of-the-week-americas-most-just-companies-are-bouncing-back-more-quickly-during-the-current-recession/.

McDonough, William and Michael Braungart. *Cradle to Cradle: Remaking the Way We Make Things*. New York: Farrar, Straus and Giroux, 2002.

McKay, Mandi, Leslie Lukacs, Dave Keeling, Sophie Hahn, Gary Liss, Joseph Burton and Claire Miflin. "Building a Circular Economy with Zero Waste Businesses." Panel at the 2020 National Zero Waste Conference, December 1, 2020. https://youtu.be/EvnUmJXkufw.

Moritz, Bob E., Kevin Ellis, Harald Kayser, Raymund Chao, Tim Ryan, Richard Oldfield, Stephanie Hyde, Bill Cobourn et al., *23rd Annual Global CEO Survey: Navigating the Rising Tide of Uncertainty*. London, United Kingdom: PwC, 2020. 37. Accessed January 5, 2021. https://www.pwc.com/gx/en/ceo-survey/2020/reports/pwc-23rd-global-ceo-survey.pdf.

Ray C. Anderson Foundation. "Ray's Life." Accessed December 23, 2020. https://www.raycandersonfoundation.org/rays-life/.

Rockström, Johan, Mattias Klum and Peter Miller. *Big World, Small Planet: Abundance Within Planetary Boundaries*. London: Yale University Press, 2015.

SaveOnEnergy. "Land of Waste: American Landfills and Waste Production." Accessed December 23, 2020. https://www.save-onenergy.com/land-of-waste/.

Schellenberger, Michael. "If Solar Panels Are So Clean, Why Do They Produce So Much Toxic Waste?" Forbes, May 23, 2018. https://www.forbes.com/sites/michaelshellenberger/2018/05/23/if-solar-panels-are-so-clean-why-do-they-produce-so-much-toxic-waste/?sh=74d3b6a3121c.

Schmidt, Carolina, Gino Van Begin, Frans Van Houten, Cristianne Close, David B. McGinty, Rachna Arora, Janes Potocnik, Noko Ishii, Peter Bakker, Mukhisa Kituyi, Feike Sijbesma, Anders Wijkman et al., *The Circularity Gap Report 2020.* Amsterdam, Noord-Holland: Circle Economy, 2020. 15. Accessed December 30, 2020. https://assets.website-files.com/5e185aa4d27bcf348400ed82/5e26ead616b6d1d157ff4293_20200120%20-%20CGR%20Global%20-%20Report%20web%20single%20page%20-%20210x297mm%20-%20compressed.pdf.

Small, Diane. "5 Brands You Think Are Eco Friendly... but Really Aren't." *Eluxe Magazine,* November 15, 2019. https://eluxemagazine.com/culture/articles/5-brands-you-think-are-eco-but-really-arent/.

TED. "Ray Anderson: The Business Logic of Sustainability." May 18, 2009. Video, 1:28. https://www.youtube.com/watch?v=iP9QF_lBOyA.

"Tide Clean." *TruthinAdvertising Blog. TruthinAdvertising.org,* September 16, 2020. https://www.truthinadvertising.org/tide-purclean/.

TRUE Zero Waste. "TRUE Program for Zero Waste Certification." Accessed February 10, 2021. https://true.gbci.org/true-program-zero-waste-certification.

United States Green Building Council. "LEED Rating System." Accessed February 10, 2021. https://www.usgbc.org/leed.

Whan, Eric and Stacy Rowland et al., *Healthy & Sustainable Living: A Global Consumer Insights Report.* Toronto, Canada: GlobeScan, 2019. 5. Accessed December 30, 2019. https://globescan.com/wp-content/uploads/2019/09/Healthy_Sustainable_Living_2019_GlobeScan_Highlights.pdf.

Zero Waste International Alliance. "Zero Waste Definition." Last modified December 20, 2018. Accessed December 22, 2020. http://zwia.org/zero-waste-definition/.

THE PURCHASER'S DILEMMA

All for Reuse. "All for Reuse Vision." Accessed February 10, 2021. http://allforreuse.org/index.html.

Duer, Jacob. "The Plastic Pandemic Is Only Getting Worse during COVID-19." *World Economic Forum: Agenda*, July 1, 2020. https://www.weforum.org/agenda/2020/07/plastic-waste-management-covid19-ppe/.

Fortunato, Piergiuseppe. "How COVID-19 Is Changing Global Value Chains." United Nations Conference on Trade and Development News, September 2, 2020. https://unctad.org/news/how-covid-19-changing-global-value-chains.

Helms, Natalie. "Ketogenic Diet: What Are the Risks?" *UChicago Medicine,* June 20, 2019. https://www.uchicagomedicine.org/forefront/health-and-wellness-articles/ketogenic-diet-what-are-the-risks#:~:text=The%20keto%20diet%20could%20cause,%2C%20liver%2C%20thyroid%20or%20gallbladder.

Institute for Sustainability, Energy and Environment. "MSW Diversion Rate." Accessed December 22, 2020. https://icap.sustainability.illinois.edu/objectives.

Librett Creative. "Marketing." Accessed February 10, 2021. http://www.librettcreative.com/marketing.

Nike. "What Is Nike's Reuse-a-Shoe Program?" Accessed December 23, 2020. https://www.nike.com/help/a/recycle-shoes.

Stephanie Sizemore. "Klean Kanteen: Bring Your Own." Accessed February 10, 2021. https://www.stephaniesizemore.com/Klean-Kanteen-Bring-Your-Own.

US Department of the Interior. Environmental Protection Agency. *Advancing Sustainable Materials Management: 2017 Fact Sheet.* Washington DC, November 2019. https://www.epa.gov/sites/production/files/2019-11/documents/2017_facts_and_figures_fact_sheet_final.pdf.

PHASE TWO

CHANNELING COPERNICUS AND CURIE

"Adidas Aims to End Plastic Waste with Innovation + Partnerships as the Solutions." News (blog). Adidas, January 28, 2020.

https://news.adidas.com/parley-ocean-plastic/adidas-aims-to-end-plastic-waste-with-innovation---partnerships-as-the-solutions/s/be70ac18-1fc9-45c1-9413-d8abaac2e849.

Alvarez, Edgar. "Nike's Chief Design Officer on Why the Company Is Going All in on Sustainability." *Input,* February 2, 2020. https://www.inputmag.com/features/nike-john-hoke-chief-design-officer-sustainability-recycled-space-hippie-tokyo-2020-olympics.

Anderson, Ray and Robin White. *Confessions of a Radical Industrialist: Profits, People, Purpose: Doing Business by Respecting the Earth.* New York: St. Martin's Press, 2009.

Ellen MacArthur (@ellenmacarthur). "Waste and pollution do not happen by accident—they're a result of the way we design things. If we can change our mindset to view waste as a design flaw, and embrace new materials and." Twitter, July 7, 2020, 5:29 a.m. https://twitter.com/ellenmacarthur?lang=en.

European Commission. "Sustainable Product Policy." Updated December 13, 2018. Accessed December 23, 2020. https://ec.europa.eu/jrc/en/research-topic/sustainable-product-policy.

"From Old to New with Looop." *H&M Magazine,* October 8, 2020. https://www2.hm.com/en_us/life/culture/inside-h-m/meet-the-machine-turning-old-into-new.html.

Green & Book Ambassadors. "By teaching children about love, listening to the homeless, and laughing while picking up smelly trash." Facebook, July 23, 2020. https://www.facebook.com/GreenAndBookAmbassadors/.

History.com Editors. "Industrial Revolution." *History*, Updated September 9, 2019. https://www.history.com/topics/industrial-revolution/industrial-revolution.

Hodges, Carl. "Eco-Scientist." Filmed at CUSP Conference 2008 in Chicago, IL. Video, 9:30. https://www.cuspconference.com/videos/carl-hodges-2008/.

Hoke, John. "John Hoke on Design." *Nike News* (blog). *Nike, Inc,.* April 11, 2016. https://news.nike.com/news/john-hoke-on-design.

ISS SRPS. "The Rise of Sustainability." July 13, 2017. Video, 30:30. https://www.youtube.com/watch?v=oOLlS2VoGLM.

Ketchum. "Innovation Is More Than a Buzzword—Consumers Are Willing to Pay 21 percent More for Innovative Brands." *PR Newswire*, March 24, 2015. https://www.prnewswire.com/news-releases/innovation-is-more-than-a-buzzword--consumers-are-willing-to-pay-21-more-for-innovative-brands-300054750.html.

Loomis, Ilima. "Jet-Setting: Turning Aquaculture Wastewater into Aviation Fuel." *Global Aquaculture Advocate*, June 3, 2019. https://www.aquaculturealliance.org/advocate/jet-setting-turning-aquaculture-wastewater-into-aviation-fuel/.

"Meet the Innovator Battling Plastic Waste in Vietnam: Trang Nguyen." *The World Bank: News*, May 31, 2019. https://www.worldbank.org/en/news/feature/2019/05/31/meet-the-innovators-battling-plastic-waste-in-vietnam-trang-nguyen.

Meha, Nelson. "Indigenous Worldviews and the Circular Economy." *Scion Connections*, June 2019. https://www.scionresearch.com/about-us/about-scion/corporate-publications/scion-connections/past-issues-list/scion-connections-issue-32,-june-2019/indigenous-worldviews-and-the-circular-economy.

Nike. "Nike Grind: A Legacy of Innovation." Accessed December 23, 2020. https://www.nikegrind.com/about/.

Oppenheimer, Todd. "Sustainability on Steroids." *Made Local Magazine*, May 2015. https://madelocalmagazine.com/2015/05/sustainability-on-steroids/.

Safronova, Valeriya. "Nike's Chief of Design Doodles All Day." *New York Times*, October 16, 2017. https://www.nytimes.com/2017/10/16/fashion/nike-nba-uniform-golden-warriors-hyperdunk.html.

Seawater Works. "Seawater Works." Accessed December 23, 2020. https://seawaterworks.com/.

SpaciousEconomy. "Farmshorts Northbay—Singing Frogs Farm." May 9, 2013. Video, 0:07. https://www.youtube.com/watch?v=8uaE5mLtFgU&feature=youtu.be.

Spangler, Adam. "The Future's Farmer." *Vanity Fair*, April 23, 2007. https://www.vanityfair.com/news/2007/04/hodges200704.

TED. "Josh Kaufman: The First 20 Hours —How to Learn Anything." March 14, 2013. Video, 9:35. https://www.youtube.com/watch?v=5MgBikgcWnY.

TED. "Ray Anderson: The Business Logic of Sustainability." May 18, 2009. Video, 1:28. https://www.youtube.com/watch?v=iP9QF_lBOyA.

The Compost Kitchen. "Our Story." Accessed December 23, 2020. https://www.compostkitchen.com/story.

Urban Canopy. "Residential Composting." Accessed December 23, 2020. https://www.theurbancanopy.org/compost-club.

TAPPING INTO CREATIVITY

Agarwal, Prateek "The Environmental Kuznets Curve." Intelligent Economist, March 1, 2018. https://www.intelligenteconomist.com/kuznets-curve/.

Clements, Ron and John Musker, dir. *The Little Mermaid*. 1989; Burbank, CA: Walt Disney Pictures. Blu-ray Disc, 1080p HD.

Diaspora Co. "About." Accessed February 4, 2021. https://www.diasporaco.com/pages/about.

Doughnut Economics Action Lab. "And Now... It's Time for Planetary Economics." June 4, 2017. Video, 0:21. https://www.youtube.com/watch?v=gxcez9kE19w&feature=youtu.be.

Ecovative Design. "Partner with Us." Accessed December 24, 2020. https://ecovativedesign.com/#.

Global Shakers. "What Makes Adriana Santanocito & Enrica Arena Global Shakers?" Updated October 21, 2019. Accessed

December 24, 2020. https://globalshakers.com/world-shakers/adriana-santanocito-enrica-arena/.

Harper's BAZAAR. "Everything Zero Waste Expert Lauren Singer Eats in a Day." November 20, 2019. Video, 6:30. https://www.youtube.com/watch?v=--f8hjw9Uiw.

"Innovation Goes Orange." Face2Face (blog). Fibre2Fashion.com, August 18, 2017. https://www.fibre2fashion.com/interviews/face2face/orange-fiber/adriana-santanocito-and-enrica-arena/1638-1/.

McCafferty, Hugo. "Matt Stone: The Future of Sustainable Living." Fine Dining Lovers, April 22, 2020. https://www.finedininglovers.com/article/matt-stone-future-sustainable-living.

Meaning Conference. "Kate Raworth L Doughnut Economics L Meaning 2017." November 30, 2017. Video, 7:15. https://www.youtube.com/watch?v=lkCiootiFWE&feature=youtu.be.

Mooney, Jordan. "Chef Matt Stone Is on a Mission to Make Australia More Sustainable." Food & Wine, accessed December 24, 2020. https://foodandwine.ie/interviews/matt-stone-interview.

Nash, Brad. "Matt Stone Wins Chef of the Year at GQ's 2019 Men of the Year Awards." GQ, November 28, 2019. https://www.gq.com.au/men-of-the-year/event-coverage/matt-stone-wins-chef-of-the-year-at-gqs-2019-men-of-the-year-awards/news-story/a364991b78223942fc824a6d4695867c.

Orange Fiber. "Who We Are." Accessed December 24, 2020. http://orangefiber.it/en/about/.

Price, Laura. "Top Australian Chef Champions Kangaroo Meat, Zero Waste and Eating Bark." *50 Best*, May 25, 2017. https://www. theworlds50best.com/stories/News/australian-chef-champions-kangaroo-zero-waste-bark.html.

Raworth, Kate. *Doughnut Economics: Seven Ways to Think Like a 21st-Century Economist*. Hartford: Chelsea Green Publishing, 2017.

Raworth, Kate. "Why We Need to Move toward an Economy That Can Regenerate Itself." *Business* (blog). *Ideas.TED.com*, April 11, 2018. https://ideas.ted.com/why-we-need-to-move-toward-an-economy-that-can-regenerate-itself/.

TED. "Kate Raworth: A Healthy Economy Should Be Designed to Thrive, Not Grow." June 4, 2018. Video, 15:10. https://www. youtube.com/watch?v=56YoTElkI9o.

TED. "Maayke-Aimée Damen: Saving the Planet by Running a Dating Site." January 2, 2020. Video, 2:50. https://www.youtube. com/watch?v=7A8x_cIjG1o.

TED. "Matt Stone: Beyond the Zero Waste Restaurant." September 17, 2014. Video, 0:16. https://www.youtube.com/ watch?v=56YoTElkI9o.

COMMUNITY MATTERS

Barenblat, Ayesha, Allison Griffin and Eleanor Amari. "Meet the Designer: Rachel Faller of Tonle." *Stories* (blog). *Remake*, April 1, 2017. https://remake.world/cambodia/meet-the-designer-

rachel-faller-of-tonle/?gclid=EAIaIQobChMIgumF7Z2v6gI
VDb7ACh3AEAHvEAAYASAAEgI4ePD_BwE.

Beals, Callum. "4 of the World's Most Sustainable Islands." *Sierra,*
accessed December 25, 2020. https://www.sierraclub.org/sierra/
green-life/2014/03/4-worlds-most-sustainable-islands#:~:
text=Because%20of%20their%20isolated%20nature,in%20
its%20use%20and%20transportation.

Beer, Jeff. "Exclusive: Patagonia CEO Rose Marcario Is
Stepping Down." *Fast Company,* June 20, 2020. https://www.
fastcompany.com/90515307/exclusive-patagonia-ceo-rose-
marcario-is-stepping-down.

Bell, Lizzie. "5 Q's with Anastasia Mikhalochkina, Founder of
Lean Orb." *Blog. Babson WIN Lab*, March 20, 2018. http://www.
thewinlab.org/blog/2018/3/18/5-qs-with-anastasia-mikhalochkina-
founder-of-lean-orb.

Bora, Chun, Richard Howard and Eric Stener Carlson et al., *Guide-
lines on HIV/AIDS in the Workplace.* Phnom Penh, Cambodia:
Kingdom of Cambodia: Ministry of Labour and Vocational
Training, June 2010. 9. Accessed December 25, 2020. http://
www.ilo.org/dyn/natlex/docs/ELECTRONIC/86087/109129/
F162133305/KHM86087%20Eng2.pdf.

de Cuba, Kevin. "Making Aruba Future-Proof through Sustainable Circular Economy." *Blog. Circular Economy Platform,*
2020. https://www.cep-americas.com/single-post/2020/03/24/
Making-Aruba-future-proof-through-Sustainable-Circular-
Economy.

"Founder's Story with Rachel Faller: Tonlé, a Zero Waste, Ethical Fashion Brand on a Big Mission." *Travel Under the Radar*, accessed December 25, 2020. http://www.travelundertheradar.com/sustainable-fashion-with-tonle.

Fox, Joe, Lauren Tierney, Seth Blanchard and Gabriel Florit. "What Remains of Bears Ears." *Washington Post*, April 2, 2019. https://www.washingtonpost.com/graphics/2019/national/bears-ears/.

Google Maps (search item "coffee shops near me"; accessed December 31, 2020). https://www.google.com/maps.

Hedden, Donnia. "On the Road with Worn Wear – 2015 Spring Tour Recap." *Stories* (blog). *Patagonia*. Accessed December 25, 2020. https://www.patagonia.com/stories/on-the-road-with-worn-wear-2015-spring-tour-recap/story-17733.html.

Jack Wolfskin. *Google Search Results: "Jack Wolfskin's."* Accessed February 12, 2021. https://www.google.com/search?sxsrf=ALeKkooBzca1UUmAbyRv5VImmkNANiw7jw%3A1612844300605&ei=DAoiYOC7JMzktQXL4LOwAw&q=Jack+Wolfskin%E2%80%99s+&oq=Jack+Wolfskin%E2%80%99s+&gs_lcp=CgZwc3ktYWIQAzIECCMQJzIECCAAQDTIECAAQDTIECAAQDTIECAAQDTIECAAQDTIECAAQDTIECAAQDTIECAAQDTIECAAQDVCQJliQJmCWKGgAcAF4AIABlAGIAaQCkgEDMC4ymAEAoAEBqgEHZ3dzLXdpZpesABAQ&sclient=psy-ab&ved=0ahUKEwjg8fWc-dvuAhVMcqoKHUvwDDYQ4dUDCAo&uact=5.

Jack Wolfskin. "Responsibly Sourced. Ethically Produced." Accessed February 12, 2021. https://hyqa.jackwolfskin.com/.

Lean Orb. "Our Pursuit of Sustainability Is Rooted in Optimism." Accessed December 25, 2020. https://leanorb.com/pages/lean-world.

MacLaughlin, Steve and Chris Clark. "Miami-Based Company Produces Biodegradable Tableware." *NBC 6 South Florida*, September 13, 2019. https://www.nbcmiami.com/news/local/miami-based-lean-orb-recyclable-utensils/1934896/.

Marcario, Rose. "Rose Marcario: Business Doesn't Live in a Vacuum, but in an Interconnected World." *Stories* (blog). *Patagonia*. Accessed December 25, 2020. https://www.patagonia.ca/stories/business-doesnt-live-in-a-vacuum-but-in-an-interconnected-world/story-31029.html.

"Meet Anastasia Mikhalochkina of Lean Orb in Wynwood." *VoyageMIA*, June 28, 2018. http://voyagemia.com/interview/meet-anastasia-mikhalochkina-lean-orb-wynwood/.

Merriam-Webster. s.v. "greenwashing (n.)." Accessed February 12, 2021. https://www.merriam-webster.com/dictionary/greenwashing.

Semuels, Alana. "'Rampant Consumerism Is Not Attractive.' Patagonia Is Climbing to the Top—and Reimagining Capitalism along the Way." *Time*, September 23, 2019. https://time.com/5684011/patagonia/.

SOKO. "Our Impact." Accessed February 17, 2021. https://shopsoko.com/pages/about-our-impact.

Sudetic, Azra. "Fashion Made from Ocean Plastic Might Not Be What You Think It Is." *EcoCult,* June 17, 2020. https://ecocult.com/recycled-ocean-plastic-fashion/.

Tonlé. "Team." Accessed December 25, 2020. https://tonle.com/pages/team.

PASSION FOR TRASH

A Fierce Green Fire. "Lois Gibbs—the Love Canal Story." April 18, 2011. Video, 0:51. https://www.youtube.com/watch?v=I1VzX5MvjXY.

Bassett, Nicole. "Is Your Business Wasting Money on Waste?" *Green Biz,* November 16, 2018. https://www.greenbiz.com/article/your-business-wasting-money-waste.

Beer, Jeff. "Exclusive: Patagonia CEO Rose Marcario Is Stepping Down." *Fast Company,* June 20, 2020. https://www.fastcompany.com/90515307/exclusive-patagonia-ceo-rose-marcario-is-stepping-down.

BLK + GRN. "Behind the Brand." Accessed February 4, 2021. https://blkgrn.com/.

Center for International Environmental Law. "Plastic and Human Health: A Lifecycle Approach to Plastic Pollution." Accessed December 26, 2020. https://www.ciel.org/project-update/plastic-and-human-health-a-lifecycle-approach-to-plastic-pollution/#:~:text=Microplastics%20entering%20the%20human%20body,outcomes%20including%20cancer%2C%20cardiovascular%20diseases%2C.

Crook, Jordan. "Package Free Picks up $4.5 Million to Scale Sustainable Cpg Products." *Tech Crunch,* September 26, 2019. https://techcrunch.com/2019/09/26/package-free-picks-up-4-5-million-to-scale-sustainable-cpg-products/.

Dr. Robert Bullard. "Biography." Accessed February 12, 2021. https://drrobertbullard.com/biography/.

GreenBiz. "How to Design for the Future." September 8, 2020. Video, 0:51. https://www.youtube.com/watch?v=I1VzX5MvjXY.

HealtheBay. "The Majestic Plastic Bag—a Mockumentary." August 14, 2010. Video, 0:21. https://www.youtube.com/watch?v=GLgh9h2ePYw.

"Interview with Nicole Bassett, the Renewal Workshop." Once. October 9, 2019. https://www.once.eco/blogs/interviews/interview-with-nicole-bassett-the-renewal-workshop.

Kondo, Marie. *The Life-Changing Magic of Tidying up: The Japanese Art of Decluttering and Organizing.* Berkeley: Ten Speed Press, 2014.

Marcel, Joyce. "The Big Buzz: Sarah Kaeck, Bee's Wrap." *Vermont Biz,* September 22, 2019. https://vermontbiz.com/news/2019/september/22/big-buzz-sarah-kaeck-bees-wrap.

OUI the People. "The Reconstitution of Beauty." Accessed February 4, 2021. https://www.ouithepeople.com/pages/reconstitution.

People for Community Recover. "History." Accessed February 12, 2021. http://www.peopleforcommunityrecovery.org/history.html.

Renaud, Chris and Kyle Balda, dir. *The Lorax.* 2012; Santa Monica, California: Illuminaton Company, 2012. Blu-ray Disc, 1080p HD.

Rodriguez, Leah. "Meet Lauren Singer, the Environmental Activist Making It Easy to Go Waste-Free." *Global Citizen,* April 30, 2020. https://www.globalcitizen.org/en/content/lauren-singer-package-free-interview/.

Solve-MIT. "Watch Solver Nicole Bassett Pitch the Renewal Workshop." October 8, 2019. Video, 3:01. https://www.youtube.com/watch?v=2yP2f68K2F8&feature=youtu.be.

Stelian, Hélène. "Nicole Bassett, Co-Founder, the Renewal Workshop." *Purpose Stories* (blog). *Hélène Stelian Coaching,* November 21, 2017. https://helenetstelian.com/nicole-bassett/.

Suess, Dr. *The Lorax.* New York: Penguin Random House LLC, 1971.

TED. "Lauren Singer: Why I Live a Zero Waste Life." May 27, 2015. Video, 0:10. https://www.youtube.com/watch?v=pF72px2R3Hg.

TED. "Nicole Bassett: The Future of Business Is Circular." August 27, 2019. Video, 13:27. https://www.youtube.com/watch?v=rUZ-fIBJHzvY.

Trash is for Tossers. "DIY and Guides." Accessed December 25, 2020. https://www.trashisfortossers.com/diy-and-guides/.

United Nations Environment Programme. "Our Planet Is Drowning in Plastic Pollution." Accessed December 26, 2020.

https://www.unenvironment.org/interactive/beat-plastic-pollution/#:~:text=Because%20right%20now%2C%20a%20lot,dumps%20or%20the%20natural%20environment.

Wasi. "How Is Wasi Clothing Sustainable?" Accessed February 4, 2021. https://wasiclothing.com/.

Weissman, Arthur. "What Is It about Humans and Waste?" *Green Biz*, May 18, 2019. https://www.greenbiz.com/article/what-it-about-humans-and-waste.

Yankovich, Gyan. "People Are Obsessed with These $18 Reusable Beeswax Food Wraps." *BuzzFeed*, June 6, 2018. https://www.buzzfeed.com/gyanyankovich/these-beeswax-wraps-mean-you-never-have-to-mess-with-saran.

SEEING IS BELIEVING

American Psychological Association. "Stress Effects on the Body." Accessed December 27, 2020. https://www.apa.org/helpcenter/stress/effects-nervous.

Ellen MacArthur (@ellenmacarthur). "What if we could build an economy that uses things, rather than uses them up?" Twitter, June 4, 2020, 5:00 a.m. https://twitter.com/ellenmacarthur?lang=en.

Ellen MacArthur Foundation. "Financing the Circular Economy." Accessed December 27, 2020. https://www.ellenmacarthurfoundation.org/our-work/activities/finance?gclid=CjoKCQjw28T8BRDbARIsAEOMBcw1UAXKWnV5SditHSbNVABJkidnczkCXlU-iVnUybez1m5T9SOUHkYaAvcMEALw_wcB.

Ellen MacArthur Foundation. "Mission and Vision." Accessed February 12, 2021. https://www.ellenmacarthurfoundation.org/our-story/mission.

Elvis & Kresse. "Our Story." Accessed December 27, 2020. https://www.elvisandkresse.com/pages/about-us-2.

"Innovator: Andrew Cooper and Alex Schulze." *Newsweek*, January 16, 2019. https://www.newsweek.com/sponsored/creative-class-2019/andrew-cooper-and-alex-schulze.

"Laureate 2011 Europe: Kresse Wesling." *Fellows* (blog). *Cartier Women's Initiative*, updated December 21, 2020. https://www.cartierwomensinitiative.com/node/158.

Lobeck, Rachael. "4ocean Co-founders Andrew Cooper and Alex Schulze Named Forbes 30 under 30 Social Entrepreneurs." *Cision PR Newswire*, November 14, 2018. https://www.prnewswire.com/news-releases/4ocean-co-founders-andrew-cooper-and-alex-schulze-named-forbes-30-under-30-social-entrepreneurs-300750165.html.

Minter, Adam. *Junkyard Planet: Travels in the Billion-Dollar Trash Trade.* London: Bloomsbury Press, 2013.

Shelton, Suzanne. "Engaging Middle America in Recycling Solutions: The Challenges & Opportunities." *Shelton Group*, September 2, 2020. https://sheltongrp.com/engaging-middle-america-in-recycling-solutions-the-challenges-opportunities/.

TED. "Dame Ellen MacArthur: The Surprising Thing I Learned Sailing Solo Around the World." June 29, 2015. Video, 1:15. https://www.youtube.com/watch?v=ooIxHVXgLbc.

Unreasonable. "Turning Trash Into Luxury Fashion Items | Kresse Wesling." December 22, 2017. Video, 1:27. https://www.youtube.com/watch?v=uIQ86NFoFhc&feature=youtu.be.

"'We Are in This for the Long Haul': Florida's 4ocean Founders Work to Save the Seas from Trash." *CBS Miami,* May 31, 2019. https://miami.cbslocal.com/2019/05/31/florida-4ocean-founders-clean-trash-oceans/.

Woods, Ross. "A Brief Review of Bali Tourism in 2019." *Hotel Investment Strategies, LLC.,* February 4, 2020. http://hotelinvestmentstrategies.com/a-brief-review-of-bali-tourism-in-2019/#:~:text=The%20number%20of%20international%20tourists,Badan%20Pusat%20Statistik%20Provinsi%20Bali.

World Wildlife Fund. "Ecological Footprint." Accessed December 27, 2020. https://wwf.panda.org/discover/knowledge_hub/all_publications/ecological_footprint2/?.

4Ocean. "About Us." Accessed December 27, 2020. https://www.4ocean.com/pages/about#.

4Ocean. "What's 4ocean Doing to Stop Plastic from Entering the Ocean?" February 14, 2019. Video, 0:22. https://www.youtube.com/watch?v=7_Mt-CNCt6c&feature=youtu.be.

RIDING TRENDS

Alvarez, Edgar. "Nike's Chief Design Officer on Why the Company Is Going All in on Sustainability." *Input,* February 2, 2020. https://www.inputmag.com/features/nike-john-hoke-chief-design-officer-sustainability-recycled-space-hippie-tokyo-2020-olympics.

Anderson, Brad. "How Are Sustainable Startups Like Pela Fighting Plastic Waste?" *Lead* (blog). *ReadWrite*, March 12, 2020. https://readwrite.com/2020/03/12/how-are-sustainable-startups-like-pela-fighting-plastic-waste/.

Ashraf, F. "Earth Day 2020: Celebrities Take to Twitter to Join the Conversation on the Environment." *Indulge,* April 22, 2020. https://www.indulgexpress.com/entertainment/celebs/2020/apr/22/earth-day-2020-celebrities-take-to-twitter-to-join-environmental-conversation-24279.html#:~:text=on%20the%20environment%20and%2020,environment%20since%20last%20Earth%20Day.

Ballentine, Claire. "Rent the Runway CEO Says Access, Not Ownership, Is Fashion's Future." *Bloomberg,* November 21, 2019. https://www.bloomberg.com/news/articles/2019-11-21/rent-the-runway-founder-says-access-not-ownership-is-fashion-s-future.

Barnhart, Brent. "The Most Important Social Media Trends to Know for 2020." *Social Media Trends* (blog). *Sprout Social,* August 4, 2020. https://sproutsocial.com/insights/social-media-trends/.

Bertulli, Matthew. "The Legacy of Retail in One Number: Zero." *Matthew Bertulli* (blog). *Medium,* July 19, 2017. https://medium. com/@mbertulli/the-legacy-of-retail-in-one-number-zero-515ef702b139.

Biel, Justin. "ThredUP's Founder Shares His Formula for Developing a World-Changing Business." *Grow Wire,* January 9, 2020. https://www.growwire.com/thredUP.

Canadian Business. "Growth List 2020." Accessed December 29, 2020. https://www.canadianbusiness.com/growth-list-2020/.

CASETiFY. "Welcome to the New Casetify." Accessed February 13, 2021. https://www.casetify.com/about-us.

CNBC. "Rent the Runway CEO: Closet in the Cloud | Mad Money | CNBC." May 23, 2018. Video, 2:00. https://www.youtube.com/watch?v=KJpqevuoKtA.

CNBC Television. "ThredUP CEO James Reinhart on the Company's New Partnership with Walmart." June 23, 2020. Video, 1:55. https://www.youtube.com/watch?v=y1eozJ-h2-E.

"Cone Communications Gives Companies a Lesson on How to Speak Gen Z." *Sustainable Brands*, September 12, 2017. https:// sustainablebrands.com/read/marketing-and-comms/cone-communications-gives-companies-a-lesson-on-how-to-speak-gen-z.

Conversocial Report: The State of Social Customer Service. New York, NY: Conversocial. 3. Accessed December 29, 2020. https://www. conversocial.com/hubfs/StateofSocialCS.pdf?t=1497783197137.

Ellen MacArthur Foundation. "Financing the Circular Economy." Accessed December 27, 2020. https://www.ellenmacarthur foundation.org/our-work/activities/finance?gclid=CjoKC Qjw28T8BRDbARIsAEOMBcw1UAXKWnV5SditHSbNVAB JkidnczkCXlU-iVnUybez1m5T9SOUHkYaAvcMEALw_wcB

Grow Ensemble. "Fueling a Circular Economy Through Sustainable Everyday Products." *B The Change* (blog). *Medium*, June 9, 2020. https://bthechange.com/fueling-a-circular-economy-through-sustainable-everyday-products-c05c369eb4d2.

INspired Insider. "Matthew Bertulli of Pelacase & Demacmedia on Inspiredinsider with Dr. Jeremy Weisz." March 12, 2020. Video, 24:20. https://www.youtube.com/watch?v=B_lUz000 Pe4&feature=emb_logo.

Jennifer Hyman (@Jenn_RTR). "I am present and doing all I can. Currently I'm doing customer service instead of playing with my 2 young babies on a Saturday so I appreciate your vocalness to improve things but." Twitter, September 14, 2019, 1:59 p.m. https://twitter.com/Jenn_RTR/status/1177457526217949184.

Leighton, Mara. "ThredUP Rewards You for Cleaning Out Your Closet While Donating to Those in Need—Here's What It's like to Use." *Business Insider*, September 11, 2020. https://www.businessinsider.com/thredUP-upcycling-review#:~:text=Any%20unaccepted%20items%20(the%20things,men's%2C%20and%20kids'%20items..

McDonald, Samantha. "Why Both Macy's and JCPenney Teamed up with ThredUP—in Less Than 24 Hours." *Footwear News,*

August 15, 2019. https://footwearnews.com/2019/business/
retail/thredUP-macys-jcpenney-partnership-1202817653/.

Mishan, Ligaya. "The Long and Tortured History of Cancel Culture." *New York Times*, December 3, 2020. https://www.nytimes.
com/2020/12/03/t-magazine/cancel-culture-history.html.

Murray, James. "Hundreds of Companies Crack down on Plastic from
Fast Fashion to Supermarkets and Beyond." *Green Biz,* March 6,
2020. https://www.greenbiz.com/article/hundreds-companies-
crack-down-plastic-fast-fashion-supermarkets-and-beyond.

Porter, Beth. "What Really Happens to Unwanted Clothes?"
Green America, Winter 2019. https://www.greenamerica.org/
unraveling-fashion-industry/what-really-happens-unwanted-
clothes.

Rent the Runway. "Our Story." Accessed December 25, 2020. https://
www.renttherunway.com/about-us/story?action_type=footer_
link.

SimilarWeb. "Pelacase.com January 2021 Overview." Accessed
December 29, 2020. https://www.similarweb.com/website/
pelacase.com/ .

TED. "Amit Kalra: 3 Creative Ways to Fix Fashion's Waste Problem." March 9, 2018. Video, 1:28. https://www.youtube.com/
watch?v=yeVU2Ff4ffc.

Wildflower Cases. "How Wildflower Cases Blossomed." Accessed
February 13, 2021. https://www.wildflowercases.com/pages/
about-us.

SIX DEGREES OF CIRCULARITY

Chicago Ideas. "Tom Szaky: Eliminating the Idea of Waste." March 7, 2013. Video, 0:55. https://www.youtube.com/watch?v=LH qwd-LBp5c.

Clasper, James. "Meet Startup Queen Mette Lykke." *Scandinavian Traveler,* August 31, 2017. https://scandinaviantraveler.com/en/people/meet-startup-queen-mette-lykke.

Crow, Daniel and Ariane Millot. "Working from Home Can Save Energy and Reduce Emissions. but How Much?" *Commentary* (Blog), *International Energy Agency,* June 12, 2020. https://www.iea.org/commentaries/working-from-home-can-save-energy-and-reduce-emissions-but-how-much.

ecosummitTV. "Eco17 Amsterdam: Maayke-Aimée Damen Excess Materials Exchange." July 10, 2017. Video, 1:22. https://www.youtube.com/watch?v=IVGViBxPBfY&feature=youtu.be.

"Exclusive Interview with Maayke-Aimée Damen – Co-founder at Excess Materials Exchange." *Blog. London Speakers Bureau,* accessed December 29, 2020. https://londonspeakerbureau.com/interview-maayke-aimee-damen/.

Gladwell, Malcolm. *The Tipping Point: How Little Things Can Make a Big Difference.* Boston: Little, Brown and Company, 2000.

Hocevar, John, Tom Szaky, Holly Kaufman and Bridget Croke. "Reusable Packaging: Scaling Past a Pandemic." Panel at the 2020 Circularity20 Conference, August 27, 2020. https://events.greenbiz.com/events/circularity/online/2020/program/next-gen-packaging#115187.

Holt-Lunstad, Julianne. "The Double Pandemic of Social Isolation and COVID-19: Cross-Sector Policy Must Address Both." *Health Affairs Blog. Health Affairs,* June 22, 2020. https://www. healthaffairs.org/do/10.1377/hblog20200609.53823.

Hwang, Tzung-Jeng, Kirna Rabheru, Carmelle Peisah, Willian Reichman, and Manabu Ikeda. "Loneliness and Social Isolation During the COVID-19 Pandemic." *International Psychogeriatrics* 32, no. 1 (October 2020): 1217–1220. https://doi. org/10.1017/S1041610220000988.

Impakter. "Tom Szaky—Full Interview." September 24, 2019. Video, 2:10. https://www.youtube.com/watch?v=U2O7IQYGMaA.

Inspiring Fifty: Nordics. "Mette Lykke ~ Denmark." Accessed December 29, 2020. https://nordics.inspiringfifty.org/mette-lykke.

"Loop Expands Nationwide to Meet Consumer Demand." *Press Release* (blog). *Nosh,* September 22, 2020. https://www.nosh. com/food-wire/2020/loop-expands-nationwide-to-meet-consumer-demand/.

Murray, Adrienne. "The Entrepreneur Stopping Food Waste." *BBC News,* January 6, 2020. https://www.bbc.com/news/business-50974009.

Ochwat, Dan. "Terracycle's Loop Platform Hits Milestone Reach across 48 States." *Store Brands,* September 22, 2020. https:// storebrands.com/terracycles-loop-platform-hits-milestone-reach-across-48-states#:~:text=The%20Loop%20program%20began%20in,signed%20up%20for%20the%20service.

Resources Passport. "Our Resources Passport Is Not Just Another Way of Storing More Data." Accessed December 29, 2020. https://www.resourcespassport.com/.

"Social Isolation and Loneliness: The Silent Pandemic." *Harris Regional Hospital*, August 31, 2020. https://www.myharris regional.com/news/social-isolation-and-loneliness-the-silent-pandemic.

TED. "Maayke-Aimée Damen: Saving the Planet by Running a Dating Site." January 2, 2020. Video, 2:50. https://www.youtube.com/watch?v=7A8x_cIjG10.

TED. "William McDonough: Cradle to Cradle Design." May 17, 2007. Video, 14:41. https://www.youtube.com/watch?v=IoR jz8iTVoo&vl=br.

"The "I Am" Q&A." *CNBC*, accessed December 29, 2020. https://www.cnbc.com/id/100000748.

Winterich, Karen, Lindsey Boyle and Brian Reilly. "Habits and Hooks: Changing Consumer Behaviors." Panel at the 2020 Circularity20 Conference, August 27, 2020. https://events.greenbiz.com/events/circularity/online/2020/program/stakeholders-storytelling#115231.

Zero. "Zero-Waste Groceries, Delivered Fast." Accessed February 19, 2021. https://zerogrocery.com/.

PHASE THREE

CONSUMER CONNECTION

Bowerman, Mary. "Man Pledges to Wear All the Trash He Produces for 1 Month." *USA Today*, September 30, 2016. https://www.usatoday.com/story/news/nation-now/2016/09/30/man-pledges-wear-all-trash-he-produces-1-month/91317682/.

Greenfield, Rob. "The Food Waste Fiasco: You Have to See It to Believe It." *Blog. Rob Greenfield*, October 6, 2014. https://www.robgreenfield.org/foodwaste/.

Happen Films. "Tips for Zero Waste Living—How a Family of 5 Makes Almost No Waste! | Life with Less Waste." June 28, 2019. Video, 1:15. https://www.youtube.com/watch?v=B5ijPk5_8pM.

Hedden, Donnia. "On the Road with Worn Wear – 2015 Spring Tour Recap." *Stories* (blog). *Patagonia*, accessed December 25, 2020. https://www.patagonia.com/stories/on-the-road-with-worn-wear-2015-spring-tour-recap/story-17733.html.

Lanier, John Anderson. "Tomorrow's Child." *Ecocentricity* (blog). *Ray C. Anderson Foundation*, August 1, 2016. https://www.raycandersonfoundation.org/articles/tomorrows-child. © Glenn C. Thomas 1996. Used by permission of the Ray C. Anderson Foundation

Meha, Nelson. "Indigenous Worldviews and the Circular Economy." *Scion Connections*, June 2019. https://www.scionresearch.com/about-us/about-scion/corporate-publications/scion-connections/past-issues-list/scion-connections-issue-32,-june-2019/indigenous-worldviews-and-the-circular-economy.

NARTS: The Association of Resale Professionals. "Industry Statistics & Trends." Accessed December 30, 2020. https://www.narts.org/i4a/pages/index.cfm?pageid=3285#:~:text=Many%20resale%20shops%20don't,shops%20in%20the%20United%20States.

Schaller, Olivia. "Green Planet—Rob Greenfield, a 100 percent Green Life." France 2 TV, November 9, 2016. Video, 0:05. https://www.france.tv/france-2/telematin/1883627-planete-verte-rob-greenfield-une-vie-100-ecolo.html.

Sedaghat, Lilly. "7 Things You Didn't Know about Plastic (and Recycling)." *National Geographic Society Newsroom* (blog). *National Geographic,* April 4, 2018. https://blog.nationalgeographic.org/2018/04/04/7-things-you-didnt-know-about-plastic-and-recycling/#:~:text=In%20other%20words%2C%20it's%20what,can%20no%20longer%20be%20used.

Sustainable Living Tasmania. "Reducing to Zero Waste! #Dontwastehobart (14/15)." November 22, 2015. Video, 2:13. https://www.youtube.com/watch?v=jhpwAo-cHNs&feature=youtu.be.

TED. "William McDonough: Cradle to Cradle Design." May 17, 2007. Video, 14:41. https://www.youtube.com/watch?v=IoRjz8iTVoo&vl=br.

Zero Waste Families. "About the Course." Accessed February 14, 2021. https://zerowastefamilies.com/about-the-course/.

Barenblat, Ayesha, Allison Griffin and Eleanor Amari. "Meet the Designer: Rachel Faller of Tonle." *Remake*, April 1, 2017. https://remake.world/cambodia/meet-the-designer-rachel-faller-of-tonle/?gclid=EAIaIQobChMIgumF7Z2v6gIVDb7ACh3AEA HvEAAYASAAEgI4ePD_BwE.

Bruce-Lockhart, Anna. "More Plastic in the Sea Than Fish? Not If We Do These 3 Things." *World Economic Forum: Agenda*, January 16, 2017. https://www.weforum.org/agenda/2017/01/more-plastic-in-sea-than-fish-3-strategies/.

Future Coalition. "Minimizing Your Environmental Footprint with Lauren Singer | Earth Day Live." May 5, 2020. Video, 1:23. https://www.youtube.com/watch?v=7psva_fs6Bc.

Gunders, Dana, Jonathan Bloom, JoAnne Berkenkamp, Darby Hoover, Andrea Spacht, and Marie Mourad et al., *Wasted: How America Is Losing up to 40 Percent of Its Food from Farm to Fork to Landfill.* New York City, NY: Natural Resources Defense Council, 2017. 4. Accessed January 5, 2021. https://www.nrdc.org/sites/default/files/wasted-2017-report.pdf.

"One Garbage Truck of Textiles Wasted Every Second: Report Creates Vision for Change." Ellen MacArthur Foundation, November 28, 2017. https://www.ellenmacarthurfoundation.org/news/one-garbage-truck-of-textiles-wasted-every-second-report-creates-vision-for-change.

Tiseo, Ian. "Volume of Household Waste Collected by Local Authorities per Capita in England from 2010 to 2018." *Statista*, June 29, 2020. https://www.statista.com/statistics/322535/

total-household-waste-volumes-in-england-uk-per-person/
#:~:text=Household%20waste%20volumes%20per%20person,
collected%20per%20person%20that%20year.

United Nations. "Goal 12: Ensure Sustainable Consumption
and Production Patterns." Accessed December 31, 2020.
https://www.un.org/sustainabledevelopment/sustainable-
consumption-production/.

US Department of the Interior. Environmental Protection Agency.
*National Overview: Facts and Figures on Materials, Wastes and
Recycling.* Washington DC, 2018. https://www.epa.gov/facts-
and-figures-about-materials-waste-and-recycling/national-
overview-facts-and-figures-materials.

Waxman, Olivia B. "Lots of People Have Theories about Neil
Armstrong's 'One Small Step for Man' Quote. Here's What
We Really Know." *Time,* July 15, 2019. https://time.com/5621999/
neil-armstrong-quote/.

BIPOC ZERO WASTE DIRECTORY

"Black & Indigenous Owned Sustainability Businesses to Support
& BIPOC Zero Wasters To Follow." *Zero Waste Blogs, Stores &
Apps* (blog). *Reusable Nation,* June 26, 2020. https://www.reusable
nation.com/zero-waste-living/black-owned-sustainability-
businesses-to-support-amp-bipoc-zero-wasters-to-follow.

Kellogg, Kathryn. "Why We Need an Intersectional, Anti-racist
Zero Waste Movement." *Blog. Going Zero Waste,* November 16,
2020. https://www.goingzerowaste.com/blog/why-we-need-an-
intersectional-anti-racist-zero-waste-movement/.

Made in the USA
Middletown, DE
10 May 2021